The author could be described as a 'veteran' in every sense of the word, even though he was only aged 21 when the war ended. Armin Scheiderbauer served as an infantry officer with the 252nd Infantry Division, German Army, and saw four years of bitter combat on the Eastern Front, being wounded six times. This is an outstanding personal memoir, written with great thoughtfulness and honesty.

Scheiderbauer joined his unit at the front in 1942, and during the following years saw fierce combat in many of the largest battles on the Eastern Front. His experiences of the 1943-45 period are particularly noteworthy, including his recollections of the massive Soviet offensives of summer 1944 and January 1945. Participating in the bitter battles in West Prussia, he was captured by the Soviets and not released until 1947.

Adventures in my Youth is a unique memoir - the author originally wrote it only for his daughter.

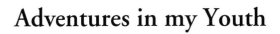

Adventures in my Youth

ADVENTURES IN MY YOUTH

A German Soldier on the Eastern Front 1941-45

Armin Scheiderbauer

Translated by C.F. Colton, MA

LONDON NEW YORK SYDNEY TORONTO

This edition published 2003
by BCA
by arrangement with Helion & Company Limited
CN 115012

Reprinted 2005

Published by Helion & Company Limited 2003

Designed and typeset by Helion & Company Limited, Solihull, West Midlands
Cover designed by Bookcraft Limited, Stroud, Gloucestershire
Printed by The Bath Press, Bath

Cover photograph used courtesy of Bildarchiv Preußischer Kulturbesitz.
Prologue written by Dr Sarah Williams.

For details of other military history titles published by Helion & Company contact the above
address, or visit our website: http://www.helion.co.uk.

Contents

Publishers' Note

Many military terms have been retained in their original German, and readers are directed to the glossary for English definitions.

The publishers' wish to extend their thanks to the author, Dr Armin Scheiderbauer, for his patience and support for this book. He has dealt with all our enquiries and requests with the utmost politeness and promptitude. Dr Sarah Williams kindly agreed to write the prologue, and the publishers' would like to express their gratitude for her accurate work.

To provide some background to the author's experiences, it was felt that a brief summary of the wartime activities of the 252nd Infantry Division might prove useful to readers.

Formation

The division was created on 26 August 1939, as a so-called '4th Wave' division, from replacement units of *Wehrkreis* VIII. At that time it consisted of:
Inf.Rgts. 452, 461, 472
All divisional-level units numbered 252

Combat history

1939

Polish campaign – formed part of *Kampfgruppe* Gienanth, seeing action at Miltitsch, Herrnstadt, Krotoschin-Lissa, Görschen, Kröben, Jarotschin and Wreschen. Security work in the Konin-Klesczew area, and Posen. Transported to the Western front, October 1939.

1939-40

West/French campaign – assigned to 1st Army, attacked through the Maginot Line at Geblingen, Schweix, Willerwald, the Saar canal. Further offensive operations in the Vosges, Badonviller and Celles. Transferred to Poland in July 1940, where it remained until the invasion of the U.S.S.R.

1941

Eastern Front – formed part of 4th Army, Army Group Centre, where it fought around Bialystok and in White Russia, June-September. In October it was with 4th *Panzergruppe* around Vyazma, and the drive on Moscow. On 11 November Inf.Rgt. 452 was disbanded, and replaced by Inf.Rgt. 7, from the 28th Inf.Div.

1942

Eastern Front – With 4th *Panzer* Army until April, around Gshatsk, then with 3rd *Panzer* Army in the same area until the end of the year.

1943

Eastern Front – Transferred to 4th Army, with which it served at Jelnja, February to October. In November it returned to 3rd *Panzer* Army, around Orsha and Nevel. Grenadier Regt. 472 was temporarily inactive between 25 February 1943 and July 1944.

1944

Eastern Front – Remained with 3rd *Panzer* Army for much of the year, through Operation *Bagration* and the withdrawal to Lithuania. In July, the Division was reorganised as follows:
Gren.Regts. 7, 461, 472
All divisional-level units continued to be numbered 252
Transferred to 2nd Army in October, around the Narev bridgehead, Poland.

1945

Eastern Front – Defended the Narev area in the Soviet Vistula-Oder offensive, and subsequent retreat to West Prussia. Although much of the remnants of the Division escaped to Bornholm, they were 'repatriated' to Kolberg, and Soviet captivity.

Bibliography

For those wishing to read more about 252nd I.D. and *Grenadierregiment 7* the following are recommended:
Walter Melzer *Geschichte der 252. Infanterie-Division 1939-1945* (Podzun Verlag, 1960)
Romuald Bergner *Schlesische Infanterie. Grenadier-Regiment 7. Das Infanterie-Regiment 7 und seine Stamm-Truppenteile in Krieg und Frieden. Eine Chronik schlesischer Infanterie 1808-1945* (Pöppinghaus, 1980)

Prologue

Armin Scheiderbauer was born on 13 January 1924 in Gröbming, eastern Styria, the eldest son of a Protestant minister. Armin's parents were Austrian, and in later life Armin himself retained a sense of Styrian identity. However, in 1930 his parents moved to Thuringia, in order to gain some experience of church life in the 'homeland', and it was here, in Germany, that he spent the greater part of his childhood.

Armin's early years were happy ones, spent in a series of small rural communities. He recalls his days in village schools and friendships with local children with considerable affection. The family was a close and happy one, and frequent visits from relatives and neighbouring ministers created a busy and lively atmosphere in the vicarage. Every aspect of daily life in the vicarage was moulded by religion. Prayers were said in the morning, evening, and at mealtimes, and from an early age Armin was actively involved in the church itself, not only attending services but acting as a bell-ringer and as an organ-pumper on Sundays. Within the family church holidays, such as Reformation Day, were important staging posts of the year. Armin's confirmation and the course of preparatory lessons which preceded it marked an important rite of passage in the boy's early life. In later life he looked back on the vicarage and its values – the emphasis on duty, positive action, and putting Christian virtues into practice in daily life - as being a lasting influence on his ideas and outlook.

Religion was not, however, the only important influence on Armin's social and psychological development. From an early age he took a particular interest in history, and his ideas about Germany and its place in the world were formed in his early childhood. The events of the Great War and the injustice of its outcome were something of which Armin was aware from his earliest years at school. In particular he knew about and was proud of the medals which his own father had gained for service in that conflict. Two events at school played a particular part in developing Armin's sympathy with nationalistic sentiments. The first was a visit from a participant in the sea-battle outside Skaggerak, who had survived the famous sinking of the cruiser *Frauenlob*. This inspired in the young Armin an ambition to join the navy, perhaps as a U-boat officer. The second was the performance of the plays *Wallenstein* and *Egmont* by Goethe, which awoke in Armin a strong admiration for military valour and an interest in 'the heroic ideal'. These impressions were strengthened by other nationalistic influences in the environment: a series of images from German history on cigarette cards made a particular impression on his imagination, as did the books detailing subjects such as the history of Germany's lost colonies which he received as school prizes. Even as a boy Armin had developed the conviction a career in the armed forces would be the most honourable path that he could aspire to.

In the later years in Thuringia political developments, as well as the general nationalistic tone of the period, began to have an impact on Armin's family. In 1931 Armin's parents joined the NSDAP. As Protestants they were attracted to the Nazi appeal to 'positive Christianity'; this appealed to their perception that the Augsburg confession as inextricably linked to the idea of German national identity.

Armin's uncle (who was also his godfather) was even more politically engaged; he fled to the Reich following the failure of the July putsch of 1934 and was a member of the Austrian legion. Armin himself was a member of the Hitler Youth, serving as a banner-bearer and later as treasurer. From 1934, however, the family found itself swimming increasingly against the political tide. As Nazi control of the church grew, and as their intrusion into doctrinal questions increased – their insistence, for example, that the Old Testament was a tainted 'Jewish' text which should not be taught in church – Armin's father felt compelled to join the 'bekennende Kirche' movement, which opposed the Nazi inspired 'deutsche Christen's' influence within the church. Although never expelled from the party, Armin's father was subjected to hostile interrogations on a number of occasions. Faced with the distrust of the Church hierarchy, and even of members of his own congregation in Thuringia, Armin's father felt compelled to seek a position in Austria. Yet members of the Protestant church in Austria felt suspicious of a man returning from the Church in the 'homeland'. It was only with some difficulty that his father found a new position, and even then it was as an assistant minister – a demotion which was not only painful to his feelings, but which also entailed a significant deterioration in the financial circumstances of the family.

As a young man Armin was only dimly aware of the political difficulties of his father. However, after the move to Stokerau, which occurred shortly before the outbreak of war, Armin had two experiences which led him to feel some discomfort with the political tone of the times. He was taken to a demonstration against the assassination of von Rath by his schoolteachers. While there he witnessed a group of demonstrators jostling and taunting some Jews who were present. A family friend who saw Armin and his classmates at the demonstration, reproached him for taking part in this harassment, a charge which left him feeling uncomfortable. In 1939, while he was boarding with a family in Sonneberg, he and a group of friends were arrested and held in the police station overnight. The youths had no idea why they had been apprehended, but in the morning were told the reason; they should not have been wandering the streets because the *Gauleiter* was due in town that day. The boys were completely unaware of the proposed visit. These two incidents left Armin with a strong sense of injustice.

Despite these negative experiences, Armin was nevertheless keen to join the army as soon as he left school in 1941. Indeed, such was his yearning for military glory, that his chief response on hearing the news of the fall of Paris was to fear that the war might be over before he had an opportunity to take part. The stories of heroism on which he had been reared led him to believe the noblest profession to follow would be that of an infantry officer. His own father had been an army officer, and he felt that this type of combat was more authentic and heroic than that found in the other forces. To him the life of an officer represented values similar to those of the church: duty to fatherland; a commitment to order and decency in society; care and responsibility for subordinates. In retrospect he also suspects that he knew that a career in the army would keep him at arm's length from the political authorities, who had caused so many problems for his family. Upon receiving his call-up papers in July, he therefore left willingly and with some enthusiasm. His only anxiety was that the war might frustrate his plans to marry his childhood sweetheart Herta, as the couple had planned during his last summer in Stockerau.

Part I

Training

1

August 1941-June 1942: Call-up and training

Aged 17 years - called-up for basic training; aged 18 years - training complete, appendicitis

On 1 August 1941, I had to be in the *Jäger* barracks at St Avold in the Westmark by 3pm. If the word 'Westmark' had not been added, I would not have had even a vague idea as to where my destination was. Westmark was the name given to that region which had been added on to the Reich after the surrender of France. Whether that included only the former German Alsace and Lorraine, or more, no one knew. In any event, I had to seek the aid of a large-scale map to find St Avold which, I finally discovered lay between Saarbrücken and Metz in Lorraine. 1 August was not a normal call-up deadline, the normal dates were 1 April and 1 October. It turned out that there were in fact only a few of us young lads who turned up on 1 August 1941, in accordance with our call-up orders. In the meantime, Mum was in the Liesertal with Rudi and Liesl, so I went for a few days to where they were staying in Zlabing Post Lieserbrücke. For 31 July they had planned a trip out to the parsonage at Eisentratten to visit the family of Pastor Schimik, a school friend of Father's.

From there, I began my journey on the regular afternoon post bus. The journey took me first as far as Spittal on the Drau, and from there by rail via Salzburg. During the night we crossed southern Germany to Saarbrücken. There I left the express train to get on an ordinary passenger train going towards Metz. On the platform I met a boy who was looking around just as I was. He was dragging along two big suitcases. I spoke to him and it turned out that we were both going to the same place. He was Ludwig (Wiggerl) Popovsky, the son of a Vienna tram driver. In him I had found my first comrade. We remained close through two years, more or less.

Neither of us knew or had any explanation why we had ended up in that particular district. We also knew nothing about the unit to which we had been assigned, namely the 2nd Company of Infantry *Ersatz* Battalion 7, nor from which part of the country its members came. Wiggerl, like me, had left it up to chance as to what infantry unit he would be assigned. The mystery was resolved shortly after we arrived. First, after getting out at St Avold station, we had to lug our heavy luggage two kilometres over a mountain, behind which lay the little town. At the edge of it was the *Jäger* barracks.

We arrived at about 2.30pm. Although we were not yet soldiers, we had nevertheless to experience for ourselves the truth of the saying that 'half his life the soldier has to wait in vain'. There are certainly good reasons for that. At 3pm, however, to a certain extent in an official manner, there began the new and serious part of my life. It turned out that altogether there were four of us soldiers who had

1

been provisionally accepted as officer candidates. Most were from Lower Silesia. One came from the Ruhr area, two from Trautenau in Lower Bohemia and the two of us, Popovsky and I, came from Vienna and the Vienna area.

The battalion stationed in St Avold was the *Ersatz* unit for Infantry Regiment 7, in peacetime based in Schweidnitz. We found out that the entire Silesian *Ersatz* Army Corps had been moved into the 'Westmark'. In the French campaign Regiment 7 had been commanded by a colonel from Vienna. At that time, replacements had been added to the regiment to the strength of almost a battalion of men from Vienna. It was the case, right up to the end of the war, that in almost every company I came across there was at least one Viennese or Austrian.

For my part I often regretted that I had made no attempt to join a unit from my homeland. Before I became a soldier I had dreamed how grand it must be to march in the victory parade through the *Ringstrasse* with the returning troops. But later my regret was because I had no close wartime comrades living nearby. That became clear to me when eventually I sat on the Linz regional high court with my colleagues Zauner and Hemetsberger. They had been in the Linz Division, the 45th. Zauner was among the men of the Linz Infantry Regiment – 'the sons of the region and of the city' – who marched off to war from the castle barracks. Hemetsberger had been an artillery officer in the Division.

Immediately after 'installation', under which general heading I include being assigned a barrack room and a bed, and obtaining items of military uniform and equipment, there began the rigorous service involved in basic training. It lasted six weeks. It turned out that this too had been a kind of test. Of the seventeen of us who had joined on 1 August, six were dismissed because they did not meet requirements. Because they were not yet of age for military service they were sent back home. We could easily imagine with what mockery they would be welcomed back to school by their classmates who had stayed behind, after their experience of a 'holiday' that brought so much trouble.

So, 'eleven' of us remained together. Our service went on, apart from the normal work of the barracks, under the supervision of a *Leutnant*, a NCO, and a *Gefreiter* who, at the same time, was senior soldier in the barrack room. The 'eleven' of us were Hans Alterman from Gottesberg in Silesia, Walter Borrmann from Breslau, Walter Henschel from Reichenbach in the Eulengebirge, Hans Bernt and Gottfried Bergmann from Liegnitz, Jochen Fiedler from Glogau, Diesel and Helmut Überla from Trautenau, Pohlmann from Wuppertal, together with Popovsky and me.

Since Popovsky had a camera with him, I have some photos. The first shows us in a group on the parade ground. We are wearing field service jackets, with our top collar button undone, our belts buckled, army boots, and the 'forage' field service caps on our heads. My hands are still stuck into my trouser pockets in a quite unmilitary fashion.

After basic training was over we were moved to Mörchingen, halfway between Metz and Saargemünd. The place mostly consisted of barracks built after 1871, after Alsace-Lorraine had reverted to Germany. Here was the staff of *Ersatz* Regiment 28, to which the two infantry regiments 350 and 461 belonged. From then on our group was part of the 2nd Company of *Infanterie-Ersatz-Bataillon* 350. I scarcely have any recollections of St Avold, because at the time, during basic training, you were not allowed to leave the barracks. I can only remember one single trip out that we used to find a photographer's studio. I recall Mörchingen as the place where all our training took place, carried out on the parade ground and on the firing range. Certainly, in St Avold we drilled on the parade ground and first practised with our weapons. That was only a little compared with the variety of the drill to which we were then subjected.

The 'Training Regulations for the Infantry' (A.V.I.), Army Service Regulations (HDV 130/2a) for *Schützenkompanie* was the 'bible' according to which our life as soldiers then proceeded. From the Individual Training I shall quote the following, concerning the 'basic position':

1)   The soldier's good bearing is an index of his training and overall physical education. It is to be improved whenever everyday service provides the opportunity.

2)   Standing without weapon to 'Attention'! In the basic position the man stands still. The feet stand with the heels close together. The toes are placed as far apart as to position the feet at not quite a right angle to each other. The weight of the body rests at the same time on the heels and on the balls of both feet. The knees are slightly straightened. The upper body is held erect, the chest slightly pushed forward. The shoulders are at an equal level. They are not drawn up. The arms are stretched gently downwards, the elbows pressed moderately forward. The hand touches the upper thigh with fingertips and wrist. The fingers are together. The middle finger lies on the trouser seam, the thumb along the index finger on the inside of the hand. The head is held erect, the chin a little drawn back into the neck. The eyes are directed straight ahead. The muscles are easy and at the same time tensed. Convulsive over-tension of muscles leads to a poor and forced bearing.

3)   Should there be heard the cautionary part of a word of command, the call of a superior or the command *Achtung!* without these being preceded by Attention! the man of course remains still.

4)   'Stand at Ease'! The left foot is moved forward. The man may move, but not speak without permission.

We had the old Kar 98 rifle. Rifle training was followed by training on the light machine-gun (LMG), the 08 Pistol, the machine-pistol, the hand-grenade and the anti-tank rifle. All that was followed by the infantryman's training in combat and field service, and training in close-quarters fighting. No less important was training in the section, the smallest unit, which consisted of the section leader and nine men.

The section leader is leader and first of his section into battle. He is responsible for:

1)   carrying out his combat task,

2)   direction of the light machine-gun fire and, as far as combat allows, the rifle troops,

3)   ensuring that the weapons, ammunition and equipment of his section are ready for combat and are at full strength.

Section training also included the section's method of combat, its behaviour under fire, working its way forward, penetration, taking and holding a position, withdrawing, as well as the group being on reconnaissance service and picket duties.

HDV 130/2a of course also covered training in the platoon and in the company. All that was contained in 670 points. Infantry officer training, however, not only required the knowledge necessary to command a section, a platoon or a company, but also knowledge of the so-called heavy infantry weapons, i.e. the heavy machine-gun, the heavy mortar, the light and heavy infantry guns, and the anti-tank gun. It covered training in horse riding and driving, the latter including driving both horse-drawn and motorised vehicles.

By listing the material it can be seen that we spent most of our service time on the training ground. We began with simply moving around the ground in the respective formation, then to march training in formations of different, slowly increasing lengths, and finally firing practice. All that was preceded by a thorough process of training in firing positions. I proved to be a good shot. I soon found out that my vision in my right eye was not as sharp as that in my left. The eye test we had when we mustered had been a cursory one. It was only much later that I became aware that I had an astigmatism, with a clear decrease in visual sharpness of my right eye as against my left. Meanwhile, after I had successfully tried shooting left-handed, I stuck with it and achieved excellent results. At the exercises at 100m range, standing offhand, and 200m range, lying offhand, I managed to score 30 and 55 respectively, and thus was in the narrow range leading the group.

Firing practice, and the marches that regularly took place on Saturday, stood out from the drill on the parade ground. Firing practice involved bodily relaxation. Marches involved particular bodily exertion. If on the first march, which lasted an hour, we covered only 5km, within a few weeks that was increased in 10km increments to 55km. It all led to the very edge of exhaustion. As proper infantrymen, on the marches we wore footcloths instead of socks, and before the march we smeared our feet with deer tallow so that, provided our boots fitted, blisters or sores hardly ever occurred. Only once did I get so-called pressure points, that is, blisters under the hard skin. They were extremely painful but at least entitled me to sit up on the horse-drawn vehicle that followed behind us.

Everyday life in the barracks began with reveille, soon followed by the duty NCO's (UvD) call 'those detailed to fetch coffee step out'. Before work began, one-and-a-half hours after reveille, morning washing had to be done, beds had to be made expertly and lockers tidied up. Inside work included cleaning weapons, and cleaning barrack blocks. The weekly hour of polishing and patching also took place as part of the daily boot cleaning and occasional uniform cleaning sessions. We pressed the trousers of our walking-out uniform by laying them overnight between the sheet and the straw mattress.

In addition to the field uniform and drill clothing, every man also possessed a walking-out uniform. It was called *Sarasani*, because in actual fact it looked by no means smart, but resembled circus dress. While the field uniform was made of single coarse cloth of a green-grey-brown colour, the walking-out uniform had two different kinds of grey cloth. The jacket was vaguely green, but the trousers were more of a blue tinge. The collar was dark green, the collar patches and those on the forearms were of silver braid trimming.

To that was added the field service cap and, best of all, the white braid, which was the colour of the infantry arm of the service. Apart from its smart and clean appearance, this colour always seemed to me to express the innocence and unpretentiousness for which the infantry was praised. Other colours used were the red of the artillery, the green of the *Gebirgsjäger*, the black of the pioneers, the blue of the medical units, the bright blue of the Panzer units, the citrus yellow of the signals units, the dark yellow of the cavalry and later reconnaissance troops, and the violet of the military chaplains. But none of them could compare with our pure white.

Outside training mainly took place on the large garrison training ground. However, especially for marching, we switched to the friendly, hilly countryside near to, or further away from, Mörchingen. Once we were resting near a large plum orchard that was far away from any village. It gave the *Leutnant* the idea that we should 'take cover' there and stuff our bellies. Some time later, before the wine harvest, our march took us past a field that was planted with vines. Here, too, the lieutenant let us 'take cover' between the furrows. As you see in old pictures of the land of milk and honey, we lay on our backs between two furrows, reaching for the nearly ripe grapes hanging over us, and contentedly ate our fill.

The most pleasant activity, because it was completely different from all the others, we had on Wednesdays. Then, from 2pm to 4pm there was riding, and from 4pm to 6pm driving. In our riding training each one of us had his own horse, mine was the mare 'Orange'. Everyone had to keep a piece of bread from his rations for the horse, to win its trust and to be able to reward it. We learned not to approach the animal from the rear, and how to bridle and saddle it. We also had to muck-out the stalls and brush the horses.

During the course of that training we learned the paces of the horse, the walk, trot, and gallop, and how to control the horse. Finally, in the riding arena we jumped modest obstacles, and performed exercises on horseback. Riding outside was more satisfying than strenuous, especially when, after our first few hours of riding, our behinds were not burning any more. Once, I must have irritated 'Orange' because she bolted with me on the training ground. She slipped into a raging gallop and I could not hold her. After almost a kilometre she had calmed down, but evidently wanted to vex me some more, because she stopped abruptly in her tracks. I had to summon up all my strength not to fly out of the saddle, which is certainly what she intended.

The driving instruction passed off without such difficulties. To drive a horse-drawn vehicle was something we learned in an afternoon, but instruction in driving motor vehicles stretched out over several months. As well as a thorough theoretical and technical training, taken with the aid of an Army service regulation book, a lot of time was spent on the driving itself. We rode motorcycles, motorcycles with sidecars, and drove a medium-weight *Kübelwagen*. On 18 January 1942, that is, a few days after my eighteenth birthday, we received our *Wehrmacht* driving licences.

On Wednesday evenings in the officers' mess there were 'Gentlemen's Evenings'. We officer cadets, in our walking-out uniforms of course, had to take part. Before dinner you would stand about aimlessly in the side rooms of the dining hall. Then the commander of the *Ersatz* Regiment would invite us to take our places.

On the first occasion we were, understandably, somewhat awkward and almost stood in ranks. That led a doctor, whom I later got to know as a very clever man, to the sarcastic remark, 'Ah, the gentlemen have turned up for confirmation'.

We did not always sit together at the end of the table, but were placed individually between officers and thus had to take part in their conversation. If I had not already learned at home how to behave at table, I would have been taught it there. It is true that I had not learned at home that you had, on occasion, to manage with only 40cm space at the table. That had to be done on Christmas Eve, when the wives of the married officers were invited to dine with us and space was tight at the table.

On those occasions, and also on the gentlemen's evenings, music was supplied by a palm court orchestra composed of members of the regimental music corps. It was frowned upon to speak of service matters. That was strictly avoided. On the gentlemen's evenings we were allowed out for longer. We were allowed to stay out after the general lights-out, I think until midnight. The food in the officers' mess was not better than that in the barracks canteen, but was cooked separately. An exception was made at Christmas and New Year, when everyone got a portion of carp or tench. But in addition, there were also *Bratwürstchen* or *Bockwurst* that assuaged our hunger and, together with the potato salad, laid down a good basis for the wine. In the Mörchingen officers' mess you could buy splendid French wine. It was there that I drank my first white and red Bordeaux and Burgundy.

In St Avold there had often been air-raid warnings that mostly lasted from midnight, until the enemy aircraft had left the area of the Reich. For that reason duties were assigned in such a way that, after reveille at 4.30am, they began at 6am. After the meal set for 10.30am, the lunch break lasted until 2pm, so that everyone could catch up the sleep they had lost during the night. There were none of those annoying disturbances in Mörchingen.

Once, in the autumn, we went to Strasbourg and saw the sights of that beautiful city, by then once again in Germany. On the platform of the Minster, from where you got the wide view eastwards into the Black Forest and westwards into the Vosges, Ludwig Popovsky took our photograph. At that time he had attached himself to Helmut Überla from Trautenau. I had become friendly with Hans Alterman from Gottesberg in the Riesengebirge. From Alterman I have a written testimony to our friendship which he wrote for me in the little book *Novellen aus Metz*, which each of us had received from the regimental commander as a Christmas present. 'Either we shall meet in victory or never again', the young man had prophetically written.

A year later, when we passed out of the War College in Dresden, of 'us eleven' comrades there only remained Henschel, Popovsky and I. Fiedler wanted to become an officer of engineers. I later chanced to meet him on Liegnitz station as a *Panzer Leutnant*. I met Bormann at about the same time, in the spring of 1944, in Mährisch-Schönberg. From the summer of 1942 he had had a stiff knee, and without attending War college had, after a long delay, become an officer. Of the others I never heard anything more. As far as my friend Hans Altermann is concerned, I am sure that he was killed in action as early as 1942.

It is time that I described our instructors, who no doubt had been selected for that duty. The *Gefreiter* and senior soldier in our block, Herbert Kräkler, was a candidate for NCO, a small, blond young man from a Silesian village. His place was shortly afterwards taken by *Obergefreiter* Wahle. I met Kräkler in the summer of 1942 at Upolosy when we were both already NCOs and could call each other by the familiar *Du*. A few days later he was killed in action. Wahle was getting on for thirty, and, to judge by his appearance and behaviour, came from a town. The NCO, August Gehle, during the French campaign had suffered a fractured pelvis from a falling tree. Like Wahle, he was a patient, self-controlled instructor who never lost his temper and carried out his duties in an exemplary manner.

Leutnant Riedel came from Bad Rheinerz in the county of Glatz. He was, as he would proudly relate, the son of a worker and had joined the Army after leaving school. He was extraordinarily agile and intelligent. Like Gehle he was a fair-minded superior officer who showed preference to no one and provided us with a thorough training. He, too, gave each of us a little book for Christmas. I corresponded later with Riedel, but do not know what became of him, or of Gehle and Wahle. Once, when I was suffering from bad toothache, I had to visit Riedel in his room before morning duties, to wake him and knock him up to ask permission to be allowed to go on sick parade to the dentist. I was not sure how he would react to being disturbed, and was pleasantly surprised when he gave me permission without question.

The two photographs of our Christmas in barracks show 'us eleven' officer cadets with *Obergefreiter* Wahle in our *Sarasani* jackets. In front of the Christmas tree in the background, there are on the left, some lockers and against the wall, in front of them, a bunk bed. In the foreground is the long table. In the second photograph we are sitting with our tunics off. In front of the darkened window is the big tree, decorated with *lametta* and many burning candles. From the ceiling is hanging the big Advent wreath and on the table, too, some lights are still burning. In front on the left sits Popovsky, beside him Altermann, on the right opposite him Überla, and in front of him is me, with a reflective-questioning expression.

Better than all the service regulations intended for training, instruction and individual study, was the *Reibert*. It was named after its author, Dr.jur.W. Reibert, *Hauptmann* and company commander. A 300-page compendium, it was entitled *Der Dienstunterricht im Heere*, i.e. Service Instruction in the Army. We used the green-bound edition for the men of the *Schützenkompanie*. The *Reibert* was an excellent systematic compendium of all the training material. As well as the introduction for service instruction, it was divided into the sections Patriotism, The Soldier's Profession and its Duties, Sense of Duty, Behaviour of the Soldier, The Army, Anti-Gas Defence, Close-Range Weapons, Weapons and Equipment, Drill, Firing, together with Duties in the Field and Combat. In addition to the oath on the colours, the words of which everyone had to know and repeat as he was sworn in, there were 'The Duties of the German Soldier', about which *Reibert* states: 'The German soldier is expected to know the following articles by heart and word-for-word'. They read:

1)   The *Wehrmacht* bears arms for the German *Volk*. It protects the German Reich and Fatherland, the *Volk*, bound into one in National Socialism, and its living space. The roots of its power lie in a glorious past, in German *Volkstum*, German soil and German labour. Service in the *Wehrmacht* is a service of honour to the German *Volk*.

2)   The honour of the soldier lies in the full and unconditional offering of his person for *Volk* and Fatherland, even unto sacrificing his life.

3)   The highest virtue of the soldier is aggressive courage. This demands toughness and resolve. Cowardice is a disgrace, hesitation is un-soldier like.

4)   Obedience is the foundation of the *Wehrmacht*, trust the foundation of obedience. Soldierly leadership rests on delight in taking responsibility, on superior ability and tireless care.

5)   Great achievements in war and peace can only come about in the unshakeable fighting community of leader and troops.

6)   Fighting community demands comradeship. Comradeship is particularly proven in need and danger.

7)   Self-possessed and yet modest, upright and true, God-fearing and truthful, discreet and incorruptible, the soldier should be to the entire *Volk* a model of manly strength. Only achievements justify pride.

8)   His greatest reward and greatest happiness is found by the soldier in the consciousness of duty joyfully fulfilled. Character and achievement are the hallmarks of his way and of his worth.

Those 'duties' hark back in their essentials to the Imperial Army and probably to still older regulations. Millions of soldiers in both World Wars modelled themselves on those regulations. In the Second World War soldiers followed their guidelines right to the bitter end. For those born after those wars it is hard to comprehend. But for me and my comrades, who willingly submitted ourselves to those duties, with all the idealism of youth, they were a kind of profession of faith.

To give an example of the sterling quality and thoroughness of the *Reibert*, I will quote from the General Principles of the Barracks, Room and Locker Regulations:

Anyone who shouts, howls and engages in tussles in quarters offends against discipline and order. Decorous singing is permitted, if barrack block comrades agree. Popular songs, hackneyed old hits, and songs of an obscene nature, are not a suitable part of a soldier's singing repertoire. In the barrack block, i.e. the soldier's home, scrupulous order and cleanliness is to be paramount at all times. The tone adopted among the block inmates should be comradely so that they can get along well with each other. Lunch is a communal meal both because of technical necessity, for reasons of military order and to cultivate comradeship. For meals the soldier will appear with clean hands, clean fingernails, and with his hair combed. At table he will sit upright, will not unnecessarily rattle about with the crockery, will be decorous, and refrain from unsuitable chatter.

There are many other examples that could be added. However, it may become clear why, in our day, the *Wehrmacht* was spoken of as the 'school of the nation'. In that school, even the 'simple man of the people' learned a lot that he had not learned from either his parents or his teachers.

At the end of 1986, 45 years on, when I read the letters that I wrote to my family from St Avold and Mörchingen, during that first period as a soldier, I was astonished by the dispassion and distance with which I regarded the business of the

Army, although I was right in the middle of it. In all conscience I had shrugged everything off. To have to learn hard lessons, to go through troubles and exertions, to have the occasional moments of harassment had never become too much for me. In any event, neither I nor my officer cadet comrades had ever been 'reduced to tears'. That was something about which the regimental commander had once asked at the gentlemen's evening. He no doubt was speaking from personal experience as he thought of his own time as a cadet. Certainly the cadets of the Imperial Army, about whom such stories were told, had been much younger. For them the seriousness of military life had begun when they were only ten years old.

In my first letter to my Mother and sisters I complained that 'we have really very little time' and that we officer cadets were given the 'most impossible things to do'. Thus, for instance, 'would you believe it', I had been ordered by the UvD to darn his leather gloves. Nevertheless, I completed it to his total satisfaction. On 4 August 1941 I had to travel to Metz to the Reserve Military Hospital for a specialist medical examination of my heart. At my recruitment medical, the unit MO diagnosed a 'serious' defect. In Metz it proved, 'thank God, to be a completely wrong diagnosis'. Otherwise I would have been sent home, which would have been a big disappointment. After only ten days we were having firing practice for the first time.

'Then was our swearing-in, a ceremonial occasion. In the afternoon we had no duties and we had our first trip out, it is true, with our NCO and *Obergefreiter*. But it was quite nice. We gorged ourselves at a confectioner's. For once at least we were full again. Otherwise we are always hungry. Yesterday we got our pay books and identity tags'. To Father I reported on 25 August that 'today we had been flushed out, quick marched with machine-gun and gas mask, and then over the 2.5m high scaling wall'. But still, 'I don't let it get me down, you needn't worry. In the group there's a lot to laugh about, and you get through everything much easier with humour than with idealism'.

On 4 September I told Mother of a stay in sick quarters. The cause was angina, from which I had suffered a lot in my youth. In that letter I was longing for my schooldays, but in the next sentence went on that 'we all really think that we've never had any other life than the one we have now in the military. Our time as civilians is only a beautiful dream. For all that we're happy and contented'. In the letter of 18 September to my Mother, I reported that 'in the last two days we have had no rest at all at night. The day before yesterday we had night exercises until 12.30am, then straight into the air-raid shelter until 2.30am. Yesterday was Gentlemen's Evening again, very jolly, then air-raid shelter again until 2am. A Gentlemen's Evening like that', I said, 'was as good as a rest, despite the tightness of space, especially the tightness of my tunic. I sat at table with the Colonel, but fortunately he left about 10pm. Then things got going. You get used to drinking. Today I can feel no ill effects at all'.

At the beginning of October, the recruits arrived who were born in 1922. They had been called up normally. For us officer cadets, who had the so-called inspection behind us, it meant that we had reached the lowest rung on the military ladder. We were assigned as block seniors and during the mornings served as assistant instructors. My nine men, all but two, were Silesian farm lads. In my letter of 18 October I answered Mother's question as to how I was feeling to be block senior. 'It was very nice', I said, 'the work was quiet and we didn't have to do any more lousy jobs. On the other hand, we didn't have any more free time for ourselves – particularly because we needed to attend the officer's mess very often'. We had to go to the Gentlemen's Evening there three evenings a week, as well as having to have lunch there on Saturdays and Sundays. At another level that made a change. Among the older officers who frequented the mess was the leading baritone of the Breslau Opera. The palm court orchestra that sometimes played in the evenings, was conducted by the Opera's first violin.

At the end of October I told Mother and Rudi of my success in pistol-shooting, that our training work was indeed easier, but not our other work. Part of that meant we had to run the obstacle course with the heavy machine-gun, the mortar, and each of us carrying 50lb weight. I also told them about essay subjects. We had to write the essays in the evenings we were not at the officers' mess. The theme, 'Loyalty is the very marrow of honour,' is something I could still write about today, unlike the question 'Why must Russia lose the war?' I give an account of the swearing-in of the recruits as a ceremonial occasion in which the regimental music corps participated. They played, among other things, the chorale *Wir treten zum Beten vor Gott, den Gerechten*, 'We Come to Pray before God the Just One', the so-called Dutch Prayer of Thanks. In a letter of 30 October to Lieserl, who was seven at the time, I wrote that snow had fallen overnight, but that I was sorry I couldn't go sledging with her, but on the other hand had to be glad if no-one was going sledging with me.

I do not remember whether at the time we actually suffered from hunger, even if I often wrote about hunger and tiredness. But it was no wonder. The unaccustomed physical strains reached the very limits of what we could tolerate. Others, thank God not me, experienced symptoms of exhaustion such as nose bleeds. The comradeship among us eleven was good, even if at first we two Austrians and the two Sudeten Germans did not feel really very comfortable together. That was why I wrote, with delight, 'now and then I meet a fellow-countryman', such as, a man from Waidhofen who had studied with our Professor Höchtl.

By the middle of January 1942 we had completed the first stage of our training, and after a successful 'inspection' we were promoted to *Gefreiter*. Then, too, came the longed-for leave, during which an event occurred that threatened to derail my plans. Literally overnight I got severe pains in the region of my appendix which required that I was admitted immediately into the Stockerau civilian hospital. In the middle of the night the consultant had to be fetched. After palpating my abdomen, to no little horror on my part, he uttered the words, 'It's too late'. In fact, the appendix had perforated, but an infection had developed which had to be cured before there was any question of an operation. I had to remain in hospital for some weeks.

On the day after I was admitted I was laid down in a small room. The only other patient there I recognised as my schoolmate, Ewald Henk. A few days previously – I had found out from Herta – he had attempted suicide because of an unhappy love affair. The object of his affections was 'Mausi' Grundschober, a really striking girl who, however, had not yielded to his advances. Standing in front of a mirror in order to give particularly drastic form and experience to the scene, Ewald shot himself through the body with a 6.35mm Flobert rifle. But he had set the barrel muzzle too low with the result that he shot himself in the left lung and spleen. After the shot he dropped the rifle and staggered wailing into the family living room where he cried: 'Help me, I have shot myself.'

My great worry was that the ill-timed appendix would throw me completely off course or else delay my training. Only at the end of March did I arrive back with mixed feelings in Mörchingen, just in time to be able to spend a few days with my comrades before they left for the field. A farewell photo shows us on the steps in front of a door in the barracks building, crowding round our Lieutenant Riedl, our NCO Gehle and *Obergefreiter* Wahle. For the farewell, which meant the end of our period of training, we received presents from the *Leutnant*. For me he had selected a small volume of poetry, *Volk vor Gott*. This showed that he had not only recognised the religious bent instilled in me by my parents, but that he also admired it. The dedication harked back to the hard period of training and also contained a maxim for my future:

'Dear Scheiderbauer. Life brings us many hardships, but it is only in these that we show our strength. We overcome! We never give up! The reward will be ours!' The little book contains -

Gebet in höchster Not, a prayer when things are at their worst, by Ricarda Huch; *Gebet der Knechte und Mägde*, a prayer of the Lads and Lasses, by Richard Billinger; *Die innere Gestalt*, a prayer, 'The Inner Form', by Josef Weinheber; *Geistiches Lied*, a 'Song of the Spirit' by Hermann Claudius; *Zuflucht*, a 'Refuge' by Ina Seidl; *Haussegen des deutschen Bauern*, 'The German Farmer's Blessing on His House' by Paula Grogger, and Jochen Klepper's *Neujahrslied*, a 'New Year's Song'. Hermann Stehr, Heinrich Zillich, Walter Flex, Bergengrün and Rilke, Agnes Nigl and Rudolf Alexander Schröder with his *Lobgesang*, a Song of Praise, were among the authors. The last page contained the prophetic dedication of my friend Hans Altermann that I have already mentioned. 'Either we shall meet again in victory – or never again! Always, your friend Hans'.

My comrades' 'assignment', the term by which it was known to us, was followed by dreary weeks for me. I was only fit for indoor duties and was employed as recruit *Gefreiter* in the 2nd Company of Infantry *Ersatz* Battalion 461, in the neighbouring barracks. The recruits, who reported on 1 April, were all from the eastern part of Upper Silesia, aged from thirty to thirty-five years, and were all members of the so-called *Volksgruppen* 2 and 3. According to that system of classification, which still covered the Reich Germans (*Volksgruppe* 1) and the Poles (*Volksgruppe* 4), there were those who professed to be German or who were still classified as Germans.

Two of these I can still see. One was a slim, sensitive cobbler Slavik, from Ornontowitz near Gleiwitz. The other was a small, black-haired and round-headed *Hilfsarbeiter* Stanitzek from Hindenburg. Slavik used to tell of his craft and how he had made orthopaedic footwear but also had made riding boots for Polish officers. He told us that he had not long been married. He had taken a kind of vow never to take off his wedding ring, and spoke of his marriage in a way that impressed me. But he was killed in Russia when he went into action for the first time. Stanitzek was a true Pjerun. I remember him as a *Schweik* character. He taught me how to drink 96% proof vodka, that is, trickled on to a sugar cube!

I then had more time for myself, and went into the officers' mess as I had before. Jochen Fiedler, who had a wireless set, left it behind for me. After four weeks I had to report to the medical officer, and at the beginning of May was sent to the reserve military hospital in Metz. For a few more days I was 'under observation'. Indoor duties such as peeling potatoes, in comparison with my previous duties, I found demeaning. If they were not on the agenda, we could go out and look around the town. I went for walks in the parks by the Moselle and even went to a concert. One afternoon I had been in a coffee-house and got into conversation with Wolfgang Schneiderhahn, the young leader of the Vienna Philharmonic. That evening he was playing Beethoven's Violin Concerto. The German cultural life in Metz was mostly provided by artists from Vienna. Later I found out that, at that time, people like Josef Meinrad were engaged in the theatre in Metz.

On 10 May I was operated on and after about a fortnight discharged back to Mörchingen. Of my fellow-patients I remember a *Feldwebel* who had a sliver of bone from his lower thigh transplanted into his lower arm in order to make the arm more mobile. The *Feldwebel* was a teacher and had an education to match. He played chess, and so we were able to pass the time playing chess and in conversation. Nevertheless, I was impatient, and would not accept my fate. I would much rather 'be in Russia in the worst muck', as I wrote to Mother. She and Aunt Lotte, she said, had 'little natural tendency or talent to be mothers of German heroes'. However, my letters spoke of little else. There was not even loving raillery, but a few reproaches that she had not written. It was rather a restrained kind of tenderness with frequent assurances that I was thinking a lot of her and my sisters and was 'her thankful son'.

In one Christmas present, the little book *Wie die Pflicht es befahl*, 'As Duty Commanded, Words from our War Poets', the editor's foreword states that "in this struggle all Germans are animated by a single belief. It is belief in the mission of the *Führer* and in the eternal nature of the *Reich*. There is a single certainty that Germany shall live, even if we must die". To the quotations from works of the war poets Walter Flex, Ernst Jünger, Baumelberg and Zöberlein, etc. was added the then well-known poem *An die Mutter* by a certain Irmgard Grosch. Its last verse runs:

If I fall, Mother, you must bear it,
and your pride will overcome your pain,
for you were allowed to bring a sacrifice
to him whom we mean when we speak the word Germany.

Such proud mourning, as was displayed in many death announcements at that time, would certainly have been beyond my Mother. I am also unable to say how she took the news of the death of my brother. He was killed in action, as late as April 1945. But the poem had little effect on me. Naturally its heroic tone, all the more so in the poetic art form, appealed to me. But the thought that it could be I who was being mourned like that did not occur to me. I never suffered from premonitions of death, but carried the conviction that it would never happen to me. I was even then looking forward with confidence to the longed-for test of the front, and left for the field with a light heart.

The Reich was in danger. It was not Germany that had declared war on England and France, but they that had declared war on Germany. But, as far as the Soviet Union was concerned, there was no doubt about what the Reich government had written, in its declaration of war, to the Soviet government: 'The German *Volk* is conscious that it is called to save the whole civilised world from the deadly dangers of Bolshevism, and to lay the way open for a true process of social advancement in Europe'. That extract from the declaration was printed in small print on the upper edge of many field postcards. Who among us could have doubted the truth of what was said there? Who could have proved it to be wrong?

Part II

From Raw Recruit to Old Hand

2

July-September 1942: First actions

Join Regiment 150km from Moscow; Officer Cadet; in action against the Russians

From 15 October 1942 *Infanterieregiment 7* was a *Grenadierregiment,* a unit in the Prussian tradition. It served in the First World War as *Grenadierregiment König Friedrich Wilhelm II (1. Schlesisches)* Nr 10. After reorganisation and re-formation it had participated from 1935 to 1939 as *Infanterieregiment 7* in the campaign in Poland. In 1939 and 1940 it fought in the campaign in the West. Within the unit of the 28th *Infanteriedivision,* to which it had belonged since the beginning of the war, it was prepared for the attack on the Soviet Union in the Suwalky sector in East Prussia.

It served in the following actions in Russia, 1941-42:

- 22-27 June 1941: breakthrough of the 'Bunker Line'

- 29 June-9 July 1941: Bialystok-Minsk encirclement battle

- 10 July-9 August 1941: advance and fighting at Smolensk

- 10 August-1 October 1941: defensive fighting on the Popij, before and around Jarzewo

- 2-14 October 1941: the Vyazma battle

- 15 October-18 November 1941: the Regiment was released from the 28th *Infanteriedivision* and placed under the command of the 252nd *Infanteriedivision*

- 19 November-4 December 1941: the attack on Moscow

- 5 December 1941-15 January 1942: retrograde movements into the *Rosa-Stellung* and trench fighting

- 16-25 January 1942: the *Winterreise,* or the winter journey (Translator's note - the term *Winterreise* ironically echoes the 19th century poet Heinrich Heine's sequence of poems under the same title, and also Franz Schubert's subsequent musical arrangement of Heine's poems)

- 26 January-28 February 1942: widespread defensive fighting to the east of Gschatsk.

It was in the *Gschatsk-Stellung,* some 150km west-south-west of Moscow, that I joined the regiment. On 2 July, in St Avold, I had begun my journey which, as a straggler following my comrades, I had to make on my own. The journey passed through Berlin and Warsaw. At first I was in trains carrying men back to the front from leave. But from Warsaw to Smolensk through West Prussia, Kovno, Vilna, Dünaburg, Polotzk, Vitebsk, I was in an empty hospital train. On 4 July I sent to my Mother and sisters 'very best wishes from the German-Russian frontier'. From Vyazma I wrote on 8 July that I was 'very impressed' by the Russian landscape and by what I had seen on the journey, and that I was hoping to arrive at my unit 'the day after tomorrow'.

At last, on 10 July, I wrote my first letter as a 'sender', with field post number 17638 C, from the 6th Company of *Infanterieregiment 7*. From Gschatsk onwards, to which goods trains were travelling, I had to march with my knapsack. At the regimental command post the commander 'even shook my hand to welcome me'. Then there was a further march via the battalion command post to the company, which was commanded by *Oberleutnant* Beyer. I was immediately assigned my post as *MG-Schütze*, Machine-Gunner 1. The company had just been resting for some days in the woods close to the regimental command post and the baggage-train village of Shabino. We were to go back up the line the following night and relieve another company. As the 7th Company was being relieved I met Jochen Fiedler and his section leader Kräkler, our block seniors from St Avold. Fiedler said that of 'the eleven' of us only six were with *Infanterieregiment 7*, the others had joined *Infanterieregiment* 232 or 235.

The relief had proceeded smoothly so that the sections, at intervals of several minutes, and of course in single file, marched away, to avoid making any noise and alerting the enemy. In the trenches during the day it was more or less quiet. The Russians fired off some shells only now and then and those were only of light calibre. By contrast, during the night the Russians did not trust the calm. So the nights were dominated by a perpetual, blind cacophony of explosions. At midnight, when the summer night was at its darkest, for the first time I went alone on sentry duty. Somewhere else and under other circumstances I might have thought of Lenau's night, 'whose dark eye was resting on me, solemn, gentle, dreamy and unfathomably sweet' (translator's note: Nikolaus Lenau, German lyric poet, 1802-50).

But then I had a redoubled sense of loneliness. I did not know my way about the positions, which were strange to me, and I had not yet seen them in daylight. I did not know where the enemy was, and could only guess where my fellow-sentries were. I only knew the way from the sentry-post to the bunker. For a short time I was overcome by a feeling of being deserted. It seemed to bode ill for my probation at the front that the company 'sarge', immediately after I arrived in the baggage-train village, had ordered that I get my hair cut. Then, at the field church service in the full glare of the sun, when I was wearing my *Stahlhelm*, I had felt ill. I felt completely alone. I had no view in the direction of the enemy, since our trenches were behind an incline. The only thing that happened during those first two hours on sentry duty was the tour of inspection by the company commander. I scarcely heard his approach. Eyes directed forward, I quietly made the regulation report: 'Nothing unusual to report'.

It was only on 14 July that I had to transfer into the first platoon of the company, to take over the section of a NCO who was going on leave. A week or so later we officer cadets were assembled in Shabino, near to the regimental command post. We had to take yet one more 'revision course' before our promotion to NCO. That was expected on 1 August. The course was given by *Oberleutnant* Steiff, the then regimental adjutant. (I met him again in 1975 in Vienna, where, as a *Brigadegeneral* in the German *Bundeswehr,* he was taking part in the negotiations which dragged on for years concerning bilateral reduction of forces in Europe). As far as we could see, the reason for the course was that the regimental commander wanted to get an idea of our theoretical knowledge and capabilities.

On 1 August I was proud to tell my Mother and sisters that, together with the five other officer cadets, I had been promoted to *Fahnenjunkerunteroffizier,* Officer Cadet NCO. On that occasion three of them received the EK II, Iron Cross 2nd Class. I was very pleased because 'my appendix didn't stop me'. Because I was a few days short of the minimum 2 months' probation period at the front, in actual fact I should not have been allowed the promotion. However, the commander, *Oberstleutnant* von Eisenhart-Rothe, a gaunt gentleman with the elegance of a cavalryman, and evidently of a similar elegance in thinking, took the responsibility upon himself. Then, I wrote to my Mother, I had a salary, and the business of 'public assistance for the children' was at an end.

The previous day we sat together and wrote to our nearest and dearest 'with liquor and cigars'. The 'official' celebration of our promotion, with the commander and some officers from the regimental Staff, was planned for the evening. Our celebration was part of it, because after the commander had left, *Oberleutnant* Roy, the commander of the 13th *Infanteriegeschütz* Company, took over the presidency of the Corona and we moved up into so-called 'increased drinking'. (I met Roy, who, despite his twenty-five years, even back then had a bald patch, at the Division reunion in Stuttgart. While reminding him of that evening in Shabino, I told him that it was he I had to thank for getting drunk worse than I ever had in my life.) It happened that Roy, himself a drinker of note, ordered us officer cadets to drink up in turn.

Finally, 'to conclude the evening', he got me to gulp down within five minutes all the drink remaining in the glasses on the table. I managed it, too, under the astonished eyes of my comrades. But after a while I had to be taken back to my quarters while being held up on both sides. But I must not have been able to manage to stay there for the rest of the night, because towards morning I found myself lying in the ferns beside the cottage in which we had our quarters. That was the end of the promotion celebrations. It was the next day, when I was already back with my company, before I got over the hangover.

I then took over the 8th section of the company again. On a piece of paper I had written down for myself the names, dates of birth, occupations and addresses of my men. The slip of paper I had folded twice and placed in my field hymn book. That little book, 5 x 7.5cm in size and ½cm thick, was an Army regulation (No. 371), in a Protestant and a Catholic edition. It contained, in addition to the professional duties of the German soldier, the oath before the colours, and also extracts from the war letters of German soldiers killed in action. It had prayers beginning with the Our Father to the prayers *In Gefahr,* In danger, and *In der Todesstunde,* At the Hour of Death, for the dying. There were prayers for burials, chorales and hymns, and finally Bible texts designated as 'essential sayings'.

My men were -

Füsilier Werner Mutz, born 30 April 1923 in Stolp (Pomerania), a shopkeeper in Stolp,

Gefreiter Helmut Budewizk, born on 4 March 1922 in Hamburg, a student
in Berlin-Steglitz,

Gefreiter Albert Vickendey, born on 3 April 1913 in Rickensdorf, *Kreis*
Helmstedt (Brunswick), blacksmith in Brunswick,

Gewehrschütze 1: Obergefreiter Anton Neumann, born on 11 December
1910 in Himmelwitz, Upper Silesia, tailor in Himmelwitz,

Gewehrschütze 2: Füsilier Wladimir Stamer, born on 26 July 1909 in
Sosnowitz, Upper Silesia, baker's assistant in Gleiwitz,

Gewehrschütze 3: Füsilier Otto Beer, born on 2 December in Süptitz, *Kreis*
Torgau, agricultural worker in Süptitz.

My deputy section leader was

Obergefreiter Rudolf Iwanek, born 20 October 1919 in Vienna, automobile
painter in Vienna.

I can see the faces of almost all those men in my mind's eye, as I read their
names, even though I have never seen any of them since. I knew that Mutz was
killed in action a few days later, and that Budewizk, a happy lad with a friendly face,
was posted missing.

Though I had reported from my post on sentry duty 'nothing unusual to report' to the company commander, the situation for the battalion suddenly changed
drastically. I quote from the regimental history:

Of the fighting in which individual units were involved with divisions other
than their own, the action of II./*Infanterieregiment* 7 (Vielhauer), parts of *Pan-
zer-Jäger Abteilung* 252, 14./*Infanterieregiment* 7, 14./*Infanterieregiment* 461
under *Oberst* Karst as *Kampfgruppe* leader should be mentioned. The alarm was
sounded on 12 August 1942.

Some 50km south of Gshatsk, in the region of the 3rd *Panzer-Armee*, and
the area of IX *Armeekorps* and XX *Armeekorps*, the Soviets had succeeded in
breaking into the positions of the divisions. They were the 183rd
Infanteriedivision and the 292nd *Infanteriedivision*. Especially in the area of the
183rd *Infanteriedivision*, the Russians had succeeded in penetrating deep into
the main combat area. A breakthrough threatened.

The *Kampfgruppe* was loaded on lorries and driven up to the main highway
leading south from Gshatsk. They were unloaded in Upolosy and placed under
the command of the 292nd *Infanteriedivision*. Marching up beside the road,
partly on 'corduroy' roads, the scattered II./*Infanterieregiment* 7 reached
Ssilenki to take a rest. A supply dump that was being dismantled served to
strengthen the unit. Hordes of Army baggage handlers were fleeing back to the
rear, parts of the baggage-train and flak units were getting ready to flee. All of
that characterised the situation. Although it all reeked of retreat in disorder, the
Kampfgruppe was in the kind of mood to advance. In a wood near Ssawinki west
of the highway, positions were taken up facing south.

To the east of the highway II./*Infanterieregiment* 131 had taken up position. That battalion, too, was placed under the command of *Kampfgruppe*
Karst. Further to the east was a gap up to II./*Infanterieregiment* 351. It appeared
that eastwards there was a coherent front, but the situation to the west of the positions of II./*Infanterieregiment* 7 was completely unclear. There the 183rd
Infanterieregiment appeared to have been broken through. Scarcely had II./
Infanterieregiment 7 hastily dug into the woodland, at about 8pm on 14 August

1942, than the enemy armoured attack began. It was beaten back with bloody casualties.

Further armoured attacks followed in which it was mostly only individual tanks that succeeded in breaking the main line of resistance. The few anti-tank weapons did not succeed in dispatching the tanks that had broken through, so the infantry had to do it at close range. After an unquiet night, on 15 August, at 6.15am the Soviets again attacked with armour and infantry. With the energetic support of the artillery, it was possible to repulse all enemy attacks. But to the west of the position the Soviets had succeeded in pushing forward through a gap towards Besmino. By striking out widely, they encircled II./ *Infanterieregiment 7*. With *Kampfgruppe* Karst taking up a position of all-round defence, it was possible to block the highway successfully further on.

On 17 August heavy fighting was taking place around the village of Ssilenki, while the 292nd *Infanteriedivision* withdrew to a line further to the north. Seriously combat-weary, completely soaked, with only cold rations, the troops were partly broken through in a very strong armoured attack. They had to make a fighting withdrawal on to the Upolosy high ground. As a result Upolosy itself was drawn in to the bridgehead position. West of Upolosy the enemy had broken through at Popowka. That was *Infanterieregiment* 19. One company of *Panzer-Abteilung* 18 was placed under the command of *Kampfgruppe* Karst and supported the infantry.

A Stuka attack in the early morning of 18 August, on Cholmino and the wooded territory to the south-east of Upolosy, won some more breathing space. Enemy armour, assembled immediately south of Cholmino, was shattered by artillery fire. The gap to the west of *Kampfgruppe* Karst still yawned. On the eastern wing *Feld-Ersatz-Bataillon* 292, then under the command of the *Kampfgruppe*, maintained the connection. Renewed enemy attempts to assemble armour were successfully opposed by the artillery. But it was not possible to prevent Soviet infantry, with armour, from advancing to the west of Upolosy northwards across the Worja. The enemy seemed from this point to have shifted the emphasis of their attack from the east, against 292nd *Infanteriedivision*. They moved opposite the sector held by *Kampfgruppe* Karst and further westwards.

The intervention of *Infanterieregiment* 82 on 20 August, and the arrival of *Infanterieregiment* 282, had a relieving effect on the *Kampfgruppe*. On 24 August it was possible to repulse a large-scale enemy attack on the Upolosy sector. But further to the west the enemy succeeded in taking Bekrino and Schatescha. On 1 September *Oberst* Karst was decorated with the Knight's Cross, for personal gallantry in counter-attacking. On 2 September fresh enemy attacks took place against the Upolosy bridgehead. But they were all repulsed. Only on 6 September were orders executed for the planned evacuation of that position. *Bataillon Vielhauer* returned to the Division with a combat strength of about 80 men. A small barracks at *Waldlager Nord* was sufficient to provide accommodation for that little band.

My personal experience was more exciting than the picture painted by the dry report from the regimental history. During the night the battalion was relieved from its position and removed from the Division's Field Reserve. I handed over my section sector and the stocks of ammunition, hand-grenades, and machine-gun belts. We thought it was a relief that those supplies did not need to be dragged along. I marched off with the section in the direction of the assembly area to which we had been ordered.

Company after company joined us on the route. Soon the whole battalion was on the march with us. We went in line, one behind the other at long intervals in order to invite as few casualties as possible in the event that we were attacked from the air, or fired on. From Shabino, the baggage-train village, the battalion went to Gschatsk, to the camp in the woods some kilometres north of the town. In the summer of 1941 that camp had served as headquarters to the Russian Supreme Commander, Central Sector, Marshal Timoshenko.

Hauptfeldwebel Melin, the 'sarge', a strict, self-possessed man, had his cross with the drivers, not only those of the horse-drawn vehicles. In a mighty voice he gave out his orders. In pure Silesian, one of them asked, 'Wot 'ave ah for't tek, *Herr Hauptfel?*' And the *Hauptfeldwebel* replied, 'Tek 't' Poischou', by which he meant a captured French Peugeot lorry. Several ways led to Gschatsk. The one that went via Staroje was the furthest, but was better for the vehicles and the Peugeot. We followed the route that had more 'corduroy' roads and was therefore better. But even so, to the accompaniment of dreadful cursing, horses and motor vehicles had to be heaved out of the sticky mud.

On the way it was passed from man to man that we had set off as Army Reserve and should be getting some rest. I believed it, the old hands did not. On 23 August 1942, in the brightness of the dawn morning, we arrived in the camp in the woods and settled ourselves down in the barracks. I slept for some hours. Towards noon there was something to eat and afterwards there was a front-line film show. While the film *Der grosse Schatten*, 'The Great Shadow', was still running, the Battalion Adjutant shouted 'Alert!' Barely five minutes later the battalion was standing ready to march. When the lorries of an Army mobile column arrived we were immediately loaded up. We were told that the Russians had broken through at Juchnow and that we were to be thrown in to the gap created by that move.

The journey through the bare countryside, only here and there crossed by bushes and woods, was not exactly pleasant. We travelled standing, squatting, or sitting on machine-gun boxes. The 'oldies' who had taken part in the advance and the winter retreat, said that it was no picnic which awaited us. We younger ones, 'dropped in the shit', again, did indeed feel the tension hanging over everyone. It could be read in the expressions of the officers. But it was more with curiosity and interest than with fear that we looked forward to the things that this 'fire brigade' action would bring.

Outside the village of Saawinki, some thirty kilometres north-west of Medyn, we were unloaded. Immediately, a security line was formed in platoon strength in the direction of the enemy. I lay with my section beside the road that led to the enemy. Somewhere in front there were still supposed to be German troops. No-one knew any more. A motorcycle with sidecar drove up from behind us. A strange officer got out. To my report he said, sounding surprised, ' *Infanterieregiment* 7! My God, that's an active regiment!' To my ears it sounded as if he had determined that from then nothing else could happen and that it was a dead certainty that the Russian breakthrough would be cleaned up.

Just as we had hastily dug in, I was taken by a runner to the battalion commander. He ordered me, and the section, to carry out a reconnaissance patrol into the woods that lay about two kilometres in front of us. The object was to find out if they were occupied by the enemy. It was my first reconnaissance patrol. It was the real thing, the active beginning of my probation at the front. On the successful completion of this depended my whole life's ambition! I instructed the men and we set off.

The first signs of dusk were just becoming noticeable when we reached the woodland. We went in line, spaced widely apart, but could see no trace of the enemy. We crossed a tongue of woodland, while I, as I had learned during training, tracked our direction of march with a compass. Finally, we marched in a long curve leftwards as far as the road and turned back. Halfway the battalion met us. In the meantime they had been ordered to take up positions in front of the wood facing the enemy. The tongue of woodland we had just crossed was the edge of a larger forest that stretched over to the right. It offered the Russians a good opportunity to take us unopposed in the rear. An attempt was then made to counter the danger by having the 7th Company take up position almost at right angles to the forward-deployed 5th and 6th Companies. We would provide cover for the battalion from the direction of the wood.

To my disappointment, my section was held in reserve. We had to dig in again, but on fairly open ground. By that time night had fallen and it seemed to me that we would not be staying in that position for very long. I had the men dig only moderately deep foxholes, just deep enough to be able to snatch some hours' sleep in them with adequate protection against shell splinters. The foxhole I had myself dug barely reached to my knees, so that my body, lying on bushes as a kind of bedding, and covered in the same way, did not protrude above the level of the ground. Within moments there crept over me the uncomfortable thought that I was lying in a coffin.

Night passed and gave way to morning. The enemy, it was said, were preparing to attack. From my 'coffin' I watched uneasily as, to the right of the sector of the 7th Company, 300m to 400m away, individual brown figures, at intervals of a minute or so, were jumping across a small clearing between covering undergrowth. To judge from the direction in which they were moving, they were evidently trying to get into the tongue of woodland lying to the battalion's rear. The Russians were demonstrating their well-tried tactic of 'trickling through'. You could work out how long it would take a company or still larger units to have gathered in the wood behind us. Those movements had been reported to the battalion.

Then the orders I had expected reached me. With my section, I had to take up position at the extreme wing of the 7th Company, facing west, in thick woodland. There was virtually no field of fire. In places it was only five to ten metres. On the left I was beside the section led by Kräkler, our old block senior. On the right there were no neighbours at all. When Kräkler and I saw each other neither of us thought of our time together being polished up into soldiers. It is true, it was a time that had not been as much an effort for him as it had for me. We just shook hands and said, as if with one voice, 'Eh, lad, what a bloody mess!'

Once again it was the old story of digging holes. After we had finished it began to rain. Thin, continuous streams of rain trickled down from the sky. Sooner or later it would have soaked us to the skin. Of the enemy there was nothing more to be heard. We could only suspect that they must be somewhere 'in front' of us in the wood, in considerable numbers. Wrapped in branches and tarpaulins we tried to protect ourselves from the penetrating rain that fell even more heavily. Soon water began to gather in the foxholes. Hours passed. Still there was no end to the rain. The sound of the rain and the wind, and the darkness of night as it began to fall, could almost make us forget that we were on the front line and had to watch out for an enemy. After I had assigned the watch I tried, as I sat on the hollow side of my *Stahlhelm* in the puddles in my foxhole, to find some degree of comfort.

I was shaken out of my chilly doze when the order came to take two men on a reconnaissance patrol in the wood. I had to find where the Russians were. It seemed pointless to me. The rain was getting even heavier. There was complete darkness. It was already midnight. I considered the task to be well-nigh impossible. I would either find out nothing at all or possibly run right through the foxholes that the Russians had dug for themselves. I could lose my way, despite the compass, or even fall into a Russian foxhole unawares. In any of those cases the reconnaissance I was ordered to carry out would show no satisfactory result. I chose two volunteers and we set off. It was so dark that from time to time each of us had to keep hold of the other so as not to get separated. Again and again we would stop, and crouch down to listen. The darkness of the wood and the crackling rain did not allow us to hear or to see anything. With my machine-pistol cocked I felt my way, and crept forwards, my finger on the trigger, always expecting to be fired on suddenly out of the darkness, or to bump into a Russian, or at least a tree.

Then, in a clearing, the existence of which was more to be sensed than seen, there was a sound that did not fit in with the 'symphony' of the storm. We dropped straight to the ground and saw a section of Russians, six or eight men, cross the clearing. I saw their silhouettes, the contours of the plain, old-style Russian helmets outlined against the sky. They came quite close to us, went past, and were swallowed up in the darkness. My two men, experienced *Obergefreiters,* did not think of giving themselves away. As for me, however, my heart stood still. I held my breath and pressed the trigger. The bolt of the machine-pistol shot forward with a crack, but no shot was fired. There was a blockage. Despite that mishap, nothing happened. In the wind and rain the Russians had heard nothing! We turned round and, with the help of the compass, searching and feeling our way, we reached our positions. I reported our observations.

At about 1.30am on 15 August 1942, the kitchen arrived after almost two days. It brought cold bean soup that had gone sour. Even so it was gulped down ravenously. In the foxhole, under the dripping tarpaulin, I dismantled the machine-pistol by the light of a tallow candle, and cleaned it with clammy, wet fingers. Sand and water had caused the blockage during the reconnaissance patrol.

In the open country it should have become light soon after midnight, but in the wood nothing could be seen of the dawning day. Only towards 3am did the coming day show itself. At the same time men's voices could be heard from the direction of the enemy. They indicated that the enemy were pushing forward. By means of loud shouts the Russians ensured that they kept together. They came nearer and nearer. We had to let them approach to within 10m of us because we could not see them sooner. Once again I went from foxhole to foxhole and gave instructions, especially to the leading machine-gunner. Both he and I were facing our first real battle. The young Pomeranian had arrived a few days before with the replacements. It was the first time since the beginning of the Russian campaign that, for the Silesian regiment, the replacements did not come from Silesia. The Russian voices became louder. There was the crack of branches. They must already have come to within fifty metres of us. Meanwhile, we stood in our foxholes, and stared into the undergrowth out of which they had to appear.

There they were – at last! The place was heaving with brown figures! The wood seemed to be spitting them out. To judge by the direction of their bodies and their eyes, they intended to push by obliquely on the right. We fired on them from the flank. The machine-gunner was scattering the first bursts of fire from his weapon. In what direction was he firing? He didn't seem to be hitting anything, because I saw no Russians falling. But he had to be hitting them, they were no more than ten paces away! This time my machine-pistol did not misfire. But I caught myself not aiming at all. I was simply pointing the gun and pulling the trigger, but I was firing too high. I pointed lower.

Out of the cluster of brown figures into which the machine-gun was spraying its bullets, a tall young Russian came forward and flung an 'egg' hand-grenade at the machine-gunner. The latter was still trying to get out and change position with the machine-gun, while I gave him covering fire. Then the grenade exploded and the poor young lad collapsed, half out of his cover, across his machine-gun. The men from my section had withdrawn. I had lost contact with them. I was standing alone, when a hand-grenade rolled up at my feet. Darting from side to side, I jumped back. There was nothing else I could do. I had to leave the dead machine-gunner and his weapon where they lay.

Quite some time later, the section was ordered back by the battalion. I reported again to the company commander, who was glad that we had been able to withdraw. He was holding the section in reserve at the command post. We took up our 'coffin' holes from the previous night and hurriedly made them deeper. Things did not remain quiet for long. The pressure on the 5th and 6th companies was even greater. One infantry attack had already been beaten off. During the next few hours it was announced that we were getting air support, and the order was given to lay out the aerial recognition cloths. Ground troops carried those cloths with them so as to identify themselves at any given time to their own air force. They were about one square metre in size, either orange-coloured cloths, or *swastika* flags. They were to be spread out on the ground, on buildings, or on vehicles. The loud sound of engines announced the arrival of the aircraft. The approaching aeroplanes gave us cause for hope.

Despite the extremely serious situation a feeling of strength overcame me, because up to then we had seen nothing of the Russian air force. First a flight of Stukas, Ju (Junkers) 87s, flew in. Almost vertically they dived down with their engines screaming. The detonations of the bombs followed. Then, a squadron of Ju 88s also attacked, and, finally He (Heinkel) 111 bombers. Unfortunately, ahead of the 5th Company sector they had dropped their bombs too short. There were dead and wounded. Among them was the excellent company commander, *Oberleutnant* Esken. Not long after that short pause there suddenly rang out shouts of 'Tanks, tanks!' and for the first time in my life, I heard the characteristic dull rumble, that unforgettable grinding noise of heavy tank engines.

A scout car was the first to drive from the left through our lines. Unconcerned, he rattled on up the Saawinki-Upolosy road. When he got as far as the battalion command post, he was polished off with one shot from a 5cm anti-tank gun. From my inactivity in the reserve, I was able to watch from the command post how the gunners let him approach and then, from 30m range, let him have it so that he lurched to a halt. With his hands in the air, a barefoot Russian, smeared with blood and oil, crept out.

Our company commander told us a few days later that the prisoner said the Russians deployed entire families as tank crews. 'The husband was the driver, the wife aimed and fired the gun, and the adolescent son loaded the gun'. You could well believe it. From the tongue of woodland where the 7th Company and my section had been, shortly after the scout car had been destroyed, a single Russian ran out with loud cries. He shouted in a hoarse voice, *Kamerad, Kamerad.* As if he himself wanted to desert to us, or wanted us to desert to his side, he held up one hand, gesticulating. But suddenly the older man pulled a hand-grenade from his pocket, pulled out the pin and held the grenade in the air. It exploded and mangled his hand. Thereupon he ran back into the woodland, wailing loudly. What he wanted remained a mystery to all of us.

The Russians again mounted a frontal attack on the main fighting line with tanks and infantry. The tanks fired with their cannon and machine-guns while we were under heavy mortar fire. In front they were shouting *Urraih*, and were already breaking through. A runner came under the heaviest covering fire and reported what we had realised without him telling us, that the main fighting line could not be held. *Oberleutnant* Bayer, the commander, without waiting for orders from the battalion, decided to withdraw some hundred metres. On his order the entire company ran across the short stretch of level ground. When they had reached the level of the command post, he, too, ran back and I with him. The *Oberleutnant*, in a bleached summer tunic with a yellow-brown belt, knew that he presented a particularly good target to the enemy. He sprinted like a runner in a race and had overtaken the company in no time.

Behind us, the tanks rattled up, firing with everything they had, while our men ran back in front of them. Where were the anti-tank guns? At the edge of a small hollow, in which the company was then to take up position, the battalion commander Kelhauer stood erect, unmoving, and without cover. Only his moist eyes gave any sign of how moved he was, and then the words: 'Bayer, lad, you can't just bolt with the lads!' From his words there spoke the complete shock that German infantrymen had given up a position without higher orders and had given way to enemy pressure. The fact that it had happened in the form of a completely orderly withdrawal, and the men had immediately taken up positions again, altered nothing of that inconceivable fact. Hitherto, there had never been such an event in the regiment's history. In December, facing Moscow, they had had to withdraw. But that was following orders. Even so, the tears had run down *Oberst* Boege's frozen cheeks, as those who were there tell with awe.

While I was running back over the level ground, the right-hand pocket of my tunic had been shot through. Even in retrospect, that discovery sent a jolt of horror through my limbs, because in this pocket I was carrying two 'egg' hand-grenades! A tank shell had lacerated the company commander's breeches. A *Feldwebel* had had a grenade in his hand shot through by a bullet, luckily without it hitting the detonator.

The fire became heavier. It even compelled those who were tired to dig in hurriedly. The hollow at the edge of which we then found ourselves attracted the enemy mortar fire like a magnet. The strikes were good. For us, they were dangerously near. I was still standing in the open. Some 15 metres from me a shell hit a fully-occupied foxhole. A *Gefreiter* with blonde hair and a chalk-white face was somersaulted by the blast of the explosion some 5 or 6 metres out of the hole. All around the earth was spraying up with the shells exploding. There rang out the blood-curdling screams of a fatally-wounded man crying for his mother. I used to think that was an invention of fiction writers. After a while, in obviously unbearable agony, he looked at Bayer, and cried, '*Herr Oberleutnant,* shoot me!' Bayer, at other times never at a loss for words, shrugged his shoulders helplessly and turned away without a word.

'God Almighty, let it soon be evening', I thought. Unsure, under the stress of being in the thick of events, and under cover in the hollow, I could see nothing of the enemy. In the immediate main line of resistance, 50 metres further forward, I would have been able to survey the ground. I would have seen them attacking and breaking through. I would have been able myself to take aim and fire. But there at the company command post, I was condemned to wait under gruelling fire unable to do anything.

Finally, the decisive attack was made. Three tanks of the types KV 1 and KV 2, the latter 56 tons in weight and armed with a 15cm howitzer, drove up the road and through the battalion's front. The anti-aircraft guns were gone, the anti-tank unit long since lost. From in front there rang out *Urraih*. Then, our men were getting out of their trenches and retreating. They could no longer be stopped. The tanks had also overrun the field dressing station where a number of wounded were waiting to be transported away. The tanks then formed up some 200 metres behind the scattering remnants of the battalion. In a triangle on the elevated open ground, each one gave the other cover.

Beside the knocked-out scout car I noticed as I passed, the dead platoon commander of the 7th Company. A man took his pay book and broke off his identification tag. I could see no outward injury on the dead man. It must have been a tiny splinter in the head, or in the heart, that had brought his life to an end. While I was standing by the dead man, suddenly I could no longer see any of my own men. The air was ringing out again with *Urraih*, the whistling and bursting of the shells and infantry guns. Even the company commander was no longer to be seen. So I hurried after some *Landser* who were striving to get across a small hollow to a wood, evidently with the intention of getting around the tanks. I caught up with them, and we hurried together along the edge of the woodland to get past the firing monsters. After we had successfully got round them, we reached a river that had overflowed its banks. From somewhere or other bullets crackled in the water.

I began to wade and sank deeper and deeper. With one hand I held my machine-pistol over my head. In the deepest places I had to move as if swimming. Soon I felt the bottom under my feet. Again and again, probably from one of the tanks, a machine-gun spat fire at us. The fellow must be able to see us. What should I do now? Inexperienced as I was, I thought myself to be the only survivor of the company. The men with me belonged to another unit. We decided to look for the baggage-trains, which surely had to be in one of the neighbouring villages.

Night had fallen by the time we found them. The 'sarge' welcomed me. There was not one word of reproach. He knew what had happened. I had to make my report. I did so and was secretly ashamed that I had run to the baggage-village instead of looking for my comrades further forwards. The 'sarge' left me no time for that. He himself gave me fresh dry clothes and ordered me to sleep in late. The next day at noon I was to go forwards again with the food vehicle. Then he took me into a floor-boarded room in a Russian house, in which nine other scattered men were sleeping. I lay down with them, my haversack under my head, on the hard floor of the farm cottage.

On the morning of 16 August 1942 I awoke from a leaden sleep with the feeling that I had only just gone to sleep. Washing, shaving, the fresh clothes without lice, what a joy! Then I inspected the contents of my pockets. The letters were washed-out, the photographs stuck together and useless. But worse still, my pay book was similarly illegible. Some of my papers, among them my driving licence, were missing. I had just put them down in my gas mask case with my gas mask and then forgotten them when the CO gave the order to withdraw. During the previous days I had not dared to think of the imminent end of my probation at the front. But the fact that the order to return to my regiment came on that very morning was a new piece of good fortune. Then I only needed to report in up front. With that relieving certainty within me, I joined the food vehicle.

The Russians were taking a breather. The company was not even under fire. The command post was based in a house, not in a hole in the ground. The CO was pleased to see me when I reported, and immediately gave notice of departure. He looked weary, and had long stubble. He had once again had 'uncanny luck', he said. When he was standing under cover behind a hayrick, a tank shell came through the several metres of hay but was slowed down so much that only its head came out on the other side. There, it was finally brought to a halt by Bayer's belt buckle. It gave him quite a fright, but nothing happened. It did not explode!

He wished me all the best for the journey home and sent his greetings to the regiment. Then I left. But however depressing the events of the last few days had been, and however much I was looking forward to getting to War College, it was not an easy thing for me to leave the company. It seemed to me undeserved that the *Scheisse* (I have to use the proper expression for the action!) should be at an end, for me of all people. Among many others, even our old friend Kräkler had been killed. The battalion of more than 500 men had shrunk to a fifth that size. The 'Sixth' then only numbered twenty-six men. With such thoughts in my mind I got in to the lorry travelling to the Division. As we were driving out of the baggage-village, rifle fire was cracking behind us into the morass of the road. The road was under enemy observation.

3

October 1942-January 1943: Training courses and promotion

Officers' course in Dresden; promoted to Leutnant; commanders' course in Berlin - aged 19 years

The effects of the Upolosy adventure were with me for a long time. To Rudi I wrote that I had experienced 'atrocious and terrible things', but where need was greatest, 'God's help was closest'. Apart from a few tiny splinters in my hands, that today I can no longer remember, I told him that I had remained unscathed. Our chaps had said that the battles of the winter had not been as bad as those terrible days. The return from Gschatsk to St Avold took us eight days. I can remember several stops that lasted many hours, first in Vyazma then in Molodetschno and Dünaburg. Only from Warsaw were regular trains running, but we had to change trains many times. In Berlin we arrived at the Silesian station and had to go to the Zoo station. From there a train went to Metz. Our destination was St Avold, where we were given a few days' leave.

From my correspondence I note that I must have visited my Father in Vienna. He was in the Reserve Military Hospital there, on the Rosenhügel. It was only while in the position at Gschatsk that I had found out he had had a surprise move to Russia. During the course of the advance in the south, which then led on into the Caucasus and to Stalingrad, his military hospital group had got as far as Stalino and Artemovsk, in the eastern Ukraine. We suffered considerable casualties in the offensive. They led to the associated overload on the resources of the dressing stations, the field and main military hospitals. It also led to the overwork of the medical officers and other medical unit staff. At the age of fifty, in a state of nervous exhaustion, he himself had to be taken into hospital. But he was able to tell of his good fortune that he was not sent back to service behind the lines on the Eastern Front. Instead he was sent to the West, to Cambrai.

On 13 September 1942 I was back in St Avold. From there we three active officer cadets, Henschel, Popovsky and I, were sent to Metz for a preparatory course for War College. About sixty Reserve officer candidates were assembled there for 'a revision of the ABC', as I wrote home. Once again it was a matter of cleaning our boots and belts. Apart from the danger of being killed, life in the field, I said, 'was far better'. I asked Mother to send me fifty marks because we were hungry, and were being 'woefully shoo'd about'. In the evening we went into the town to eat un-rationed standard meals in the inns. The course was supposed to last until 9 October and the course at the War College to begin on 12 October. But we still did not know to which school we would be sent. On 29 September I asked Mother to send immediately, and by registered post, my certificate of Aryan ancestry and my fifth-form German essay exercise book. Father sent me a textbook on stenography

29

on which I worked from time to time. At the grammar school I had not taken that option so as not to further increase my workload. The course in Metz 'gradually petered out' at the beginning of October. In the mornings we were supposed to undertake duty with a company, but 'since no-one is bothered, we lie in really late in the morning and then go into town'.

We three from Regiment 7 were ordered to 'School I for Probationary Officers of Infantry' in Dresden. It was the War College for the active junior infantry officers and could be found in Neustadt under the really civilian-sounding address of 11 Marienallee. I arrived early on 12 October and as the first to arrive had rung them up. Then in the afternoon I went out by tram to the War College. I did not meet the prescribed requirement of at least two months' probation at the front, so at first it seemed doubtful whether I would be accepted. It was with relief that I noted the positive decision. Part of that was doubtless due to the fact that the regiment, which knew what the entry requirements were, had sent me there nevertheless.

It was a pleasant surprise for Popovsky and me that almost half the course participants and a large part of the teaching personnel were southern Germans. I even found a room with Popovsky. In fact it was an apartment. The rooms, each provided for four men, consisted of bedrooms and living rooms. As it was war-time, by means of double beds they were occupied by twice the normal complement of men. So there were eight of us. As well as the two of us there were six more *Gebirgsjäger*, among whom we immediately felt at home.

I can still remember Ernst Lauda from Kapfenberg, Hubert Melcher from Obdach, Adolf Aschauer from Goisern, Dauth from Munich, Jakoby from Konstanz, and Zilinski from Stettin. The man from Stettin had reported to the mountain troops for the same sort of reasons that many southern Germans and Austrians went into the Navy. At the War College I also met Bäuerl from Stockerau, the brother of one of Rudi's classmates, and my fellow-pupil from Sonneberg, Klausnitzer. Once again, I wrote urgently for my *Ariernachweis*, because non-Aryans, covering those who were up to one-quarter Jewish, were not allowed to become officers (translator's note: the certificate of Aryan ancestry required under the National Socialist racial laws before an individual could be admitted to many institutions).

The accommodation was unbelievably comfortable. We had white bedclothes, running water in the bedroom and the rooms were cleaned by cleaning ladies. I wrote that the War College was 'the best time I had had as a soldier so far'. It required not only physical, but also mental and spiritual qualities. The superiors, all officers, were selected men. The head of the *Inspektion* was a *Hauptmann* from *Infanterieregiment* 19 Munich, the Group Officer *Oberleutnant* Maltzahn. I also recall the tactics teacher, *Major* Rousen from *Infanterieregiment* 49 Breslau. The *Inspektion* corresponded to a company, the Group to a platoon. The aim of the course was to train us to become platoon commanders, the normal function of a *Leutnant*. The exercises took place on the famous Dresden troop training ground, the 'Heller'. We had little free time. What little time I could spare I spent with my relatives, mainly with Uncle Rudolf and Aunt Hanni Löhner. At that time Rudolf had much to do. He was working on commissions for the memorial to Richtofen, the fighter pilot, at the *Invalidenfriedhof* in Berlin. He worked too on figures for the Dresden Opera and the *Reich* War Ministry.

In our room we often had a 'beano', to which the Styrians, Ernst Lauda and Hubert Melcher from *Gebirgsjägerregiment* 28, especially contributed. Their *Ersatz* troop unit was at that time in Marburg on the Drau. A short time previously they had heard a production there, of Verdi's *Traviata*. Erni Lauda was really taken with the champagne aria and sang, over and over again, 'Up, drink in thirsty draughts from the glass that Beauty presents to you'. The two of them teased each other with the amatory adventures they had had in Marburg. It emerged that Erni had once spent the conclusion of such an evening in the Marburg municipal park. He had got so hot that in no time he had taken off at least his field tunic, as well as his belt.

Ernst Lauda was killed in April 1944. Hubert Melcher lost a leg. Adolf Aschauer survived the war in one piece. (Once after the war I looked him up in the *Rassingmühle* in Goisern, his home. Ernst Lauda's father at one time entered into correspondence with me and I met him in Schweidnitz.) He was at the time on the Staff of *Heeresgruppe Süd* with *Feldmarschall* Kesselring and he told me of one absurd order from the *Führer*. This order required that the sarcophagus of the *Hohenstaufen* Emperor Friedrich II be brought back with the Army on the evacuation of Sicily. However, Kesselring refused the order on the grounds that he needed every cubic metre of ship for troops and ammunition.

The star of our group was Arnold Suppan, a smart Kärntner with brown hair and brown eyes. He already held the Iron Cross First Class and the silver *Infanteriesturmabzeichen* (Infantry Assault Badge). The *Gebirgsjäger* told a lot about the Murmansk front from which they came, about the bright summer nights and the dark winter days in the Arctic Circle.

The weeks passed quickly and in the middle of November we heard the great news that the course would finish on 16 December. The best group of students, to which I too belonged, would be promoted on 1 December to *Fahnenjunker-Feldwebel*. The majority of the candidates were handed out their uniform chits. My request to Rudi was to the effect that he should obtain a sword, an officer's belt and a holster, because it looked as if there were not any in Dresden. In actual fact, a sword was never required. In any event, I would only have been able to wear it on very few occasions. My first officer's uniform I had made by Uncle Rudolf's tailor. He rejoiced in the cosy name of Trautvetter. For my overcoat and the second uniform I waited until my Christmas leave. I had them made at Splinar in the Theobaldgasse, by the tailor of the Steinbach family. The tunic was of better material, and the overcoat displayed all the skill of a Viennese Bohemian tailor.

Our instructor, *Oberleutnant* Maltzahn, professed himself to be very satisfied with us from the *Ostmark*. On the occasion of our promotion to *Feldwebel* he told us the notes he had made on our assessment. He found me, among other things, 'very intelligent'. I had never before been praised in that way. It certainly said a lot for his judgement! He himself was of above average intelligence and culture, and in addition showed us a lot of what it means to live like an officer. Our promotion to *Leutnant* was to take place on 12 December. I announced that I would be arriving home on 16 December, a Wednesday. I asked Rudi to collect me, and I ordered a 'celebration meal', of whatever Mother wanted to rustle up. Before then, however, we had the trip to Berlin. There, in accordance with tradition, the *Führer* was to speak to us in the *Sportpalast*.

The entire War College marched from the Anhalt Station. We were divided into several groups and went by different routes. On one we passed through a quarter of Berlin which showed city slums that shocked us. The event took place in the *Sportpalast*. Several thousand young officers were assembled there. At first there was a long wait for Adolf Hitler. After some time it was announced that, in Hitler's place, *Reichsmarschall* Hermann Göring would speak to us. After another long wait, Göring came hurrying in. He gave the impression that he was under severe psychological pressure which the content of his address underscored. We later found out that it was on that very day that the tragedy of Stalingrad began to loom. It explained why Hitler had not come, and made it disconcertingly clear why Göring praised the death of the Spartans at Thermopylae under their king, Leonidas. 'Wanderer, should you come to Sparta, tell them there that you have seen us lying dead as the law ordained'. The *Reichsmarschall* simply substituted the word 'duty' for the word 'law' and almost punched it at us. 'As duty ordained, as duty ordained'. At the end of his address we were immediately marched off to the station and straight away began our return journey to Dresden.

It had been the previous day when the names of those who had been promoted were read out in the gym. It began with the members of *Infanterieregiment* 1 (Königsberg) and ended with those in the *Gebirgsjägerregiment* who were last in the numerical series. We from Regiment 7, in alphabetical order, were Henschel, Popovsky, and Scheiderbauer. We soon had our turn. Afterwards Wiggerl and I dozed off in a half-sleep of emotions of release and tiredness.

The night before, following an order given by our *Leutnant* Riedl, we had hoisted 'the white flag' on the chimney of the boiler house. To accomplish that, one of our bed sheets had to be brought along, we had to cobble together something to raise it, and the 20 metre high chimney had to be scaled. Since you could climb the chimney on iron rungs on its inside wall, it presented not too much difficulty, but nevertheless it required some courage. It was Popovsky who volunteered to take up the duties of the climbing party and not one of the *Gebirgsjäger*. It might be imagined that the task would fall more easily to them because of the arm of the service they were in. *Oberleutnant* Maltzahn was pleased that his group, the twelfth group in the third *Inspektion*, had carried out the task.

With my promotion to *Leutnant* I was then to a certain extent 'grown-up'. I was not then nineteen and would not come of age for a long time. I had already been an *Unteroffizier*. But then I was capable of supporting myself and was in receipt of a salary with my own account at the Stockerau savings bank. At that time a *Leutnant's* salary was 220 *Reichsmarks* per month. It was a considerable sum for a grammar-school boy, but also for a soldier who had to live only on his service pay and that meant from his additional front-line allowance. In any event, the *freie Station* was guaranteed. It guaranteed a barracks roof over your head, and military rations that were more or less adequate and digestible for a young stomach. As well as our salary we got a one-off 'clothing payment', the enormous amount of 750 *Reichsmarks*. My kind Aunt Lotte had given me an additional 50 *Reichsmarks* for my *Equipierung*, an expression she used from the old Imperial Army. In a letter to

Mother she wrote about it and told her, quite touched, that I looked 'like a young nobleman'. Father, with great seriousness, had written me the following:

> ... Now you have your own independent profession. This gives you the authority to make your own independent decisions in forming your future life. I most fervently wish you one thing, that it will always be given to you to make use of this freedom in a wise and appropriate way. A great deal is demanded of you for your age. I also hope just as fervently that in the future you may also not disdain the advice of your parents. Of course, the plans and thoughts of parents can also be wrong and we must leave it in the hands of God to whom, of all those involved, he grants the best thought. From my experience, however, I can tell you one thing, that in my life something has always gone awry whenever I forgot, from time to time, to pray regularly. May this never happen to you! Especially in these present times that will bring many serious dangers for you. Don't forget to pray, and to pray for better days! Perhaps in some way you will have to go through again the whole process of choosing and preparing for a career. I do wish that you might be spared that. But God alone knows. My blessing and prayers will always be with you!

The Christmas leave passed off harmoniously, even if the atmosphere was really not Christmas-like. There was no snow on the ground. I had missed Father. He had been given a short period of special leave from his post because his brother, my Uncle Erich, had been killed in action, on 29 November, by Lake Ilmen in the Northern sector of the Russian front. Thus he was able to visit his brother's widow, Anneliese. She was in Eisting, near Schwertberg, with her three small children, Theja, Harald, and Ute. He also visited his mother who lived in Hadersdorf-Weidlinggau.

I got angry about grumbling townspeople who were losing nothing and from whose families no-one had joined up, but who still grumbled about the situation. From my class Iwan Wagner, who was also an infantry *Leutnant*, as well as Erhard Hameter and Friedl Schiffmann, both *Fähnriche* in the Navy, were all on leave. With Friedl Schiffmann's sister, Heidi, I struck up a fleeting and short-lived friendship. However, by the summer Herta had turned away from me. Admittedly, I visited the Henk house. When I was visiting one afternoon I left my officer's cap, overcoat and dagger in the hall. That 'con-man' Ewald took possession of the uniform and had his photograph taken, dressed in it, in his father's studio.

The course at the War College was followed by a company commanders' course at the Infantry School in Döberitz near Berlin. I arrived there after New Year. Popovsky and I were given a double room together in the bleak barracks. There, in contrast to the luxurious conditions in Dresden, unfavourable conditions prevailed. The barracks were unheated and therefore 'perishing cold'. The food was 'terribly little, bad, and cold'. At night we had to sleep in our underwear, pullovers, and training kit, or else the cold would have 'done you in'. We were allowed to go to Berlin only on Saturdays and Sundays. I immediately suffered a bout of angina, which when I was young I got almost every winter.

On my birthday, 13 January 1943, which I designated as the saddest in my life up till then, while in a foul mood, I wrote a letter to Rudi. Like me he wanted to become an active officer. I asked him whether he had sent off his application, because if not, he should think it over very carefully. I said that at such a young age one could not always make 100% correct decisions, i.e. decisions that affected one's entire life. I told him there was nothing worse than a life that was ruined by choosing the wrong profession. I said there was one thing he had to give particular thought to, something that I unfortunately had realised too late, and that was the mostly spiritual hollowness and emptiness of the service. For that reason I doubted whether the profession would satisfy my brother. With me this was, I confessed, not the case, and perhaps after the war I would still change professions in some way.

Aunt Lilli, Father's eldest sister, had at that time been living in Berlin with her family. Uncle Leopold Pohl was a clergyman in the Neukölln area of the city. In fact I turned up at their house, to the horror of my Mother. My parents had quarrelled with the Pohls over Grandmother. However, I was cordially welcomed, and they were obviously glad I had taken the step, especially as the argument had been Uncle Pohl's fault. Against Mother's reproaches I justified myself – not very seriously – by saying that it was of because of our need for heating that I had been directed to them, but also said that Uncle Pohl had lent me an immersion heater and had offered an electric heating stove. I said that I would therefore prefer if they began to get along together again, even if only under the motto of 'coals of fire'. In actual fact the contact with my relatives was a gain for me, since I could spend the night there from Saturday to Sunday.

One Saturday I heard in the Neukölln parish hall the lecture of a Rostock university professor on the subject of 'The Johannine Testimony to Christ'. The lecture took place in the air-raid shelter because of a British air-raid. We felt like the first Christians in the catacombs in Rome. During the lecture the anti-aircraft shells were crashing outside and there was a hail of shrapnel on the roofs. The following Sunday I was at the service in Uncle Pohl's church. After a long absence it was spiritually edifying for me. I was able to sit down at the piano and to play as my fancy took me. The two Pohl lads, at that time 15 and 13 years old, were not at home. Wolfgang had not changed schools when they moved to Berlin, and was visiting his grammar school in Schleusingen. He was at boarding school there and only came home in the holidays. Helmut had been taken out of the city with the so-called *Kinderlandverschickung*.

Only Ilse was in the house with her parents. She sang with the Philharmonic Choir. Son afterwards, a performance of the 'St Matthew Passion' took place in the Berlin Garrison Church, she took part and I listened to the concert. In the row in front of me there happened to be sitting *Grossadmiral* Raeder and his wife. At that time Raeder was Supreme Commander of the Navy.

One Saturday evening, my uncle treated us to a bottle of wine. It had been given to him as a present, shortly after the war began, by a former member of his confirmation class. He had, in the meantime, been killed in action. We drank the wine, as Uncle Pohl said, '*in memoriam* Eduardi Feldmann'.

Rudi took many photographs and even, by using an automatic shutter release, did his own portrait studies of himself. In those pictures he showed an inclination to clowning and to elegance. My classmate Novak wrote to me that Rudi was one of the 'best-dressed, most charming, and thus also one of the most popular' young men in Stockerau.

The work was hard. On Saturdays we worked till noon. On the other weekends we worked nine to ten hours a day. Of course, infantry matters were in the foreground, i.e. how to lead a platoon was then followed by how to lead a company. We had instruction in tactics, combat, weapons instruction and firing. Once again the officer-instructors were excellent people. The head of the *Inspektion* was a sensitive, seemingly vulnerable aristocrat, *Hauptmann* von Koenen. One of the tactics instructors was a young holder of the Knight's Cross, *Hauptmann* Johannsen, and our *Inspektion* officer was a Viennese, *Oberleutnant* Brucker. (I also recall another Austrian, *Major* Watzek, whom I happened to meet after the war in the street in Vienna. He ended his career as the Austrian *General und Kommandant* of the Vienna Neustadt Military Academy.)

Once we took part as spectators in a production of the *Infanterie-Lehr-Regiment*. It portrayed the attack of a reinforced infantry battalion, supported by a battery of light field howitzers, i.e. 10.5cm, four assault guns and aircraft. Heavy and light infantry guns, i.e. 15 and 10.5cm, also supported the attack. The exercise was completely true to life. Naturally the shooting was accurate and the system of command of classical precision! In the audience were twenty Army Generals, five from the *Waffen-SS* and three from the *Luftwaffe*. There were some 100 staff officers and some 20 *Luftwaffe Leutnants* to whom the spectacle was completely new. With their Leicas and other cameras, they all snapped simultaneously every exploding shell.

While the instructional element was really interesting, I was still disturbed by the 'exaggerated *Preussentum*, as always and everywhere'. With this I meant, and still mean, not the spirit of Prussia in itself, but the way in which many small people believed they had to express this spirit. The spirit of Prussia had its home to a certain extent in Potsdam, which we visited one Sunday. The unassuming old houses, the small well-known Garrison Church and the summer residence *Sans Souci*, itself so modest, showed us that the Prussian kings obviously always knew their limitations. As one of the officer instructors, *Hauptmann* Schubart, quoted, 'little things made Prussia great'.

The training was mostly based on the *Heeresdienstvorschrift* (Army Service Regulations: H.DV. 300/1) *Truppenführung* (i.e. Troop Command), Part One, vulgarly known as *Tante Frieda* or Aunt Frieda. The introduction to these regulations is classical in its clarity and reminds one of sentences from the seminal work on warfare *Vom Kriege* by General von Clausewitz. I quote it as follows:

1.   Warfare is an art, a free, creative activity that rests upon a scientific basis. It makes the very highest demands upon the individual character.

2.   The business of war is subject to constant development. New means of warfare are constantly providing it with new and changing forms. When these forms will come into use must be accurately predicted, their influence correctly assessed and quickly evaluated.

3.   The variety of situations in war is limitless. They change often, and suddenly, and are only seldom to be seen in advance. Unpredictable quantities often have a decisive influence. The individual will comes up against the will of the enemy outside its control. Frictions and mistakes are everyday occurrences.

4.   The tenets of warfare cannot be exhaustively summarised in the form of regulations. The principles that such regulations provide must be applied as cir-

cumstances dictate. Simple action, carried out consistently, is the most certain means to achieve the desired end.

5.   War provides the individual with the hardest test of his mental and physical powers of resistance. Therefore, in war, the qualities of character carry more weight than do those of intelligence. Many an individual is outstanding on the battlefield, but would be overlooked in peacetime.

6.   The command of armies and troops requires judicious, clear-thinking and foresighted leader personalities, autonomous and firm in decision, persistent and energetic in carrying it through, not over-sensitive to the changing fortunes of war, and with a distinct sense of the high responsibility which rests upon them.

7.   The officer is, in all disciplines, a leader and educator. In addition to knowledge of men and a sense of justice, he must be distinguished by superiority in knowledge and experience, moral seriousness, self-control and high courage.

8.   The example and the personal behaviour of the officer and of the soldiers used in officer posts have a determining influence on the troops. The officer who in the face of the enemy displays *sangfroid*, resolution, and daring sweeps the troops along with him. But he must also find the way to the hearts of his subordinates. He must win their confidence by understanding their feelings and thoughts as well as by tirelessly seeking their welfare. Mutual trust is the surest foundation for manly discipline in time of need and danger.

9.   Every leader, in all situations, should bring his whole personality into play without fearing the responsibility that is his. Delight in taking responsibility is the noblest quality of leadership. But this is not to be sought in taking arbitrary decisions without regard to the whole picture, or in not meticulously following orders and allowing a nit-picking attitude to take the place of obedience. Autonomy must not become high-handed arbitrariness. On the other hand, autonomy properly exercised, and within proper limits, is the basis for great success.

10.   Despite technology, the value of the man is the deciding factor; scattered fighting has made it more significant. The emptiness of the battlefield demands those fighters who can think and act for themselves, those who exploit every situation in a considered, decisive and bold manner, those full of the conviction that success is the responsibility of every man. Inurement to physical effort, to self-regard, willpower, self-confidence and daring enable the man to become master of the most serious situations.

11.   The value of the leader and the man determines the combat value of the troops, which finds its complement in the quality, care and maintenance of weapons and equipment. Superior combat value can compensate for numerical inferiority. The greater the combat value, the more powerful and mobile the warfare that can be waged. Superior leadership and superior combat value are reliable foundations for victory.

12.   The leaders must live their lives with their troops and share in their dangers and privations, their joys and sorrows. Only then can they come through

their own experience to a judgement of the combat value and the needs of their troops. The man is not only responsible for himself, but also for his comrades. Anyone who can do more, who is more capable, must guide and lead those who are less experienced and weaker. On such a foundation there grows the sense of true comradeship, which is as important between leader and man as it is within the unit.

13.   A unit that has been brought together only superficially, not through lengthy work of instruction and training, easily fails at serious moments and under the pressure of unexpected events. Therefore, from the beginning of the war, the need to promote and maintain the inner firmness and the manly discipline of the troops, as well as to train them, has been regarded as being of decisive importance. Every leader is obliged to intervene with every means, even the most severe, against any slackening of manly discipline, against acts of violence, plundering, panic and other harmful influences. Manly discipline is the cornerstone of the Army, and to uphold it strictly benefits all.

14.   The strength of the troops must be kept fresh to meet the greatest demands in decisive moments. Anyone who exerts the troops unnecessarily sins against success. The use of forces in combat must be proportionate to the desired goal. Impossible demands damage the spirit of the troops and their confidence in their leadership.

15.   From the youngest soldier upwards, men must everywhere be encouraged to bring to bear, of their own accord, their entire mental, spiritual and physical strength. Only in this way will the full potential of the troops be brought out to the full in consistent action. Only then will men grow up who, even in the hour of danger, will keep courage and resolution and sweep their weaker comrades along with them to bold deeds. Thus resolute action remains the first requirement in war. Everyone, from the highest commander to the youngest soldier, must always be conscious that omission and negligence will place a greater burden on him than mistakes in the choice of weapons.

I have not yet mentioned the marching songs, and other songs that played a significant part in my training period. The character of the soldier's song had changed. Certainly there was still in use a series of songs that the German Army had sung in the First World War. Those were to be sung as *Volkslieder* in a march rhythm. But in the period between the wars, and through the Hitler Youth, new songs had come along and, above all, many songs were sung 'more snappily'. Most comrades, however, did not like that way of singing, and that also expressed itself in the choice of songs. In the Dresden War College we had caused something of a sensation, because our group, with its many *Gebirgsjäger*, used to sing some Austrian soldiers' songs. Our favourite was the *Südtirolerlied* with its completely un-Prussian yodel at the end of the verse. *Die blauen Dragoner, sie reiten, Ein Heller und ein Batzen, Schwarzbraun ist die Haselnuss, Es klappert der Huf am Stege, Ich bin ein freier Wildbretschütz, Jetzt kommen die lustigen Tage, Weit ist der Weg ins Heimatland, Wer recht in Freuden wandern will,* are a few of those songs. I particularly liked *Es klappert der Huf am Stege*.

True, we were not cavalrymen, but it matched our youthful spirit when it said, 'We ride and ride and sing, in our hearts the bitterest distress. Longing seeks to conquer us, but we ride longing down'. In the final verse, 'We ride and ride and hear already the battle afar. Lord, let us be strong in the battle, then our life will be accomplished!' Of the songs that were sung in our room in the evening I will mention *Heilig Vaterland, Du voll Unendlichkeit, Kein schooner Land in dieser Zeit,* or 'Nothing can rob us of love and faith in our land, to preserve it and to form it is what we are sent to do. Should we die, then to our heirs will fall the duty of preserving and forming it. Germany will never die'.

'Belief in Germany' was the title of a well-known and much read book from the First World War. Belief in Germany had seized us all, whichever Germany that meant. It also played a part in the letter that Uncle Erich's battalion commander had written to Aunt Anneliese after Erich had been killed in action. The letter was doing the rounds of the family. Erich's death touched us all to the quick. We were glad, that as a fanatical National Socialist, who had left the church, he had still become reconciled with my Father. It moved me deeply and I wrote home about it. In February, in a large parcel from Aunt Anneliese with apples and other things, I received a tin of marmalade that had been meant for Erich. It had already been to Russia, but was too late to reach its recipient.

4

Spring/Summer 1943:
Platoon commander in Silesia, trench warfare at Nemers

Platoon commander in Silesia; journey to the front; trench warfare at Nemers

When the course finished at the beginning of April 1943, we got 14 days' leave. After that Popovsky and I had to report on 15 April to the *Ersatz* unit, *Grenadierersatzbataillon 7*, in Schweidnitz/Silesia. The Silesian *Ersatz-Armeekorps* had a few months earlier been moved back from Lorraine and Alsace to the home garrisons in Silesia. We then came for the first time into the place that had been talked about by our comrades. We believed that from then on and even after the war, the place would be our home. Schweidnitz was called the Potsdam of Silesia. Before the war it housed the Staff, the first and the third battalion of *Infanterieregiment 7*, the Staff and the first and second *Abteilungen* of *Artillerieregiment 28*, a medical unit, District Military Command, Military Records Office and Army Ancillary Office.

Schweidnitz was the *Stadtkreis* and *Kreisstadt* in Lower Silesia, principal seat of the principality of the same name. It lies in a fertile valley between Zobten and the Eulengebirge. The city has two Protestant and two Catholic churches, among them the *Pfarrkirche* founded in 1330 by Duke Bolko II. It has the highest (103m) tower in Silesia with a triple crest (1613). There is a synagogue and an old Town Hall with a famous cellar, and various monuments.

Economic activity comprised the manufacture of electricity meters, machines, furniture, gloves, tools, terra-cotta and pottery ware, feather edging materials, vehicles, cigars, needles, paper and paper goods, bricks, iron casting and textiles. Long since famous was also the beer brewery (Schweidnitzer *Schöps*). In addition, the city possessed a chamber of commerce and a *Reichsbank* office. There were two grammar schools, a theological institute, an agricultural winter school, two orphanages, an educational institute, a theatre, and an archive. It was the seat of a district court, a magistrates' court, a *Landkreis* administrative office, a motor sport school and several technical schools.

The early fortifications were removed in 1868, and transformed into beautiful parks. The Neptune Well, four market wells and a *Neopomuk* Column of 1718, enlivened the picture presented by the city. The residential houses originated in part from the eighteenth century. Of the royal castle only the *Renaissance-Portal* of 1537 was retained. The town of Schweidnitz was founded during the first half of the thirteenth century as a town laid out on a grid pattern between two roads. In 1260 it was granted its town charter. It was the residence of the first *Piasten* and an important festival ground in Silesia. In the later Middle Ages Schweidnitz developed into the second-largest trading city after Breslau. The principality of Schweidnitz was founded in 1291, and joined with Jauer in 1326. Through the marriage of the heiress Anna with *Kaiser* Karl IV, it passed in 1368/69 to the crown of Bohemia. In 1526 it went to the Habsburgs, and in 1742 to Prussia.

In 1427, Schweidnitz was besieged, in vain, by the Hussites. In the Thirty Years' War (1642) it was destroyed by the Swedes under Torstenson. In 1747 it was taken by the Prussians and developed as a fortress. In 1761 it fell once more by trickery, into the hands of the Austrians. Then it was retaken in 1762 by the Prussians, after a stubborn defence, remained under Prussian control and was significantly reinforced by four forts. In 1807 the French took possession of them and razed the outworks to the ground. In 1816, after the fall of Napoleon, they were rebuilt, but completely flattened again in 1867. According to the census of 17 May 1939, Schweidnitz had 39,100 mostly Protestant inhabitants. According to the regimental history that was the past of Schweidnitz.

The officers' accommodation in the barracks was insufficient, therefore many officers were quartered in hotels. Popovsky and I had a room in the *Hindenburg-Hof,* evidently the first house to hand. It was next to the railway station. The square in front had a small park, on to which we looked down, from our first-floor room. As far as work went, there was not much to do. We were simply waiting for our marching orders. After Popovsky left on 29 April, I felt a bit lonely. I became accustomed to the feeling. But I soon found a few good comrades. One was a chap from Linz, one was from Franzensbad in Bohemia, and there was a *Feldwebel-Offizier* candidate. He was a clergyman in the Confessional Church and, at forty years old, was waiting for his promotion to *Leutnant.*

From a letter to Father, I find that I gave him the 'Stalingrad Letter' to read and copy out. That was the shocking letter of a clergyman to his congregation who had remained in Stalingrad. (I still have the copy). In the same letter I asked Father urgently for cigarettes. Mother still kept her cigarette ration card 'z.b.V.' i.e. *zur besonderen Verfügung,* for special use. With cigarettes she could probably obtain food or could meet other obligations on which she depended.

The food in the barracks was frugal. Once I succeeded, on a forty-kilometre march, in getting into a village inn and in eating there, 'naturally for nothing', i.e. without having to hand over any *Reichsmarks, Eierspeis* or *Eröpfelschmarrn.* I remember my conversation with the landlady, who thought I was from Schweidnitz. As a result of a musical ear I could get the Lower Silesian accent very well. She was amazed when I told her that I came from the Vienna area. On such marches through the countryside around Schweidnitz I often had leisure to indulge in my thoughts. From Breslau, Silesia, in 1813, the War of Liberation began against Napoleon. King Friedrich Wilhelm III had founded the Iron Cross. The simply-styled decoration can be traced back to a design by Schinkel, the brilliant Berlin architect. Few people know of that connection. During my time in Schweidnitz I found out that the Zobten had played a similar role to the Wartburg, and that the students of Breslau had once made pilgrimages there.

As in St Avold and Mörchingen, in the buildings of the barracks in Schweidnitz, in passages and over doors there hung the various coats of arms of the places of Lower and Upper Silesia. It meant that in every place a piece of the Fatherland should be looking down on you. The *Haus Vaterland*, in Berlin was a large room in that gigantic establishment dedicated to every German region. There was a similar one in our barracks for the Silesian homeland and its sons. The fact that the character of the *Wehrmacht* was based on the wider concept of Greater Germany had at least loosened a little the principle of local allegiance. It had by no means got rid of it. After all, I then knew what Schweidnitz was like and how our regiment belonged there in peacetime. It was, as the old soldiers' song says, 'my real home'.

The wait for my marching orders did not, thank God, last much longer. I was glad when it was time and I could set off via Breslau to Minsk. There I had to report to the *Führerreserve* of Army Section Centre. On that journey to Russia I did not have a 'goal' in the same way as I had had the year before. I did not have the prospect of being sent on a course after a few months. My real probation at the front was just beginning, and all the more important since I was then an officer. Strangely, I did not think of the possibility of being wounded. A *Heimatschuss*, i.e. wound necessitating evacuation home, could bring the coming experience on the front line to a speedy end. In the First World War the Austrians had called it a *1000 Gulden Schuss*. It was more as if I felt myself travelling to meet an uncertain future. The recollection of Upolosy joined itself to that feeling. It was a kind of fear of being tested that weighed upon my spirits.

We soon got to Bialystok and Stolpcze, formerly Polish border crossings. With me in the compartment of the leave train returning to the front were sitting a senior MO and two paymasters. The MO was going to a military hospital, the two paymasters were in other lines of communication posts. The gentlemen were carrying much more luggage than I. I only had my miserable *Wehrmacht* haversack. Dawn broke and the train crawled at about thirty kilometres per hour through a region where there was the threat of partisans.

Suddenly, an explosion shook me out of my doze, and the train lurched to a halt. It threw me off the seat on which I had been stretched out. The senior MO's case fell out of the luggage rack and hit me on the back of the neck. From outside could be heard the crack of rifles. Bullets crashed through the walls and the windows of the carriage. In the train there was considerable excitement. The people from 'behind the lines' reacted with panic. One paymaster fired with his 6.35 pistol through the closed window. I spoke to him and asked him to be sensible.

Then I got out of the carriage and jumped into the ditch beside the tracks. I waited under cover until the rifle fire had ceased. It could have only been a few partisans who had been firing. But the damage was considerable. The empty carriage pushed in front of the locomotive, and the locomotive itself, had been blown off the tracks. The forward half of the first of the long express carriages had been compressed as if it had been made of plywood. There were dead and wounded.

Hours later a fully manned handcar came from the next post up the line. In the morning we were at last able to continue our journey. Meanwhile, the cause of the explosion had been discovered. The Russian improvisers had managed, by means of a much cobbled-together wire, to detonate an obviously home-made mine placed under the track. Then they had made off, not without first having put the fear of God into a couple of travelling paymasters with a bit of rifle fire.

That experience caused me, at least for the next twenty years, not to get in to the first carriage of a passenger train. From Minsk the journey went on to Vyazma.

There the line ended. Gschatsk, after the 'Buffalo' withdrawal movement in the Spring, was no longer in German hands. I had to continue on towards Spas-Demensk and get off in Jelnja. Many houses had been destroyed. Only a few remained intact and were the distinguishing characteristics of that village in the lines of communication. The *Soldatenheim* was housed in the one single storey building. The next day a vehicle was to travel to the Division. So I reserved a straw mattress for myself as the last soft bed before I arrived at the front. Then I visited the overcrowded front-line cinema, to see the 'Judge of Zalamea'.

The film had not finished when suddenly there was the roar of enemy aircraft. While bombs were already falling round about, the cinema was hurriedly evacuated and everyone dived into the cellar. Experience teaches that it is a good sign if you can hear the whistle of the bombs because then they explode further away. But in those moments it was poor consolation. There remained the dreadful feeling of having to crouch in the overcrowded cellar without being able to do anything. Getting on for 150 *Landser* were together in that one room of about seventy square metres. The ceiling was supported by only one column. More and more bombs whistled and exploded.

I was already considering whether I should get out into the open in one of the pauses between two waves of the bombing. Then a *Feldgendarme* from the Division spoke to me and suggested that I run across with him to the *Felgendarmerie* bunker. He had recognised me as being from the 'Seventh' by the white tabs on my epaulettes. We ran off straight away and we were both glad to have escaped the cage down there. The air-raid carried on until 1am, but claimed only a few victims. Above all, the direct hit on the cinema that we had feared did not happen.

On 23 May I had set off from Schweidnitz, and after two eventful days and nights had arrived with my company. I had travelled with the *Feldpost* vehicle from Jelnja to the Divisional command post at Alexandrino. The main dressing station was there and was working at full pressure. A battalion from '461', our sister regiment, had the previous night carried out an assault operation in which half the battalion had been lost. The road forward continued past scented meadows and shining silver birch and over long, carefully laid 'corduroy' roads. In the evening I at last arrived at the front line where, compared with the adventures of the journey, peace reigned.

On 25 May I wrote to Father that my welcome to the regiment had been 'cordial and very nice.' I had already met many people I knew. The quiet in our positions was 'doing me good.' I was quite tense. Only now and then was there individual fire from artillery or mortars. But soon, I said, I would have 'got used' to life at the front, and the necessary calm would return. I thanked Father that he and Mother had taught me to make the right, true Christian faith part of my life, because its true value is best learned at the front. I said that I was really helped by the New Testament that Father had given to me. He had written the dedication to me from Psalm 90, verse 10: 'A thousand shall fall beside thee, and ten thousand at thy right hand: but it shall not come nigh thee'. Therefore, I wrote, I was 'completely confident.' God would see that all was well.

Our company commander was *Oberleutnant* 'Schorsch' Hentschel, from Upper Silesia. *Kompanietruppenführer* was *Oberfeldwebel* Thalige from Troppau. Both were reservists and as early as 1942 had been awarded the German Cross in Gold.

My comrades Walter Henschel and Ludwig Popovsky were platoon commanders in the 11th and 7th Companies, and I was platoon commander in the 10th.

The length of the trenches in the company sector was one kilometre. The right-hand edge was formed by the 'post road' in the village of Ivanowo. Only charred beams and remnants of walls were left of the few remaining houses. Two platoons of the company were in the trenches in the main line of resistance. The third was in front of them on outpost sentry duty. The distance of the enemy from our sector was 1,800 metres. The outpost sentries were 800 metres in front of our main line of resistance. That was how the notional line between the muzzles of the most forward rifles was defined. The Russians now and again fired a shell from their mortar, or a *Ratschbum*. *Ratschbum* was the name we gave to the light Russian infantry gun, an anti-tank gun that fired directly at its target, so that the sound of firing and that of impact followed in quick succession. It was a sound described by the word *Ratschbum*.

The mood of the men was excellent. Winter was past and they had survived the retreat. The awareness of a solid superiority was beginning to root itself once again. 'We can hold out in a war like this for years', they felt. Only the second battalion had participated in the Upolosy adventure, but not the third, in which I then was.

Frivolously I had taken my gold pocket watch with me into the field. I carried it in an aluminium container that had a cellophane pane on one side through which you could see the watch face. But every time it was difficult to get it out of the little pocket, sewn into the waistband on the right next the button. Since I could get a waterproof service wristwatch, with luminous figures on a black background, I ventured to send the pocket watch home. It actually arrived. That was by no means certain, for in spite of draconian punishments there were many instances of theft. Even the *Feldpost* was not proof against thieves. It was the watch that I got as a confirmation present from Rudolf Löhner. It has been for many years on the writing desk in Thussi's ordination room.

One day the Divisional Commander, *Generalleutnant* Melzer, toured the positions. He was satisfied with the state they were in, but he reproved me since he believed I was not wearing a collar sash. Actually I did not have one, but instead had a beautiful purple silk scarf. However, in order not to be 'bawled out' for wearing it, I had pushed it under my collar. To wear such neckerchiefs in the garrison would have been unthinkable, but here in the field the superiors turned a blind eye. The fact that the General had caught me out irritated me for quite some time.

However, it was a peaceful day with glowing sunshine that prompted me to sunbathe on the grassy sloping back of the bunker. But soon that was too insecure, because I feared I might fall asleep. If a shell had struck, I would have been lying out in the open without cover. Another day the Russians, instead of disturbing us with shells, fired all their infantry weapons for a quarter of an hour, as if possessed, for no apparent reason. The fire could not hurt us in the cover of the bunker or in the trenches. But there was an uninterrupted chirping, buzzing and whistling and, because no shells were exploding, it was a particularly unique sound. When the firing began, the company commander's *Putzer*, i.e. batman, was outside his bunker and was wounded in the foot just as he was having a pee.

In such trench warfare, which in itself was quiet, there was the institution of the *Zugführer vom Dienst*. When it was my turn at night, I had to inspect the entire company sector and the outpost sentries. I had to check the links between our company and the neighbouring companies. Those excursions out in front of the line were exciting and not without danger. At any moment you could bump into a Russian reconnaissance patrol. On dark nights, it was said to have happened that the Ivans captured *Landser* by throwing a blanket over their head. As far as possible you had to tread quietly, often stopping and listening.

An additional task was assigned to me. I had to develop lectures for 'military moral support' on the basis of material supplied to me. Then I had to go round lecturing from bunker to bunker. The subjects were:

1.   The soldier and his political mission in the East.

2.   The soldier and the woman of a different race.

3.   The *Feldpost* letter – a weapon!

Considering that in the other battalions of the regiment the lectures were considered to be the task of a *Hauptmann*, whereas I as a mere *Leutnant* had been selected to deliver them, I felt proud. 'Only you would have to tear yourself apart', I wrote on 3 July to my Mother.

Monotony and relative peace were a breeding ground of sometimes endless rumours. In the Ivanowo days the word went round persistently that the Division would be withdrawn and transferred to Greece. As always, the rumour came to the front from the baggage-train. The 'sarge' had bet the *Kompanietruppenführer* a barrel of Smolensk beer and of course had lost. Whether he ever settled his bet with the sceptical Palige, I never found out.

At that time an appeal was suddenly made to the troops to take part in the competition for the formation of a *Frontkreuz*. The front itself was to make recommendations for the order. It was to take the form of a cross. By small variations it would indicate whether the holder had served with the fighting troops, or in the lines of communication, and how many years he had served. Commander Palige and I industriously drew up our proposals, mostly inspired by a bottle of cognac that the *Oberleutnant* donated from his own Sunday afternoon supply.

There were many indications that the Russians were planning an offensive. They were firing 'registration' fire on our positions, using targeted fire with premature detonation. Such shells exploded while still in the air. In that way it was possible to assess the accuracy of the fire. From our side, a Focke-Wulf twin-fuselage aircraft was in action over the enemy frontlines. It was carrying out close reconnaissance by means of photography. The aircraft flew over in broad daylight and was only moderately troubled by enemy fire. The Russians were asleep at that time of day.

Over Whitsun I went with my platoon on outpost sentry duty. For the men, it meant crouching in the same small hole for ten days and nights. From the outpost sentry position, the ground extending over to the enemy looked like a tightly stretched, flat tarpaulin. To lift a head above the parapet by day would have been suicidal. The position was excellently camouflaged, but the enemy was supposed not to discover it until the last minute. Flat trenches, scarcely knee-deep, connected the individual machine-gun and foxholes of the *Igel-Stellung*. The movement of a man in the daytime, even if he ducked down, could not be camouflaged. To get to such a foxhole was only possible by creeping or crawling along on your belly. Of the 24 hour period only four or five gave sufficient darkness to be able to stretch our legs and move our limbs. During those hours the units bringing food came up to the lines with rations and post for the men on the line. There was no water for washing. Washing and shaving were impossible. We had to clean our teeth with coffee. In a 2 x 2 metre hole in the ground, as deep as a man's height, was my command post. It was covered with a layer of beams. Over the entrance was fixed the end of a wire by means of which a *T-Mine,* twenty metres from the *Igel-Stellung* in the direction of the enemy, could be set off.

On Whit Sunday night it was as if the Holy Ghost was truly appearing to us. On the stroke of midnight a considerable barrage rumbled off, covering the lines of the 1st and 2nd battalions directly behind us and to the right of us. Multiple mortars, called 'Stalin Organs', also joined in. It was a fascinating sight every time the 24 or 42 shells hit, spraying fire. By then it was clear that an attack on the sentry outpost was imminent. Whether it would be my post, or that of the 3rd Battalion placed to one side was not yet clear.

Meanwhile, the sound of tanks was suddenly to be heard. That indicated the Russians intended to attack the neighbouring position. The next night we learned that, in fighting off the attack poor Popovsky got shot in the lung, but had been brought back to the rear in time and otherwise was well. It was said to have been a whole battalion. His platoon had borne itself bravely, but still had all kinds of casualties and lost one wounded man as a prisoner. When the Russians had got hold of him, they withdrew, together with the tanks.

After almost four weeks at the front, I at last got some post from home. But there was nothing from Father in France. Rudi was waiting to be called up, having been accepted into the *Panzerkorps Hermann Göring*, which made him really proud. Amusingly, he described the chaos in the school. No-one in his class wanted to learn any more, but only play truant and, with their school-leaving certificate in their pockets, go to join up. Something that he had not told me before was that in February some trains with remnants of the 6th Army had passed through Stockerau and had stopped. 'But that was quite something, a battlefield taken all together, so to speak. Ruins, destroyed tanks, guns, horses and soldiers, and among them the straw everywhere which gave the whole thing even more of a sense of doom'.

One night the comforting petroleum lamp in my bunker could have caused a disaster. A platoon runner had inadvertently bumped into it and knocked it over. The overflowing petrol was soon caught by the flame, which spread out over the little table. We had trouble getting the boxes full of ammunition safely out of the bunker, including the box that served me as a pillow, while at the same time extinguishing the fire. Unfortunately my fountain pen, a confirmation present, fell victim to the flames.

On the night of 23/24 June the battalion was unexpectedly relieved by a battalion from 461 and moved into the Nemers sector. The Division was shifted a battalion width to the right, with us thus becoming the right-hand linking battalion. The march of only 10km did everyone good. To be moving, despite the pack and large amount of ammunition that had to be carried, was a refreshing change. The new sector was excellently constructed. The bunkers were deep in the ground and were covered with roofs of thick beams. There were many machine-gun and rifle positions, all correctly placed. The trench was as deep as a man's height. Only the barbed wire obstacles were incomplete. A road, overgrown with grass, to the remnants of the village of Nemers passed through the main line of resistance in the middle of the company sector. In the middle of my platoon sector was a 50 metre wide area of woodland, with the trench at the forward edge. Tall spruce trees, together with lower undergrowth and patches of grass in between, made the landscape look more like an English park, than something you would have suspected to be in the heart of Russia.

The disadvantage of the sector was a right-angled field, beginning 50 metres in front of the trench. It then extended at that width some 200 metres towards the enemy. On the farther edge of the right angle there used to be sentry outposts, but they were withdrawn because at night they were too much at risk. Whole companies could have slipped into the brush. For that reason, every night, reconnaissance patrols had to go out to check the area.

One night, when I had once again gone round the field, I ascertained that the Russians had settled themselves in the foxholes of our earlier outposts. As we reached our barbed wire on the way back, the Russians mounted a machine-gun attack on the passage through the minefield and through the barbed wire. Evidently they had been observing us slipping through the wire, for the heavy machine-guns, which they must have fixed on the target during the daytime, fired with pinpoint accuracy. We were not able to press ourselves close enough to the ground until the attack was at last over. After calm had returned and we had taken a long jump into the trenches, the runner Grimmig said that it would have been the right time to get a *Heimatschuss* by raising your hand. He had missed the chance yet again! Grimmig was a Gerhard Hauptmann-type figure who actually did have a grim expression, but was full of native wit, goodness, loyalty and courage. The humorous talk of a *Heimatschuss* was a manifestation of the so-called *innerer Schweinehund*. The Prussian Army creation was so splendid because it had such insight into the character of even the simplest man.

My kind Aunt Lotte sent me a whole lot of literature in small *Feldpost* editions. Apparently, hovering in front of her eyes were pictures of the trench romanticism of the First World War, the 'good fathers with their front-line beards', giving themselves to edifying reading by the flicker of a Hindenburg lantern. So as not to upset her, I thanked her effusively, but sent the little books straight home. Certainly, I would have had time for reading, but I did not have the necessary calm. The impressions of life at the front were still too new and too various, and life in the trenches, even in trench warfare, were too exciting for me to be able to immerse myself in reading. Much time was taken up in writing. There was Mother who formed the central core of the family, and Father in France. Rudi it is true, was still at home, but I wrote separately to tell him things that I could not, nor would not, write to Mother, so as not to worry her. But there were also friends and finally the girl. My affection was then fixed upon the *Skorpil-Mädi*. However, she had soon turned her affections away from me, again, even though I still carried a candle for her.

I shall give a short account of the Skorpil family, with whose son Erhard I went to school. Erhard and his elder brother Hannibal were both killed in action with the *Waffen-SS*. The husband of the eldest daughter was an *Oberleutnant* in the Stockerau cavalry. In 1941, he was wounded and fell into the hands of the Russians and murdered in an atrocious way. It became known through his comrades and the whole town knew of it. All five Skorpil children were good-looking. Elfriede, the youngest, was blonde and blue-eyed like the others, and with her long, thick hair was the picture of feminine grace. She was artistic, wrote calligraphy, and played the violin. At that time she did not know whether she should go to the academy of music or the academy of art. She later became a painter.

During our nightly work on the barbed wire we suffered many casualties from mortar fire. We worked on setting up *spanische Reiter* and trip wires. Accelerated completion of the work had been ordered because of the expected enemy summer offensive. We also had to provide greater security against assault and the capture of troops. The word was that specially trained Russians had been recently creeping through the lines to capture prisoners alive. At least ten men had to work at the same time at any one place, it was said. If not the enemy would grab one or other of them as they were stretching the wire.

The roof of my bunker, with its three layers of beams 1.2 metres thick in total, gave enough protection to be able to sleep in peace. A cannon stove, a nailed-together little table and two birch-wood stools completed the 'day room'. Behind a stretched piece of thin sacking were the bunks. The current state of trench technology was also displayed in the construction of the wooden beds. As well as the usual planks which had the advantage that you lay level, there was also the wire bed which bore some similarity to a hammock. Particularly nice was my bed of young birch trunks, which dipped way under my weight and feathered like a mattress. Sometimes, when I lay down to sleep after dawn had broken, I even allowed myself the luxury of taking my boots off in order to enjoy my feathery bed even more.

Trench culture also flowered in other ways. On the table in front of the bunker window, situated on the back wall of the bunker, one and a half metres underground, in front of a light shaft half a metre square, 'Mädi's' picture was resplendent. A 'specialist' had coloured it by hand, mounted it in a birch frame and covered it with cellophane instead of glass. Nickel, the platoon medic, gave me a home-made watch-hanger. It consisted of a star shell cartridge, filed off flat on the floor, the edges of which had been made jagged and bent round the photograph.

But from time to time the quiet life in the bunker was interrupted. Once the Russians must have seen smoke. They fired exactly 75 shots from a *Ratschbum* on to the bunker. The shots were all on target. Two of them scored direct hits on the bunker, but luckily did not hurt us.

The Nemers position had the advantage that you could get from the rear up to the most forward trenches without being seen by the enemy. Thanks to that, a warm lunch was actually able to be brought forward at lunchtime. But the Russians must have got wind of the time when food was distributed. On two days in succession they 'signalled' with pinpoint accuracy with a mortar. The lunchtime had actually been put back an hour, from 12.30pm to 1.30pm. While the soup was pouring into the dishes, up above there was the 'glug' of the mortar firing: 'Plop, plop, plup, gluck'. For the men who had brought the food, who had already had their portions, the interruption was doubly unpleasant, because with the full canteens in their hands they were additionally hindered in taking cover. If they had spilled any food, they would have had a rough welcome from their comrades.

Thus it seemed to be a fact that the Russians were listening in to our field telephone conversations by means of earth lines. The listening lines were nothing more than wires fixed into the earth by an iron rod. They were brought up as close as possible to the line to which they were to listen in, that is, as close as possible to our trenches. At the other end crouched a Russian, listening in on his listening set. Despite the fact that code names were constantly changed, for instance I was 'Rucksack' for the first week in July, the listener must have been able to learn enough from the conversations to which he listened. More than anything, the tone of military respect could not be hidden. It was true that you were supposed to leave out service ranks, but habit and drill often made you embarrassed when, instead of *Jawohl Herr Major*, you were supposed to answer with a straight civilian *Ja* or *Nein*. If the Russian could hear clearly and understood German well, he could soon draw his conclusions from the unabatedly obedient tone of the one participant in the conversation, and the commanding tone of the other.

One night I tripped over a wire in the area in front of the lines. Shocked, I thought at first that an S-mine laid by us had had a Russian line attached to it. It could have gone 'sky-high' together with me. But, thank God, that was not the case. It must obviously have been a listening wire. We reeled it gently in, which was not an easy job with a total length of 600 metres of wire. Particularly at the start, you could feel resistance. Perhaps a listener was sitting at the other end. As Grimmig said, 'the eyes must have popped out of his head' when his listening set began to move!

On the night of 5/6 July, a battalion from our neighbouring division attacked the 'Ascension heights' that lay in front of their sector. The attack took place after ten minutes' preparatory fire. Nemers in particular was fully 'covered' with 80 *Do-Geschosse*, the mysterious devices I had seen from a distance a few days previously near to the battalion command post. They looked like angled wooden frames resembling easels, half the height of a man. The projectiles were ignited like rockets, and when they were fired gave a loud screaming sound. The success of the operation must in any event have been nil.

Through the regiment we heard that, of the total of eight men in the Russian outpost on the heights, only a single man had been captured. He was an eighteen years old Uzbek who could not speak Russian. The nearest interpreter for Uzbek was at Army HQ. The interpreter thought that the lad was feeble-minded, since he was not even able to say when he came into the position, nor did he say to which unit he belonged. Perhaps he decided not to say!

The one subordinate with whom I had problems was *Unteroffizier* Brinkmann, leader of the 8th section. He did not keep his trench in order. Sometimes a duck-board was not mended, or a piece of camouflage or cover was not put right, despite the fact that I had complained about it. Those were the 'little things which made Prussia great'. Brinkmann was a 'watersider' with the walk and the look of a seaman, who used to smoke his pipe reflectively. I did not dislike him, but I had obviously not handled him properly. I had a good understanding with the

Silesians and Sudeten Germans. However, I just did not have that understanding with Brinkmann. Perhaps I was too young for him.

In 1943 a lot was already being said about the new weapons that were supposed to decide the war. But they were taking a long time to come. The MG 42, which the Russians called the 'electric', and of which there were a few in the company, was only a modest foretaste. Certainly, compared to the MG 34 it was a considerable improvement. The rate of fire was markedly higher and it had hardly any recoil. So there were many sarcastic remarks and mischievous jokes when at that time we received a *mitrailleuse*, a French machine-gun from the First World War. The monster was several times heavier and also more complicated to operate than our own machine-guns. The only thing 'fine' about it was the shining golden brass handle. The machine-gun had cartridge packs of 20 rounds each. When you inserted them and pressed the trigger, it went tack-tack-tack and pounded away, in a leisurely fashion, out into the world.

On Sundays the food was better and there was even a small ration of schnapps. It was simple hooch, often sweetened with artificial honey. When the commander had been drinking, in the afternoon he ordered me to the company bunker. Part of the equipment of the company troops was a field wireless receiver, usually carried on the back. It was possible to listen on Sunday afternoons to the popular *Volkskonzert*. Requests from the front were featured on it. As I was missing music very much, on those visits to the company command post I felt myself to be on a higher cultural level.

Oberleutnant Hentschel enjoyed Sunday as much as he could by having his horse brought with the food vehicle. He rode to the baggage area, going into the sauna there and in that way 'having a nice day' on the lines of communication. Of course, it was quite right and proper if the commander went to the rear now and again. Except that things did not go too smoothly for the workmen and clerks. He had cognac sent up from the canteen stock for Patige and me, and that made us very merry.

One time, Patige and I had a bit of a binge together which led us to be giddy enough to walk up and down, with no cover, outside the trench along the parapet as if on an esplanade. It set a bad example to everyone and was against all orders. Obviously the Russians must have been drunk too, or at least asleep, because they let slip the chance of some competition shooting, with us as two targets. As the high point of the lark, towards evening we fired off red and green flares. Red usually meant 'Defensive fire, enemy attack', and green 'Lift artillery fire'. Of course the flares had been noticed and we had a hard time pacifying the questioners on the other end of the line. To this day I am still amazed that we got away with it. A letter from Father at the beginning of July read:

> Now I am able at least to imagine a little of your daily and nightly life. Your description reminds me very much of my own experiences from 1915 to 1918. A quiet position is a first prize, only I think that especially in Russia you will never be able to rely on it staying that way. Build a wall around us so that the enemy will look at it in horror. What your former section leader said, that a decent soldier always carries his field hymn-book in his breast pocket, is something I shall tell to some people here. Here in the West things are not easy. In most cases I am dealing with really indolent sensualists for whom things are going far too

well for them to think of anything serious. If my health would stand it, I would far rather be serving in the East than here.

5

Summer/Autumn 1943: Trench construction and positional warfare

Positional warfare - joining the Regimental staff; on the trench construction staff

When I had travelled to the front in May, I noticed in the train some gentlemen dressed in civilian clothes. It was said that they were members of an international commission who were going to Katyn to examine the traces of the massacre. Katyn lies twenty kilometres to the west of Smolensk. I quote now from *Meyers Enzyklopädische Lexikon*, 9th edition.

> At the end of February 1943, German soldiers discovered in mass graves in the forest the bodies of over 4,000 Polish officers. They had been taken as prisoners of war by the Soviets, in eastern Poland in September 1939, and had been held in the Kozelsk camp. On the basis of various investigations, including some during the war and some later in the 1950s, the then Soviet Government is held responsible for the murders. After German troops evacuated Katyn in 1944, the accusation was made by the USSR that the crime had been committed by the Germans. That was not regarded as having been proven.

Significantly, the matter was not dealt with at the Nuremberg war crimes trial. However, at the time, in May 1943, we learned that the written notes found on the bodies ended precisely at a point in 1940 when the Poles were in Russian hands.

During the quiet period of trench warfare it was arranged that as many German soldiers as possible were to be taken to see the mass grave. Therefore, from our company too, a man was designated to visit it. After three days he returned and gave us his impressions. He still had 'the smell of putrefaction in his nose'. That was how he closed his account.

At the end of July I suffered another deep disappointment. On regimental orders I had to leave my platoon and report to the regimental staff at the Führer-Reserve. The order came just at the moment when the offensive might start and the enemy open fire. I had my platoon under control. I had won the confidence of my men. The opportunity to prove myself as a front-line officer seemed to have arrived. It was no help at all to me that the commander said, consolingly, that 'I should be pleased'. He said it was 'a kind of honour', that they wanted 'to protect me', because they believed me capable of more than commanding only a rifle platoon.

I spent the following days in anger and defiance. Still, I was pleased to a certain extent that, by way of compensation, I was assigned to the regimental adjutant. At

least I did not have to just sit around on my backside. The activities in the regimental staff, and the people who worked there, were interesting. *Oberst* von Eisenhart-
Rothe was tall and gaunt, but I did not see a lot of him, and thus could not get a
proper picture of him. After the autumn offensive he was transferred to the Staff of
Generalfeldmarschall von Weich in Belgrade. Some time later he shot himself because of a disagreement over a horse.

The regimental adjutant, *Hauptmann* Stockter, was an expatriate German
from Mexico and was an actor by profession. Accordingly, he spoke faultless
Hochdeutsch, was a lively mimic, and was always a bit over the top. However, he
gave me a good introduction to my new job. I studied in detail the entire regimental sector and prepared all the paperwork. I drafted orders and birthday greetings.
So I came, on paper, to address majors as 'My dear so and so…'. If I imagined
something would come of it I was, at the same time, angry at my foolishness. Had I
left my platoon 'for this'!

In the evenings I squatted in the bunker of the pioneer platoon commander,
Leutnant Uxa. He was a Viennese from the Postgasse in the 1st District. I also
found another Viennese soldier in the pioneer platoon who was studying piano at
the Conservatory. Before his call-up he had been practising Beethoven's C Minor
Concerto. With *Leutnant* Franke, my companion in suffering from the Führer-
Reserve, I often sang in the bunker. I remember his favourite song, the hit song *Sag
schön gute Nacht*. Franke was a teacher and was getting on for 30. He had an unusually friendly nature and must have been a good man. He had only been married a
short time, but was killed in action soon afterwards.

On a visit to the 2nd Battalion sector, the commander of the 7th Company,
Oberleutnant Becker, offered me a cigarette from a great package of cigarettes of an
unknown kind. To my surprised enquiry as to where they came from, he told me
that the company had a Bulgarian 'godmother-aunt'. She was a rich old lady from
Sofia who had lived in Germany, and loved Germany, since her youth. He said she
had selected the 7th Company of the 7th Regiment to be a benefactress to its members. She sent substantial 'love-gifts', and in that way combined her superstitious
belief in her lucky number, with deeds friendly to the Germans.

In the trenches of the 5th Company and on the barbed wire in front of them
lay six dead Russians. They had mounted an assault at dawn. Those who were still
alive, were driven off by the platoon leader *Leutnant* Ast, after a short exchange of
hand-grenades. *Leutnant* Ast, an old war-horse known throughout the regiment,
was tall, had a prominent Adam's apple and, as befitted his name, gave the impression of being knobbly. He said that it was 'not worth burying those few, since anyway more would soon be coming'. He said a prisoner had told him that the attack
was to begin the next day. A complete contrast to Ast was his company commander, Hain. Generally called *Freund Hein*, at 5ft in height, he was really small.
From his round, friendly face and little eyes there showered wit and jollity. As I was
accompanying *Oberleutnant* Rauprich from the 2nd Battalion of our artillery regiment, Hain gave us a large measure of schnapps, because, he said, we were his 'last
visitors before the attack'.

On the presumed last day before the expected attack, some aircraft were sent in
to attack the enemy assembly areas. Some squadrons of Ju 88 and He 111 bombers
flew in, in large numbers, and dropped their bombs on the Russians. The Russians

had sent up a surprisingly large amount of flak, which maintained uninterrupted fire. One He 111 received a direct hit and disintegrated. We watched it with *Oberleutnant* Hain, in his sector of trenches. Our artillery had also put down fire over the Russians.

On the way back to the regimental command post we passed the firing position of the 8th Battery. The gunners were working stripped to the waist, a *Leutnant* helping them to load. At the regiment, too, they were working on the basis that the enemy would attack the next day. The army high command had given orders to withdraw the sentry outposts during the coming night. That order was as clear as the regimental orders drawn up by *Hauptmann* Stockter, which closed with the words: 'And so, with all our trust in God, we shall do our duty!'

I woke in the night, roused from my sleep by the rumble of deafening thunder. At precisely 3.40am the bombardment began from 500 gun-barrels. There were howitzers, cannons, light and heavy mortars and rocket launchers. It was as if a supernatural drummer was vertiginously beating his drum. Right there, two kilometres behind the main frontline, you had the impression that the frontline trenches were being ploughed up. Our regimental command post was at the edge of the woodland, in the hollow behind the artillery firing positions and all were similarly under heavy-calibre fire. Whenever a 17.2 or 20cm shell exploded nearby, a shudder went through the ground and among the gigantic spruce trees where our bunkers were scattered. Massive splinters whizzed through the air, crashed into the wood of the trees and tore terrible gashes in the earth.

At 6.20am there was quiet. It would be seen if the two and a half hours of murderous bombardment had been effective, if the men in the trenches had survived and if they were still able to put up resistance. Perhaps the Russians would stroll through the woods unopposed. But only seconds after the barrage had finished, you could hear small arms fire. Through the clear sounds of the Russian machine-pistols came the chattering of machine-guns belonging to our lads. In the regimental bunker there was plenty to do. All the lines to the battalions, and the lines leading from the battalions to the companies, had been cut by shellfire. The first reports could only be obtained by wireless. Signallers were sent out to repair the telephone lines.

We learned that the main line of resistance had held in an outstanding manner. In the 10th Company, Schorsch Hentschel, only just promoted to *Hauptmann*, had thrown back the Russians in a counter-attack. Only on the post road had they penetrated into the remnants of the village of Ivanowo. There, the badly wounded *Oberleutnant* Mallwitz was encircled with only parts of the 6th Company. Behind the battalion command post of 2nd Battalion, the enemy had been brought to a halt. A counter-attack by 1st Battalion had a certain amount of success. From our Reserve bunker I had seen parts of the battalion that had been in reserve moving forwards. *Oberleutnant* Klaus Nikolai, commander of the 3rd, and *Fahnenjunker-Unteroffizier* Eberhard Kern were with them. Kern limped because his right big toe was missing since the winter of 1941. But he preferred to be there at the front rather than at home. Towards midday, after sending back many wounded, *Leutnant* Ast came back, shot through the shoulder. 'The damned sods', he swore. He said that, to be sure, the Russians had broken into his trench as they had the day before, but had been thrown out again by him and his men.

It was said that, during the two and a half hours' heavy barrage of 6 August, the Russians fired 50,000 shells on the Division's sector. They then attacked with nine infantry divisions and two armoured brigades. In front of the regiment's main line of resistance, and in the places where they had broken through, 3,000 dead Russians were said to have been counted. *Oberst* von Eisenhart was proud of his regiment's achievements. He drove to the front every day, standing in his *Kübelwagen*. My request, that he should take me with him one time, he declined. He said that I would get there 'soon enough'.

In the meantime, *Leutnant* Franke had left, and I was the last of the Führer-Reserve to be with the regiment. Again I had a disappointment. I received an order to ride to a village ten kilometres behind the regimental command post. My task was to guide baggage-trains through a busy junction. They were to be moved further to the rear. It was the village in which, before the attack, the Division's pioneer battalion and *Panzejägerabteilung* had been located. So, in a peevish mood, I rode overnight to the rear, accompanied only by a chap from the regimental riding platoon. When we reached the highway, a Soviet aircraft was already clattering over us. Expecting to be bombed, I was holding the horse on a very short rein, and managed to control it. But then a bomb fell very close by and the nag, terrified by the crash and the lightning flash of the impact, bolted with me so that I had great trouble bringing it under control again.

After I had guided the baggage-trains through the junction, as ordered, and before riding back, I looked for the commander of the self-propelled gun company. He was proud of his men's successes. Of the almost one hundred tanks destroyed in front of the Division's sector, a large number was down to them. However, the fact that the baggage was being moved to the rear was a sure sign that the front was soon to be pulled back. The surest sign was my new mission, to go as adjutant to the trench construction staff of the Division who had been hastily formed.

I learned from the Divisional history that, under the code name 'Panther', it was intended to withdraw, within two weeks and in two stages, from the Büffel position, to the Panther position. The new line ran approximately along the line Jelnja-Dorobusch-Spasdemensk. The final position ran approximately along the line Gomel and the course of the Pronja-Lenino east of Vitebsk. The Division's *Stellungsbaustab*, i.e. trench construction staff, was under the command of *Hauptmann* Müller. Until then he had been commander of our 2nd Company.

Müller was a tall, good-looking man, with dark brown eyes and hair, and heavy eyebrows. *Oberst* von Eisenhart called him 'glowing eyes' or 'Greyhound Müller', and in actual fact his appearance could remind you of a noble greyhound. As a student at the Tharant Forestry College near Dresden he had got the daughter of a professor pregnant, and married her forthwith. At the time, that went without saying. You could well imagine that he was inclined to be extravagant, even though he had his batman write his letters to his wife. The batman was *Obergefreiter* Petzold. He had been brought along and used as the clerk.

The staff also included an officer from, respectively, the artillery, the *Panzerjäger* and the pioneers. The officer of artillery was the congenial *Oberleutnant* Rauprich whom I had got to know before the attack. Müller and I determined the course of the trenches in accordance with the infantry point of view that regarded the representatives of the other service arms as providing the supporting weapons, so to speak. In that scheme, Rauprich's task was to fix the points for the 'B', i.e. the observation positions for the forward artillery observers. We had at our disposal an Adler-Trumpf *Kübelwagen* in which we drove around the terrain. The driver was *Obergefreiter* Moravietz, who had been detached from our 14th Company together with his vehicle. The actual work on constructing the trenches was carried out by the Division's so-called *Baubataillon*, of which I will speak later. That battalion also included two horse-drawn mobile columns. One was commanded by the dark-skinned elderly *Hauptmann* Focke, a Sudeten German and an hotelier by profession. In the evening, when I was issuing orders on behalf of my *Hauptmann*, I felt like the proprietor of a small construction business, planning from day to day how best to use his foremen, his workers, and his materials.

My displeasure over the lost opportunity to prove myself in a large-scale action had vanished, and I was even then able to see good points in the 'business' of trench construction. It was not to be sneezed at that here, at the rear, you could sleep at night, take off your tunic and even your trousers. That was all the more the case since calm had returned to the front line. I had not had it so good for a long time. Our base was in the little village of Lyadi and we lived in a clean, two-roomed farm cottage. The man of the family had been with the Red Army since the beginning of the war. Since then his wife had heard nothing from him. She did not know whether he was still alive, but bore it with resignation and equanimity. In a corner of the room stood the icon. It had always been there, even under the Bolsheviks. The village commissar had made fun of it, but otherwise found no fault in it. But the villagers had not taken him seriously, said the woman.

In a frame without glass were stuck some photographs, including a picture of a dead person of a kind known in Russia. The relatives were crowded round the dead man, in an open coffin. The women were wearing headscarves and the men long, white wide smocks.

The woman lived alone with her child on the small estate. The girl, perhaps eleven years old, was called Schenia. Mother and child had brown eyes and brown hair. The child had an innocent angel's face. We were touched to see how her face lit up when we gave her some of our scanty confectionery. She was amazed, as was her mother, at the pictures we showed her from home. The woman gave us a lot of the bread that she regularly baked. It was coarse, moist, heavy and full of spelt. We knew that in doing this she was treating us as her guests, and we gave the two of them what we could spare.

The attractions of our construction sector were the Vyazma-Jelnja railway line and a collective farm that lay in front of the future frontline. The extensive State property was administered by an agricultural *Sonderführer*. He had a couple of *Landesschützen* to provide military cover. For the rest he had obviously lived up till then 'like a king'. The yield was poor, he said. There was a shortage of workforce and machines to work the land more intensively. In front of the farmhouse was a ravaged German military cemetery from 1941, which partisans had destroyed. I wondered why the *Sonderführer* had not had it restored.

On 22 August, Rudi's eighteenth birthday, I got a concerned letter from Mother. She wrote that for about a week mention had been made every day in the Army news reports of 'west and south-west of Vyazma', and she suspected that they were talking about the district where I was. On top of this, she said, mention was made once of a 'Silesian infantry division': was this mine, she asked? She was obviously worrying about me more then she needed to, but how could I have said to her that her worries, at least for the moment, were unfounded?

A few days later there was great consternation among the inhabitants of the village. The *starets*, the village elder, had got news that the 18-year-olds, born in 1925, were to be rounded up and sent to forced labour in the Reich. Since all the young men were with the Red Army, only three girls were affected. No-one could respond to the village elder's plea for help. It could not even be ascertained from which authority he had received the order.

The countryside around Lyadi could, in different circumstances, have been described as lovely. Woodland, bushes, marsh, meadow, and a small river in a deep gully offered a constantly changing picture. Seen with a soldier's eye, the 'terrain' had disadvantages, and in places even was 'shitty'. Several hundred square metres of undergrowth had to be rooted out to provide a field of fire. In another place the unavoidable change from the position on the upward slope to that on the downward slope presented a puzzle. The problem would only be able to be solved by the relevant sector commander deploying outpost sentries. He would not be envied. The comrades would not be edified over some irreparable corners that would involve close quarters combat.

In our walks over the terrain, stepping through some tall bulrushes, we came across parts of a human skeleton. The gnawed bones, shining and bleached by the sun, had evidently been scattered over a wide area by birds. The skeleton had to be that of a soldier killed in action in 1941 in the fighting in the Jelnja arc. But it was not a German but a Russian. A little further on we found the hollow skull, still covered with a Russian helmet and with the chinstrap under the chin. However, we had no time to reflect on the mythical image of a soldier's death. In looking around for more bones, I noticed two half-overgrown, square plywood boxes in the form of oversized cigar boxes. They were more or less covered with moss and overgrown. They were Russian anti-tank mines. We had stumbled into an old minefield! Virtually on tiptoe we felt our way out of the field, using the open areas as if on a chessboard to get out of danger.

Those mines would make the trench construction work considerably more difficult. At any time, members of the work units could stumble across mines, and vehicles drive over them. Casualties were to be expected. In the absence of a precise map, danger loomed practically everywhere. In addition, we would not even be able to give a guarantee to the unit that would next move into the position that the area to their rear was free of mines. If it were only a matter of anti-tank mines requiring the imposition of a certain minimum weight before they exploded, the danger would have been less. But there was no reason to assume that that was the case.

As if to confirm our worry that there were also anti-personnel mines in the area, one day after the minefield was discovered a vehicle from the light column drove over a mine on a road and was blown to pieces. In another place a Russian civilian stepped on an anti-personnel mine. Afterwards the poor devil must have lain the whole night, far away from anyone, with his foot blown off, and so met his death. Inspection of the place where the horse-drawn vehicle had driven over the mine revealed that the tyre tracks of my *Kübelwagen* were only 10cm away from them. A special angel must surely have been holding his hand over Moravietz. I ordered him from then on only to use well-worn tracks.

Some days later, I was a guest of *Hauptmann* Kriegl, the 'commander' of the famous *Baubataillon*. He lived alone in a little house. He did not have a batman, but instead was served by a local woman. Vera was a nice and intelligent technical draughtswoman from Bialystok. She made no secret of her Bolshevik convictions and her belief that the Soviet Union would win the war. But this did not prevent her from living with Kriegl, who was in his mid-forties, in a relationship similar to marriage. Vera was chubby-faced, red-cheeked, had an ample bosom, and was always in a good mood. Even if those characteristics were not in her nature, she would have had every cause to be cheerful because the only work she was required to do was to look after *Hauptmann* Kriegl.

Not only I, but also the local commander was struck by the shameless outspokenness with which Kriegl defied our notions of clean living and marital fidelity. Moreover, it was the same with the men under his command. The civilians were all women and young people who were not particularly kept under watch, but merely supervised by members of the regimental band. I heard then that every one of these *Feldwebeln* and *Unteroffiziere*, active military musicians, was said to have had a 'wife' among the women workers. The sobering realisation for me was that even among us there was luxuriousness in the lines of communication, and that these *Etappenschweine*, who had left their mark so deeply in the literature about the First World War, had evidently still not been eliminated by the spirit of the new Germany.

Still, I also participated in the amenities of the lines of communication when Kriegl had cow's liver prepared, and had roast goose served to the members of the trench construction staff. During the meal, Kriegl told of a man from the company whom he had had under his command at the beginning of the Russian campaign. That man, shot through his skull through both temples, had not only lived to tell the tale, but had been returned to the active list!

Around 10 September the trench system of the Hubertus position was practically completed, and there came the order to move the staff to the rear. *Hauptmann* Müller had to go up the line to take over command of a battalion of Regiment 461. With him went his batman, *Obergefreiter* Petzold, who looked like a middle-aged official, i.e. about 35. Petzold even wrote his boss's letters to his *Ehemädchen* , as Müller called his young wife. While Müller and I were out in the field fixing positions, Petzold would write precise descriptions in clear script, like the company secretary of a building concern. In doing so, he always spoke of 'us' and wrote in the name of 'we' and Müller signed the letters after adding a short personal note. The young wife soon had to mourn for her husband, because Müller was killed in action the following November at Nevel. He was said to have been shot through the neck and thus to have bled to death.

For a few days *Oberleutnant* Gräbsch took over command of the staff. He was an extremely ambitious, impersonal and unfriendly man in his early thirties. By profession he was an optician from Beuthen. When he left, I took over command of the staff.

At that time an armoured train used to travel on the railway line near the State farm. It was said to have been captured from the Russians in the 1941 advance.

Certainly, I had no idea how that train was adjusted to run on European gauge tracks. It was equipped with German anti-tank and anti-aircraft guns, and it was interesting to inspect it. But it was no place to be for an infantryman. We did not feel at all happy in such a steel coffin. We preferred a trench in the womb of Mother Earth.

The front was on the move again. We knew that because the roads in our sector began to fill with baggage-trains. The baggage troops were supposed to carry in their vehicles only things that were important for the war effort, such as ammunition, food, and fodder. But I saw a lot of other things that the 'high-ups' were still bringing with them. There was upholstery on lorries with women sitting on top. Their 'lordships' could make themselves really comfortable again at their next location. They had everything you need, *was man braucht*, as the song goes.

For a long time there had been much air activity. Enemy bombers, fighters, and reconnaissance aircraft were hampered by a few aircraft of our Luftwaffe. It was said that Novotny, the fighter pilot, my fellow-countryman from Vienna, was in action in that area. If it was he, then on that day I saw three aircraft shot down by him. It was the day on which we left our cottage in Lyadi. Schenia and her mother, the warm-hearted, artless woman, had tears in their eyes when we said farewell.

The withdrawal of the front pushed my trench construction staff ahead of it. In the villages there began a fight for quarters. Sometimes I had trouble in claiming a room just for my staff activities. I could find no other way of doing it than to scatter maps over the entire floor of the room in order to distinguish the importance of our work from that of the various baggage units. Only when up against a main dressing station, the place where a regiment's wounded were treated, did I, quite rightly, have to give way. But I was more than a match for other lines of communications units in asserting our importance to the fighting troops. The people from the bakery, workshop and other companies could sleep outside in the fine summer weather or, if it rained, put up tents. But I could not have my trench diagrams prepared in the rain.

Line by line, trench by trench, I laid them out. Our civilians had to almost double their daily output. One officer after the other was taken away from the trench construction staff and went back up the line. I was then the specialist for observation positions and artillery gun positions. Often I only had time, as I stood in the vehicle, to 'draw' the line of the trench, using the wheel tracks. The trench was then dug out following in my track. My 'eye' for the terrain had become so sharp that even with such provisional procedures there were never any 'blind corners'.

The roads that I encountered on my journeys around the terrain were the routes of retreats, with all the signs of retreat. Abandoned vehicles, carts with broken wheels, destroyed equipment, bomb craters, shrapnel and many dead horses lined them. There were horses with bloated bellies and glassy eyes and their cadavers spreading a pestilential stench. In Russia, 2.7 million horses were deployed by the German *Wehrmacht*. Of those, 1.7 million fell victim to the war. They too we considered to be our comrades. Many of us were cut to the heart when a horse was wounded and, gripped with deadly fear, it faced the bullet that would put it out of its misery.

From then on, each day I expected an order dissolving the trench construction staff. Everything was, in a way, flowing to the rear. Land and people seemed to be on the move. The front, the lines of communication, and parts of the Russian civilian population were flooding back. Other civilians were setting off eastwards again. Evidently they wanted to walk through the lines, or take cover and let the retreat pass them by. When a couple of women from the *Baubataillon* wanted to stow away, the *Musikfeldwebel* fired a couple of times into the air, whereupon the *Mankas* hastily turned round and told their 'guardians' they were sorry.

6

Autumn/Winter 1943:
Company commander, the Russian offensive, wounds

Made company commander; the Russian offensive - withdrawal and retrograde actions; wounds, convalescence, home leave

On 20 September the order finally came dissolving the *Stellungsbaustab*. What was left of it went back to their units, and the *Baubataillon* set off again westwards. On the way to the front, at the Division and at the regiment, I heard news. Losses had been heavy. *Oberstleutnant* Nowak had taken over command of a regiment in another sector. Ours was under the command of a newly arrived *Oberstleutnant* Dorn, a Rhinelander. *Hauptmann* Krause, previously commander of the 11th Company, had taken over command of 3rd Battalion. Nowak had called him and *Hauptmann* Hentschel, who both held the German Cross in Gold, the *Korsettstangen des Bataillons*, the battalion's 'corset stays'. I took over command of my 10th Company, in which in the summer I had been a platoon leader. But there were only a couple of men left from that time. *Hauptmann* Hentschel had been killed in action, *Oberfeldwebel* Palige and the grim *Obergefreiter* Grimmig had been wounded. Even my 'glowing eyes', *Hauptmann* Müller, was to meet a hero's death in his 'splendid Orlog', as he put it. More than the other pieces of Job's comfort, however, I was saddened by the news of the death of Walter Henschel, who was killed in action on 5 September.

How proud Walter was, when in summer 1942, after his probation at the front he was the only one of us to go back home with the Iron Cross! The *EK* had compensated him for a great deal of disadvantage and injustice. He had put up with much during his time as a recruit, by laughing and clenching his teeth. He was not a good looking chap, but was of small stature, and always held one shoulder and his head somewhat crooked. He had a round face with prominent cheekbones and acne. What most caused him to be made fun of, were his large sticking-out ears. 'Walter, lay down your ears', or 'Henschel, just see that you keep your glider's wings under your steel helmet', joshed his comrades and instructors. From exaggerated 'snappishness' he spoke quickly and indistinctly. That way of speaking sometimes degenerated into mumbling, and that brought him further reproval.

With such physical characteristics he was bound to create a negative impression, which as a rule was bad news for any soldier. That was the case with Walter. He attracted the jokes of his comrades and the lightning bolts of the instructors. But at the same time he was the best lightning conductor in diverting them from us. The high point of the harassment, which he bore with apparent calm, happened one Sunday. Since his uniform had not been in order, from reveille onwards he had to report every quarter of an hour to the *Unteroffizier vom Dienst,* i.e. the duty NCO, alternately in marching kit, in walking-out uniform, and in sports kit. At the time we gave him all the support we could, helped him change and distracted him so that he did not burst into tears. Then, after lunch, the *Leutnant* relented and let him off the remaining parades. But Walter, even without our moral support, would certainly not have come to tears. He did not feel himself that he was being harassed, just as we others would not have felt harassed if it had happened to us. He bore unpleasant things because it was part of the job.

Anyone who wanted to become a Prussian officer knew that the way to that goal was no bed of roses. He knew that before it was his turn to be allowed to give orders, he had to learn to obey and would be drilled more than the others. Walter was the son of a blacksmith from Reichenbach in the Eulengebirge. For him, the career of an officer offered an unparalleled opportunity to rise in the world. For the inspiring prospect of being able to become an officer with his Field Marshal's baton in his knapsack, he, whose father was serving as master blacksmith in a baggage-train, would have taken upon himself more than such trivial and short-lived moments of disapproval. For him it was true when he said, *Wer auf die preussische Fahne schwört, hat nichts mehr, was ihm selber gehört,* 'Whoever swears on the Prussian colours no longer has anything he can call his own'.

At New Year 1941 he had had one over the eight in the officers' mess in Mörchingen. A comrade, just as drunk as he was, smeared boot polish on his face. After reveille for the New Year parade, two hours later, he had trouble getting rid of the biggest smears. The half-hour march through Mörchingen with 'dressed' rifle had been a sobering experience for us all. On our return to the barracks, the commander of the *Ersatz* unit carried out the inspection of the New Year parade. But since the 'old man' was obviously 'sozzled' himself, he had not, luckily for Walter, discovered Walter's face covered in boot polish. So, at least that time, Walter did not attract attention. But then, in September 1943, I realised he would never again rub his sleepy eyes and, as he once did, enthusiastic and happy, shout down from his bunk into the room, imitating the radio announcer: 'Good morning, today is Tuesday, the 6 September 1943...'

It was about 20 September when I took over command of the 10th Company that I had left at the beginning of August as a platoon leader. The company had shrunk to less than the size of a platoon. I arrived in the middle of the withdrawal. At that moment the Russians were not pressing and the withdrawal movement could proceed by day. Reconnaissance patrols tentatively feeling their way forward could be seen through the binoculars. Since the type of terrain allowed it, we withdrew in broad formation just as we had advanced to attack in the opposite direction. A line of field grey, a kilometre wide, was striding over the steppe-like landscape. The men were holding their rifles over their cartridge cases, the gun barrels, like their faces, lowered. From time to time officers stopped, turned round, and looked through their binoculars. Like an unfolded fan, drawn along by an invisible hand, we left the silent land behind. We could not suppress a feeling of saying 'farewell'.

Having been ordered to, I had to look around once more in order to scout out a village that was slightly to the side of our route. I had to see if it was occupied by the enemy. When I arrived within 300 metres of the village with my two volunteers, we came under rifle fire. Bullets whizzed into the damp grass. It was friendly of the Ivans not to let us come any nearer to the edge of the village. But because of that our task was quickly done. We had ascertained that the village was occupied by the enemy, and were able to withdraw, darting from side to side. It was not easy because the terrain offered no cover.

The Division's route led southward past Smolensk. I could no longer hope to be able to visit the town a fourth time. I regretted my laziness that had prevented me from looking around properly on my previous visits. I would never again be able to wander up to the cathedral of the Assumption of Mary, and I would never again be able to sit down against the eastward-facing fortifications of Boris Godunov. That was something which I had always intended to do, inspired by Napoleon's equerry Coulaincourt. Then I should have wanted to look down upon the burning city, just as a Wurttemberg artillery major had looked, in 1812, from the walls of the fortifications. He had seen and drawn it with the mighty towers and delicate battlements. Whoever holds Smolensk holds Russia, was how the saying had gone in those days. Then the city had been alternately Russian, Lithuanian, Polish, and Russian again. To draw lessons from history was not for me at my age. That the fortunes of war had changed was something that I would not have been able to judge.

On the night of 25 September we moved through Monastyrschtschina. Here and there a house was on fire and in the light of the fire could be seen a former church and many clean little wooden houses. On the western edge of the little town we stopped for a short while. There I took over command of the 3rd Company. It too was then only 28 men strong. The 1st Battalion, to which the company belonged, was under the command of *Hauptmann* Beyer who in summer 1942 had been my company commander.

Beyer was determined to let the exhausted men of his battalion sleep for the rest of that night. For weeks they had only had on average two to three hours of sleep. Even then all that could be expected was scarcely likely to be more than four hours. The next village, Worpajewo, was our destination. Each of the weak companies took a card, and the men, who were dead tired, immediately fell to the ground. The company commanders still had to go off for a meeting at the battalion. They were told that the withdrawal was continuing and they would be moving off again in the early morning.

The meeting was interrupted by a *Feldwebel* who had gone down a little way towards the village in order to 'organise things'. God knows what the man had hoped to find. In any event he reported that out of the darkness he had been greeted with a shout of *Stoj*, whereupon he had withdrawn. This was obviously a damned nuisance to *Hauptmann* Beyer, because he said in his dry, Berlin way: 'Oh, get away with you, man, they were volunteers whose nags had bolted, stop the bother'. None of those present could bring themselves to contradict him. They did not want to disturb the longed-for peace and quiet. I assigned the watches and lay down with my men on the flat tiled floor, my head in the hollow of my steel helmet.

At 3.30am, the time we were ordered, the battalion assembled on the village street, the companies in ranks, one behind another. We were not even out of the woods when shots whipped along the village street. Men were falling, others were crying out. Panic took hold of the mass of men, who were still drowsy with sleep. Everybody was running and no one was listening to my command. As I ran I snatched a machine-gun belt from the ground and hung it round my neck like a scarf. During the one kilometre flight I turned round several times and saw some cavalry and infantry, perhaps dismounted Cossacks. It was incredible that a handful of enemy had actually put us to flight. But still there was no stopping. Some swine of a machine-gunner had dropped the belt that I was then carrying round my neck. Another whom I overtook, I caught throwing away a box of ammunition. 'You lousy sod', I bawled at him and gave him a kick in his behind. When he picked the box up again, I kept him with me with the intention of getting hold of a machine-gun. But still the mass of men had not been brought to a halt. I saw the battalion medical officer, Dr Kolb, shot down as he was struggling to bring a machine-gun into position.

A quiet unheroic man had done what it was our job, the troop officers, to do. Violent rage seized me. Finally I managed to get hold of a machine-gun and the two gunners. I snapped at them, 'We three are now staying here, even if we have to die here. Do you understand?' *Jawohl, Herr Leutnant,* they answered, shocked. Behind a low rise in the ground we went into position. With a few spadefuls the machine-gun position was improved and a small amount of cover was produced. In the complete calm that then gripped them, the two machine-gunners carried out their well-drilled handling of the weapon. The Russians were leaving some time before they followed up. The last stragglers of the battalion passed, then the first gunner let fly with his first bursts of fire. The Ivans went to ground and disappeared behind undulations in the ground. Fifteen minutes later the formation of the battalion was re-established. *Hauptmann* Beyer had had a line drawn up. When at last the first machine-gun began to chatter behind us we three were able, alternately running and jumping, to withdraw to the battalion line.

A MG 42 and 15 men were all that was then left of my company. We crossed the highway from Smolensk, and the anti-tank ditches that ran to the west of it. In the next village my company and I had to remain behind another two hours, as a reguard, until 2pm. On both sides of the village and the road along which we were withdrawing was open steppe. Whether and where there were rearguards was unknown. In front of the two houses right and left of the village street at the outskirts of the village I had a start made on digging foxholes. The comrades were not so keen on digging and said that we would have to weather out the two hours over midday. I gave way to them and we left it alone.

For an hour everything remained quiet and no enemy showed themselves. A man kept a look-out, while I sat with some others on the bench in front of the house. The sun was shining and the autumn sky was a cloudless blue. In that contemplative position I stretched out my legs in front of me, pushed my hands into my trouser pockets, and nodded off. Out of a deep sleep of only a few minutes, I was wakened by shots. The sentry ran up and made his report. From the hollow with the anti-tank ditches at the side of the highway, he said that cavalry had appeared. They had turned round when he fired on them and disappeared back into the trenches. The tense waiting and watching lasted about a quarter of an hour, until the cavalry once more came out of the hollow. They were wearing brown Russian uniforms, but with square caps on their heads. First there were 10, then 20, and then more and more, all forming up into a front, and at a gallop storming up to our village.

It must have been a squadron of about a hundred coming closer and closer. The anachronistic picture fascinated and hypnotised me. The last time that cavalry had attacked was the Polish cavalry in the Poland campaign. But in seconds I was awake and gave my order. It could only be to fire at will. They had already approached to within 300 metres of us when from the right flank, apparently from a neighbouring village, the flak of an unknown unit opened fire. While at first only individual horses reared and only a few cavalrymen fell, our rifle fire too was then beginning to hit. The remnants of the hundred or so drove down on us in a confused tangle. We had climbed out of the foxholes and were firing at will into the mass of them.

The attack collapsed, and soon riderless horses were chasing over the field. Some cavalrymen managed to turn round and to reach the hollow. Dismounted wounded Cossacks dragged themselves back. Injured horses were lying on the ground and thrashing about, whinnying. Because we had to save ammunition, we ceased fire, and fired no more after the stricken cavalrymen. The main responsibility for our success doubtless belonged to that flak unit. It certainly had rescued us from an uncertain fate. But the episode reminded me of those Cossacks, who with their skirmishing, wore down Napoleon's *Grande Armee* on the retreat from Moscow.

Soon after we had evacuated the village as ordered, we passed a herd of cattle. While the animals were grazing on unsuspectingly, the machine-gunner let fly some bullets into the herd. It followed the order that nothing that could sustain life was allowed to fall into enemy hands. Anywhere that could be used for accommodation was to be burnt. Food, weapons, and equipment were to be destroyed, under the name of 'scorched earth'. That followed the example set by the enemy in 1941.

I was back once again with the unit. After a fortnight during which I had my boots on day and night, my feet were so swollen that I was not able to get the boots off. I had ordered that the *Kuchenbulle* should bring me a pair of rubber boots and footcloths with the food vehicle. When he brought what I had asked for, the operation could begin. I had feared that the boots would have to be cut off, but things went well. Four men got hold of me, two of them pulled at a boot each and two of them held me by my shoulders and arms. As if they had wanted to pull me into four, they pulled me apart in opposite directions. But it worked, and my swollen filthy limbs were free.

Meanwhile, the autumn had begun. The so-called mud period was imminent. If it was not raining, the days were still hot, but during the night the temperature fell by 20 degrees. We were freezing, and the 'oldies' were no longer so easily dried. To warm ourselves we hoped for burning villages. Units operating in the rear saw that the villages to be evacuated were burnt to the ground. Night after night was bright. From the glare of burning settlements we would have been able to recognise our direction of march, even if we had not ourselves possessed maps and compasses. It seemed remarkable that the earth on the road along which we were retreating was burnt. It was not as if we had burned our bridges behind us.

I remember stopping one night in a burning village. While we waited in front of the fire, we dried our feet in the warmth of the glow, and rubbed our hands as a kind of recuperation. It seemed as if a watch fire of *Prinz* Eugen was warming us and illuminating the scene. For a short time we behaved as if the enemy were not already close behind us. We fancied ourselves in peace and security. All that remained of the entire battalion, officers and men, stood around the burning beams. We stared into the glowing element, smoked, drank schnapps or tea from our field flasks, chatted, or reflected on our forthcoming departure. Wood and straw crackled and the horses of other units snorted uneasily. In the warm air from the fire you breathed in the musty smell of old wood and rotten straw. Only the lime oven with the chimney resisted the fire.

It did not yet rain for days and nights on end, but in fits and starts, and for only hours at a time. But that was enough to swell the streams. Where otherwise the water might have reached to our ankles, we had to wade through fords up to our knees, or up to our bellies. In the twilight I observed a battery crossing. The path led steeply down to the water and just as steeply back up again on the other side. It was time for the gunners to get their horses to give it all they had. With *Karacho*, as we said at the time, the team of six stormed up the stony path. 'Gallop!' was the command. The gunners in the saddle hit at the horses, and those who were sitting on the gun-carriage clung to each other. While the rain spattered on the water of the swollen stream, the dauntless animals dragged the teams with the howitzers through it and up the slope on the other side. It was a kaleidoscope of power and movement that an artist might have been able to fix on paper.

A new platoon leader joined our company for 48 hours. *Leutnant* Bertram, who was about 40 years old, was a '12-ender', recognisable by the two blue bands. He had only recently been caught by the *Heldenklau*. That was what the commissions were called who were combing through the home front troops to find men who were capable of serving at the front. He had served in General Meltzer's company when Meltzer was still a *Hauptmann* in the 100,000-man Army. But then that was no use to him. His parade-ground snappishness, his dreadful Saxon and his clear air of anxiety cheered us up. As suddenly as he had come he disappeared again for no apparent reason. At that time it was said that the life expectancy of an infantry lieutenant, that is, the time in which he could expect to remain with his unit without being wounded, amounted to 13 days. *Leutnant* Bertram's life expectancy had therefore been significantly shorter.

On the evening of 30 September we crossed the Dnieper, which in its upper reaches was a modest river. I climbed down the bank, thirsty. I scooped some up with the hollow of my hand. I had drunk water that tasted of the earth. On the western steeply climbing bank we found a position ready constructed. It proved to be a considerable disadvantage that the trenches ran at a point half way up the incline. There it had been hoped to stabilise the front. The trenches had been drawn in such a way, that blind corners were avoided in the field of fire in front of the position. When we evacuated it in the afternoon the disadvantage of the position became apparent. The enemy had already occupied the opposite bank and had brought some *Ratschbums* into position. With them they could fire almost directly down into our trench, which we would immediately have to evacuate again. It was a strenuous and exciting operation, to rush uphill in the trench accompanied by the impacts of that unsavoury weapon.

After we reached the top the reason for the sudden order to evacuate became apparent. On the left, to our rear, there were already Russians whom we could see advancing to a bridge. That bridge led over a tributary stream and also had to be crossed by us. As we realised the situation, we ran at the same time as the enemy, racing to see who could reach the bridge first. If the Russians had simply opened fire on us, we would have not reached the bridge alive. But since the enemy did not fire I did not take the trouble to bring the men to a halt. After the experiences of Woropajewo, I thought that to construct the security position on the other side of the bridge would be hard enough in itself. In the event I succeeded, but only with difficulty. My voice was hoarse from shouting commands, and cursing those running away. A portly *Obergefreiter* claimed he had a bad heart and had to go back. I answered him that he should not be running and had all the more reason to stay where he was, rather than go into the position. Then, when the pursuing Russians received our first aimed rifle fire, they gave up their pursuit and we had quiet until the evening.

During the night we retreated further. The company had loaded its goods on to a horse-drawn vehicle. Machine-guns, ammunition, blankets, and a couple of men with bad feet were loaded on one wagon as they had on previous nights. The little animal, in itself tough and more efficient than our thoroughbred army horses, was nevertheless at the end of its strength. Through deep mud and over bumpy 'corduroy' roads it pulled with its last ounce of exertion, urged on by cries, and beaten on by blows from sticks. Then it stopped with quivering flanks and collapsed on its knees. But the *Landser*, whose load he was helping to carry, did not give up. While one of them spoke to the animal lovingly and kindly in German and Russian, the other was already holding a stick ready to drive it on again. They continued until the horse once again moved forward with the courage and the power of desperation.

Then the nag collapsed again, for good, out of sheer exhaustion. The men began to curse and it took a long time until weapons and equipment were unloaded. When, years later, I read Dostoevsky's 'Crime and Punishment', when I was reading of Raskolnikov's dream I had to think of that image. The devastated Nikolka with blood-rimmed eyes swings the jemmy over his horse, breaking out into the cry of 'It is my property, it is my property'.

My voice had become so hoarse that it was hard to make myself understood. It was the result of continually shouting out orders. For the longer my voice lasted the less the runners needed to run. Marches went on throughout the night, often as much as 30 kilometres. That meant even further for the runners, for in addition to the march that the unit had to make they had to cover even more ground in carrying messages. At the start of a march people still carried on conversations, but gradually the men fell silent, silent as the night.

At that time I was proud of the state of my feet. They showed no blisters or bruising and had nowhere been rubbed raw. To a certain extent I was an infantryman from the top of my head to the soles of my feet. In fact the soles of my feet were even more important than the top of my head. To the difficulties of the marches was added hunger. At one time it happened that for two days and two nights the field kitchen had not come forward. The baggage-trains lay too far to the rear so that in the heat of the day, and as a result of the long transport distances the food became sour. The bread and the *Schmiere*, proper margarine, had run out. The 'iron rations', a small tin of fatty meat and a little pack of hard tack, were not allowed to be touched. That would only have been allowed in difficult situations. In the villages, in so far as they were not already on fire or had already burnt down, there was nothing to find. The poor inhabitants had nothing to leave. One morning, one bright spark found some beehives. The company, that is we 20 men, licked and slurped with our bare hands at the sticky sweet mass. The powerful bitterness penetrated into your teeth and at first made your empty stomach want to throw up. At other times I can recall myself beside fences on which tomato plants were hanging. The tomatoes were green showing no red at all. We ate gherkins and *kohlrabi* raw, and hardly cleaned of earth, without ever the dreaded 'shits' setting in.

One day the men had sorted out for me a 'beast of burden'. The 'beast' had a string as reins, but neither halter, bridle nor saddle. At first it quite docilely let me get on to it and with one jump I was up. At that time the battalion was marching in ranks through the night. To sit comfortably on the smooth horse's back and to be carried by it was an almost uncanny feeling. But my satisfaction only lasted until we reached the next village. As I was riding past one of the burning houses, a glowing beam fell down and sparks flew up. My horse took fright, gave a jerk and bolted with me. It charged off at a gallop. I passed other fires and passed the long ranks of the battalion, marching slowly one behind the other. I was not able to subdue the nag and losing my balance came off its back. Slipping to the left I was simply unable to let go of the string that served as reins. With my right foot I hung over the crupper and held myself under the horse's neck as it raced through the village with me. Then it calmed down or else the load on its neck had become too heavy. Snorting, it finally stopped, was calm again and let me remount as if nothing had happened. But the involuntary and dangerous comedy of my situation had a cheering effect, and the good-natured ribbing that I received did not upset me.

On 4 October, word came that we were reaching the final line and the withdrawal was completed. That news gave new life to our tired bodies and spirits. The battalion commander announced that the new position was well constructed and that the field kitchens were waiting with masses of food. Front-line combat packs and fresh lice-free underwear were to be issued. There were also additional rations and a few sweets. Still more important were the announcements that there were replacements for the company. We would once again be topped up to full company strength.

Two kilometres from the new main line of resistance there lay in our sector the little village of Puply. Because it could offer accommodation to the enemy and could affect our line of sight and field of fire, military necessity required that it should be destroyed. Such unchivalrous business had not, until then, been part of our war. But where was there room for chivalry in that war? My company was ordered to set fire to the houses on the right-hand side of the street. There, in the vicinity of Smolensk and the *Bolschaja*, the highway, the little wooden houses showed more signs of civilisation then we had seen until then. It was evident that we were close to the city, as indicated by a brass bedstead that I saw in one house.

Apart from a few old people, the inhabitants had left the village. Tears were running over the lined faces of those who had stayed behind. An absolutely ancient man, who had recognised me as an officer, raised his hands. He moaned, and asked me to spare the house in which he had lived all his life and where he wanted to die. The old man moved me. It was strange that intensive propaganda, and the manifold impressions of the ruthlessness of that campaign, had not been able completely to suppress sheer human sensitivity. I struggled with my feelings of duty, and was relieved that my men sympathised with me when I ordered them to spare the house of the old man.

My company went forward and set fire to the next wooden house with a bundle of straw. The old man tried to kiss my hands, and wished me a long life. Waving away his thanks, I stressed to him that he should take care that the flames did not spring from the neighbouring house on to his. If among the men there had been a 'bigwig' or a 'fanatic' I would have risked a court martial on account of that old Russian. But there were none of that kind among us. Once a man was among frontline soldiers, he soon relearned his true values.

In the evening we moved in to the new position. The company sector was well located. The position, on a low slope, had a good field of fire and line of sight over a depression in the ground. On the other side the terrain climbed again, flat, towards the smouldering village. Whether the old man's house had remained intact could not be seen because of the smoke and the trees that were still in leaf. To a certain extent the trenches were reasonably well constructed, but in numerous places really flat. There had not been enough time to construct bunkers such as we had been accustomed to in our trench warfare. Nevertheless we found some quite large holes in the ground, about the length of a man and 150 centimetres deep. Many had been covered with a thin layer of wooden beams. I set up my command post in such a 'hole'. In it there was room for three men. A couple of arms full of hay saw to it that there was a bit of warmth in the early autumn nights that were becoming chilly.

The field kitchen had actually arrived. There were gigantic portions of warm *Leberwurst* with *Stampfkartoffeln*. Since the amount of rations in combat did not match the current complement of the unit, the portions for dead and wounded comrades were given to the living. That had less of an effect in the case of food, as in any case you could not eat more then your fill. But in the case of schnapps, tobacco, and frontline combat packs those who remained enjoyed the extra. Not a few fathers of families sent home their surplus food. I sent a parcel of it to my nine years old sister Liesl.

It was a special blessing that the field post was then distributed. During the withdrawal it had not reached us. Within three days I received 25 letters. On 8 October I was able to reply to five letters from my Mother. In that letter I wrote that the physical exertions were soon likely to be at an end. But we were still living without any extras. For four weeks I had not been able to wash, shave, or clean my teeth.

Replacements had also arrived. To my surprise, among them there were men from Lorraine and Luxembourg. Their homeland was then part of the *Reich* and they had become eligible for military service. They did not seem too enthusiastic. Most of them seemed anxious and were obviously badly trained. A tall blond man from Düdeling made an optimistic impression and found his feet straight away. On the other hand it seemed that during the night another *Unteroffizier* had disappeared. No one had seen him go and nowhere had he given any hint of leaving. Kaczmarek, an Upper Silesian who was about 40 years old, spoke Polish and Russian well and had only been a few weeks at the front. Otherwise he had always been with the baggage-trains. It was painful for me to realise that the man must have gone over to the enemy.

In the early morning of 5 October, I was wakened by the rattle of our MG 42s and the clear sound of Russian machine-pistols. With my two runners I jumped up to the main trench. A *Fahnenjunker* came running to meet me with the words 'the Ivans are here'! I took him by his lapels, said that he should come with me, and hurried on. In the trench there lay a dead Russian. With my machine-pistol drawn I felt my way around the corners of the trench, the runners behind me. One of the runners shouted 'there they go'! We had come a little too late to repulse the assault unit. Our reliable *Feldwebel* Geissel had been there before us.

The last two Ivans fled, then collapsed under our rifle fire in the area between the lines. Two gave themselves up. Three lay dead in the trench, among them the leader, a junior lieutenant. We examined his papers. The newcomers to my unit, who had not yet seen any dead Russians, approached the bodies with curiosity. They were surprised at the primitive nature of the Russians' equipment. We 'oldies' were surprised by the oversized officers' epaulettes that the junior lieutenant was wearing. The previous year they had not had those historic Russian insignia of rank. But by then the 'Great Patriotic War' declared by Stalin had begun. By then it was no longer the workers' Fatherland, but Mother Russia who was in danger, and who had called her sons.

In the meantime, *Oberstleutnant* Dorn had relieved Nowak in 3rd Battalion, and had taken over command of the regiment. In the evening he inspected the sector and received reports about the morning visit of the enemy. It is true that he did not call me *Bubi*, as Nowak had done in the summer, but like Nowak he was really paternal. On his belt buckle he had a field flask dangling from which he offered us drinks. It was good warming cognac.

The hope for a period of rest in the Puply sector had proved impossible. On the night of 12 October we had been relieved and had moved into the baggage-train village some 10 kilometres away. Until midday we had been able to sleep without the disturbing influence of the enemy. Transport, on lorries northwards to the 'taxiway', was planned for the afternoon. There, one of the combat actions was underway. In the history of the war in Russia, they were called the 'Smolensk highway battles'. The Russians had continued to attack and had made critical breakthroughs.

We spent the night of 13 October in the village of Lenino. The company had been topped up to 70 men and I had found them quarters in two rooms of a Russian house. The conditions were dreadfully cramped. The only way get some sleep was side by side, all huddled in one direction. It was impossible to turn over, because the whole chain would have become tangled up. The stench, the cramped conditions, and the lice saw to it that our rest did not develop into a recuperative sleep. Again and again a man would start up, tormented by lice. Then, in addition, there was an 'owl' in the night. It was a Soviet biplane, well-known to us from our trench warfare. Since my night ride in Jelnja I was sensitive to that aircraft, so there was to be no hope of falling asleep. In actual fact the 'owl' did drop some shrapnel bombs. One of them, a dud, stuck in the thick thatch of our house. There would have been a bloodbath if that bomb had exploded.

During that day *Leutnant* Rauprich, my acquaintance from the trench construction staff, came past with his battery. I stopped him and asked how the situation was going. He said that the artillery commander had ordered his regiment to take up preventative firing positions. Rauprich also had some other bits of news. He said the third Smolensk highway battle was underway. Not far from there the Polish Division *Thaddeusz Sikorsky* had been sent into action, and also Soviet female units. He said that he himself had seen female prisoners of war. Rauprich was not surprised that the Russians were able to stand the tempo of their advance, but at the same time were carrying out offensive battles. He also told me that, as the result of a shortage of transport, the enemy was having containers of petrol rolled westwards, on the highways, by women, children, and old men.

As dusk fell, I moved forward as ordered with my company. It was necessary to form a kind of second line behind the point where a breakthrough had been made. We dug our foxholes and the men fetched hay and straw so that the foxholes could be made warmer and softer. Though at that season the sun could still shine strongly by day, the nights were already getting cold. In the meantime, from the baggage-train we had received overcoats. We could not take off our overcoats during the day. Where could we infantrymen have put them! Therefore we were exposed, in the same clothing, to a difference in temperature of 20 degrees.

It must have been three kilometres to the main line of resistance. From the front line there rang out now and again the sound of artillery fire and the impact of shells as well as the sound of some infantry fire. Knee to knee I crouched with my runner in our two-man hole. We were freezing and could not get to sleep. At 10pm a battalion runner took me to the command post of the local unit, where our staff was already located. Freezing and swearing, I followed him.

Hauptmann Beyer had taken over command of a battalion of our sister regiment 461. So I was received by the new commander, *Major* Brauer. He had just come from Norway. He had taken part in the First World War, had no experience of the Eastern Front, and seemed anxious and awkward. In actual fact, the battalion was being run by the Adjutant, *Leutnant* Buksch. I was ordered to bring the company forward immediately in order to clean up the breakthrough area. It was about 220 metres wide and 100 metres deep, at the centre of which was a cemetery. With my company, and supported by three assault guns, I had to mount a frontal attack. From right and left assault troops of the 1st and 2nd companies were to move up the main trench. From 10.35pm to 10.40pm the artillery was to lay destructive fire on the area of the breakthrough. Then my company, with the assault guns, had to work its way forward as close as possible.

With a *Leutnant* of the unit in whose sector the breakthrough had taken place, I gave notice of my departure. The *Leutnant* went ahead in order to brief us. In ranks separated by intervals of five paces the company moved forward. I wanted to attack in two wedges. One was to be led by me, and the other by Geissler. That arrangement was necessary because in the darkness of the night I would not had been able to view the entire sector and so I relied on Geissler. Meanwhile, time had moved on, and from behind us the dull roaring of the assault guns could be heard. 300 metres separated us from the place where the breakthrough had taken place. It was the target of our attack. The *Leutnant* from the other company set off, after another handshake. He pointed me in the direction of the cemetery of Asowowo.

It was time to brief the section leaders. With lowered voices, as if the enemy were already in earshot, they passed on the orders. Then the barrage began. 'Section by section', that is, salvo by salvo, our heavy and light artillery struck where the cemetery must be. The assault guns rolled up with the grinding sound of their engines. We pulled in our heads and ducked under the trajectory of the howling shells. Then we pushed up to the place where the breakthrough had occurred. During the five minutes of our own barrage we had approached to within 100 metres. At the end of that time the enemy barrage began. We then lay in the hail of shells from their artillery, the *Ratschbums* and above all the mortars. The Russians fired one flare after the other.

The terrain, which until then had been in dull moonlight, was bathed in the distorting glare of magnesium. The men had already clustered like grapes around the assault guns. They believed that behind them they were safe from shrapnel and shot. But then it was a matter of taking cover and working our way forward, metre by metre, and from crater to crater. During the preparatory barrage by our heavy weapons we had got to within 100 metres. It seemed an eternity since the assault guns had stopped. The enemy defensive fire continued undiminished. The earth seemed to be being ploughed up by it. In the light of the flares could be seen the crosses, and the mounds of graves. Among them were figures like ghosts, who fired their machine-pistols upon us. They were the attackers. The high 'barking' of their fire again and again broke through the thunder of the heavy impacts.

In this inferno I was compelled to come to a decision. 50 metres still separated me from the cemetery. Our attack was still under way and the men were on the move. I did not know how many men there still were. My orders were to clean out the area of breakthrough. Only one last decisive leap separated me from my goal. Should I, this close to the goal, give the order to withdraw? That order would cost just as many sacrifices as the attack. I decided to carry on. It only needed one more dash forwards. I jumped up and cried 'Hurrah'! Still shouting 'Hurrah'! I sprang forwards without knowing how many of my comrades would follow my lead.

A stabbing pain in my body caused me to fall in the crater. 20 metres in front of me I had seen an enemy aiming at me with a machine-pistol. If his shot had not stopped me, I would certainly have run on like a madman. Then the Russian threw a hand-grenade after me. It exploded on the edge of the crater in which I was crouching. Earth crumbled down upon me. I had to go back, twisting and rolling. Then I raced and limped, bent and ducking, from crater to crater. I heard a piece of shrapnel whizz up. It tore my cheek open. It was already flying too slowly to be able to hurt me seriously. My right eye could have copped it, but the splinter penetrated the flesh a little bit below.

The attack had been repulsed and the enemy were firing no more flares. In the pale moonlight while I jumped from crater to crater I kept my eyes open for the remnants of my company. As well as dead men I saw wounded men curled up in craters or crawling back. In twos and threes some of them crouched under cover and joined together. '*Herr Leutnant*', one of them called to me. I pressed my hand on my burning stomach and decided that I must only be slightly wounded. '*Herr Leutnant*, over here!' I was called again. While I was listening for the voice and moving in its direction, I was brought down by another bullet. I slid into the nearest crater. Wailing voices were calling for the medics. The enemy was still maintaining barrage fire. I had no time to check on my third wound. I only felt relieved that it too could not be serious.

As I pressed myself against the edge of the crater, a mortar shell burst very close to my cover. A man dived into the crater howling with pain. His voice I recognised as that of the man who was crying out earlier, an old *Obergefreiter*. 'I've lost my hand', he groaned. I saw it dangling in his glove. Groaning, he asked me to open his belt buckle. My hand felt over his body. As I was groping for the buckle, I was seized with horror. I felt the warm soft flesh of his intestines. My hand went into his belly. It was torn open across the width of his body. 'I'll go and fetch the medic', I said to him, knowing he was beyond help. But I could not just go and leave him to die alone. After all, he had followed my orders.

Minutes passed. It seemed like an eternity, although it was not long after midnight. The seriously wounded *Obergefreiter* had become still and his breath was coming in gasps. I saw the white of his eyes glistening and felt his sound hand feeling for mine. Then a sigh was wrung out of the dying man. 'Ah, *Herr Leutnant*', he said. His head fell to one side. Again, I was shaken by a feeling of horror. Finally, I made off from crater to crater.

At the unit dressing station I found half of my company. Only 15 men out of 70 had remained unwounded. 20 must have been killed. I myself had been incredibly lucky. The first shot had clipped the surface of my stomach in two places. The second had neatly gone between two ribs over the spleen. I just about managed to walk unaided, with my upper-body bent forward. The wounded were driven back on the assault guns. I was lifted on, with *Feldwebel* Geissler, whose forearm had been lacerated by an explosive shell. At the regiment we were unloaded into *Sankas*, the medical motor vehicles that took us to the railway at Gorky. There a hospital train was standing ready. I had found time to report to the commander over the failed operation. I learned that the 1st and 2nd companies had not reached the trenches of the main line of resistance. *Oberstleutnant* Dorn shook his head sadly over the badly prepared and precipitate adventure. It had been taken out of his hands as a commander. The battalion had been put under the command of the second unit.

I can still remember the feeling of indescribable relief as I lay in the moving hospital train. The train's destination was Vilna, and was reached via Minsk. During the journey I looked out through the porthole of the wagon, a converted cattle truck. I saw an unforgettable picture. From the West shone the setting sun. In its reddish light lay a broad land, with no houses, no trees, no bushes. On the northern horizon there was the wall of a thunderstorm, blackish violet. In front of it, lonely and distant, there rested a whitewashed stone church.

I wrote home about my two shots in the stomach and that I did not expect a lengthy stay in hospital. But after 10 days, the wound made by the shot in my stomach had become inflamed and had to be operated on. The surgeon was a staff medical officer of about middle age, red-haired, small and compact. He made fun of my officer's 'snappishness', as I woke from the effects of the ether. Still under its influence, I rambled on about how nice it had been to pass, fully conscious, into unconsciousness. All responsibility was taken from me, and all thoughts of duty and compulsion fell away. The sceptical expression on the surgeon's face told me that he did not know what I was talking about. He probably had no idea of the burden of responsibility placed on the shoulders of a 19 years old company commander. After leaving the operating table, I said 'thank you, sir', as was appropriate. But he was none the wiser. 'Don't mention it, my boy', was his answer in reply to the thanks which I had meant so seriously.

The military hospital was in a convent hospital, an old building with thick walls. I have a fleeting recollection of Halina, a Polish medical student, who was on duty during the day. On the other hand I can still clearly picture the night sister with whom I had conversations every evening. She was a 70 years old nun, who 'belonged to the House'. She was a cultured lady from the Polish nobility, and a widow of 44 years. In fluent German she told me, her interested listener, of her short youth, long ago. She had lived in Warsaw and had stayed in Paris and London. For years she had done only night duty. Perhaps, in that way, she felt closer to the 'eternal night'. Every day an eleven years old girl came into the hospital selling newspapers. The child was obviously undernourished. Somehow she affected all the comrades in the room. We joined ourselves together into a 'benevolent society' for her family by always paying ten or twenty times too much for her 10-pfennig newspapers. Her eyes shone with thanks. On 3 November when we were loaded up into *Sankas* and driven to the station, 'our' little girl waved after us for a long time.

To my delight, the hospital train travelled to Wernigerode in the Harz, a lovely spa town. In its situation, and because of the Harz landscape, it reminded me of Sonneberg and the Thuringian Forrest. On the way, some of the wounded were unloaded in Halberstadt. I have no recollection of the town, but I certainly do recollect that a *Gigant* flew over it. That was the *Wehrmacht's* new large transport aircraft. A tank or a whole company of soldiers could be transported in it. The gigantic plane with its six engines, three on each wing, made a lasting impression on us wounded men, particularly because of the noise it made. It seemed to us to be a sign that the power of the *Reich* was anything but broken.

Wernigerode was the earlier residence of *Prinz* Stolberg-Wernigerode. His great castle was situated above the town and towered over it. Noble hotels and old half-timbered houses were characteristic of the town. It was a home to a series of sanatoria, into one of which I was sent. It was the house called 'Dr Kaienburg'. Evidently it was named after a doctor, but was run by his widow. In it 20 officers were accommodated whose wounds were not particularly serious and who were all capable of walking. The doctor came every day on his rounds from a military hospital. A full sanatorium regime prevailed. To me it was an unaccustomed 'feudal' environment. There was a radio in the room, a balcony with a view on to the Brocken, and billiards in the billiard hall. The food was good, but there were 'only a few cigarettes', I complained in a letter to Father.

Of my officer comrades, of all ages, I still remember three. My room-mate was an Augsburg clergyman's son *Leutnant* Uttmann. After me he was the youngest. A cavalry *Oberleutnant* of the Bamberg cavalry was *Herr* Langen from Munich. He was from the publishing family 'Langen and Müller', and very cultivated. A friendly man was the reserve *Oberleutnant* Dr Wutzl. He was a German scholar and an art historian. He was from the 45th Infantry Division, the Linz Division. He later received the Knight's Cross and after the war was a *Hofrat* in the office of the Austrian provincial government.

To get from the sanatorium into the town, we travelled one stop on the Brocken railway, a narrow-gauge railway. It travelled from the Wernigerode main station to the Brocken, the highest mountain in the Harz. We often went to the café in the afternoon or evening. Once we even went up the Brocken thinking, as we did so, of Goethe's *Faust* and the witches on the Blocksberg. In a letter of 5 December, from Wernigerode to Father, I note that I had been at home in Stockerau on a short special leave. I told him of a fine performance of *La Traviata* in the State Opera. However, I added that the only problem was that the tenor had been rotten, 'as is almost always the case in Vienna'.

But I did not like at all what was going on around my family at home. I liked it so little that I often said 'you would really like to punch them'. It was the moaners on the home front that I cursed in a Christmas letter to Rudi. 'Their 'lordships' do not deserve the sacrifices made at the front', I wrote. 'It has the effect of throwing me into a screaming rage! Then I begin to mock them. So I get dreadfully on the nerves of many people, especially girls!'

I told Rudi that I had been together a lot with two of his classmates, Egon Papritz, nicknamed Kitty, but who was later killed. The other was Ernst Vogl, nicknamed Avis. After the war he became a factory owner and a well-known contemporary composer. With those two friends I joined in one evening in a poker game. But I was a beginner! In fact I gambled so badly that at the end of the evening I had lost an entire month's salary. The main complaint of my letter was about the fact that my girl was 'not there for me'. I closed the letter asking when we would see each other again, 'because I had the feeling that the war would only last another year at most - God willing'.

In Wernigerode I had another letter from the company clerk, *Unteroffizier* Wolf. In it he told me about what had happened to my company after I left. Wolf wrote that, in accordance with my letter, the recommendations had been made for decorations for the men, namely the two medics. In the barrage fire in front of the cemetery at Asorowo they had heroically done their duty. It was the chaplain, *Unteroffizier* Jaschek, whom I had put in for the Iron Cross First Class, and *Obergefreiter* Beuleke whom I had recommended for the Iron Cross Second Class. Wolf continued:

…after the heavy casualties of 15 October, the company was topped up again. At the end of November we were taken back by rail to Nevel. From 8 November we had more heavy casualties, 20 dead and 50 wounded! *Leutnant* Ludwig, who had taken over command of the company, was also wounded. *Major* Brauer and the battalion Adjutant, *Leutnant* Buksch, were killed in action.

'I wish the *Herr Leutnant* a really good convalescence and I hope to see you again soon. Company leaders of your calibre, with a fresh and daring spirit and filled with concern about the welfare of the men in the trenches, do our people good. Then it will be easier to master the difficult tasks that face us.

Part III

The Tide Turns

7

January-July 1944: Officers' course, Operation *Bagration* - the Russian summer offensive

Aged 20 years - officers' course; 'Enjoy the war, the peace will be terrible!'; Operation Bagration - the Regiment begins a withdrawal of 500km

In Wernigerode I had already found out that, after my Christmas leave, I would be sent on a course for convalescent officers. Such courses were held in all *Wehrkreise*. The Silesian course, the one appropriate for me, took place in Freiwaldau-Grafenberg. Freiwaldau, at that time in the Sudetenland, is in the Altvater mountains, and it is also a spa. We were therefore quartered in the Altvater sanatorium, otherwise a tuberculosis sanatorium. We had duties in the morning for only three to four hours in the form of lectures or sand table war games. On the course I met the very comradely young *Hauptmann* Hein. Since the spring he had been in command of the second company as an *Oberleutnant*. From Hein I learned that of the 40 officers in the regiment, at the beginning of the enemy offensive on 6 August, only three were still with the regiment. All the others were dead or wounded. All the battalion commanders had been killed in action, as were many other good comrades. On 11 January I wrote to Father, quite shaken. 'In March we will be off to Russia again. Sometimes it gives me the shudders, but I put my trust in God'.

In the sanatorium there were skis. So some of us went skiing when the weather permitted and the snow was right. The mountain countryside offered many opportunities for skiing, and also for walking. I remember one trip, on which we came through the long *Strassendorfer Oberlindewiese* and *Niederlindewiese*. Their names were as quaint as was the landscape. 'The food', I wrote to Mother, 'was not particularly copious, but we discovered the existence of a decree. According to it those under 21 years of age were entitled to 200 grams of sausage, per man, per day, in addition to their other rations! The flabbergasted paymaster immediately authorised the addition!'

Freiwaldau was not so noble a spa as Wernigerode. It offered no diversions at all. After dinner, Hein and I, together with the artillery *Oberleutnant* Sylvester von Glinski from our Division, stayed together for a while, and then went to bed. The almost superhuman exertions that had gone on for weeks and months resulted in an enormous need to sleep. Sometimes, after I had slept 10 hours during the night, I went to bed again after lunch and slept another four hours until dinner. So the actual purpose of the course, our convalescence, was achieved. At least in my case!

After five weeks in Freiwaldau I arrived in Schweidnitz, where I met many old acquaintances and good comrades in arms. Amongst them, was *Oberleutnant* Klaus Nicolai. In August, as commander of the third company, he had been wounded. I became friendly with him and we often went to the theatre and frequented the Hindenburg-Hof in which I had lived the previous year. As head of the convalescent company, Nicolai had rooms in the barracks. I had a private room in the house of innkeeper Pöttler. Another acquaintance was *Leutnant* Heckel, member of a well-known family of hatters in Neutitschein.

One Sunday, I went from Freiwaldau to Mährisch-Schönberg, to visit my officer cadet comrade Bormann from Breslau. He had been wounded during his first period of probation at the front and had come away with a stiff knee. Another time Nicolai, Heckel and I went from Schweidnitz, in the company of two actresses, on a trip to the dam at Frankenstein. Schweidnitz possessed a quite good provincial theatre. When I heard Flotow's *Martha* the tenor part was played by a certain Alexander von Krüdener. He was a fairly old gentleman and, so the story went, had many children.

The commander of the *Ersatz* battalion was a *Hauptmann* Brandt. Nicolai and I called him 'SA man Brandt', after a novel from the *Kampfzeit*, i.e. the 'period of struggle' before the Nazis had come to power, well known at that time. The battalion adjutant was *Leutnant* Dr Waller, who in civilian life was an attorney from Eger. To a certain extent Waller seemed to me more of a business manager to the battalion. At any rate he was more of a businessman than an officer. He had gained his *Leutnant's* rank in the Czech army.

At that time a marching company went every month to France to the Atlantic Wall. There the mostly recently enlisted older and quite young soldiers were given further training. In April Waller assigned me as transport officer. After I had received the papers, he took me to one side. He made the remarkable suggestion that I should travel from St. Maixent near Poitiers, without marching orders, and without a leave permit, and go to Bordeaux to buy some things for him. Such obviously irregular suggestion I brusquely declined, without even asking for the details. However, Waller accepted it with just a shrug of his shoulders.

The railway journey, through Germany and half of France, was naturally more pleasant than the journeys through Russia had been. There was much more variety in terms of landscape. I did not even know the Rhineland through which I then travelled and had never been any further west than Metz. In Verres, the massive freight station to the south of Paris, there were troop trains. Among the goods transports there were many wagons carrying wine. Word immediately got round that a unit had succeeded, with the help of a shot from a pistol, in 'nabbing' a huge wine container. In a flash the *Landsers* on our transport had run with their canteens to the place where the 'nabbing' had occurred.

When the military police arrived, it was no longer possible to find out who had done it. As long as the hole was not stoppered the best thing was to hold the canteens under it and fill them up. The wine soon began to take effect and the accompanying personnel, again and again, had to take care that there was no rowdiness. The men lay on straw in the goods wagons, each with a little cannon oven. For the accompanying personnel there was a passenger carriage available. While unloading in St Maixent, an oven fell over in one of the Schweidnitz wagons. The straw immediately caught fire and the men had to hurriedly evacuate the wagon. 'Heaven help us', I thought, if this accident had happened during the rapid journey through France.

On the journey back, we went past the Loire castles spread out in the sunlight. The barracks of St Maixent, the French infantry school, had no attraction for me. My journey back was uneventful, apart from the fact that it passed through strange country, which was an event in itself. But the main event was Paris. At that time, there was an order that every member of the *Wehrmacht* who was travelling officially, to or through Paris, was allowed to stop there for 48 hours to see the sights of the city. With a *Pionierleutnant* from another Silesian garrison town I too made the visit. We were accommodated in a double room of the *Grand Hotel de l'Opéra*. It was the hotel requisitioned for officers' accommodation. To our pleasant surprise there was running, even if only lukewarm water.

It was a Sunday and Monday that we spent in Paris and we raced through the main sights of the town, as I wrote on 9 April to Father. We saw *Les Invalides*, the cathedral of *Notre Dame*, the *Louvre*, the *Champs-Elysées* and the *Trocadéro*.

On the *Arc de Triomphe*, where the changing of the German guard was just taking place, I discovered, among the names of Napoleonic battles and engagements engraved there, the name of Hollabrunn near Stockerau. Father had climbed the Eiffel Tower two years previously, in two and a half hours, counting the steps up to the top. However, at that time, we could only climb up to the restaurant on the first storey. But the view from there over the huge city was overwhelming and confirmed my impression that Paris was far greater than Vienna and Berlin.

In my Easter Sunday letter to Father, I told him of a good Easter sermon by a preacher from the Confessional Church in the Schweidnitz Parish Church. I thought that Father would have a lot to do over the Easter holiday in Cambrai. I reminded him of Mother's birthday on 11 April, as I knew that Father easily forgot such family events.

On the journey back from Paris I managed to trick myself a day out to Stockerau. It had been easy, because the army leave trains from the Paris *Gare de l'Est*, left in the evening after 7pm, with a quarter of an hour interval between them. The train to Vienna was the later of the two. So because I did not catch the Breslau train, I 'had to' travel with the Vienna train, so to speak. I was able to make this easily understood to the railway authorities, and the guard, an old Austrian *Reserveonkel*, nodded understandingly.

When I arrived back in Schweidnitz I learned that the father of my comrade, *Leutnant* Ludwig, had died suddenly. With *Oberleutnant* Liebig who was also from Lignitz, I travelled there in order to attend the burial. The Ludwig family owned *Vaters* Hotel in Lignitz. The mourners assembled there in the salon. *Oberleutnant* Liebig was a '12-Ender'. A former *Unteroffizier*, he had risen to the rank of officer. He had married in Lignitz, but only seldom visited his wife. In fact he had a relationship in Schweidnitz with a singer at the Theatre. Paulchen Vogt had a small voice, was thin in build, but had a lovely nature. In *Martha* she had sung the part of *Frau* Flut.

Liebig was commander of the so-called *Marschkompanie* of the *Ersatz* battalion. All officers and soldiers passed through there after they had been wounded and had been in the convalescent company. Once they had been certified fit for combat again, they waited there to be sent back to the front. Liebig himself suffered from a stomach complaint. He and the core personnel were 'GvH', i.e. *garnisonsverwendungsfähig Heimat*, which meant they were fit for garrison service at home. Unfortunately, to my disappointment, I was the same. I was longing to be at the front and did not much enjoy life in the barracks.

Meanwhile, I had found an enjoyable activity. I was responsible for the war training of a *Marschbataillon* that had just been formed. It was composed of people who had not been old enough to fight in the First World War. They had only just been called up. The platoon and company commanders had no experience of the Eastern Front. I had to set up the service plan and supervise the training operations on the training ground and shooting range. Men from those age groups formed the 'secret weapon', was what we said mockingly. But the new weapon that would decide the course of the war, for which everyone was hoping, was nowhere to be seen.

In my service in connection with the *Marschbataillon* I was under no supervision. For example, I could allow myself the advantage of prolonging the lunch break. I spent it in the officers' mess, followed by a visit to a coffee-house. How important those few visits to the coffee-house became, I will relate later in another connection.

I got to know the commander of the *Marschbataillon* that I had to train. He was a man with a remarkable history. *Major* Norbert Freisler was born about 1890 and came from Neutitschein in Moravia. He had already been an active officer in the old Imperial Austrian Army. In September 1914, something of which he was proud, as an *Oberleutnant*, he had been awarded the *Militärverdienstkreuz III Klasse*. But at that time he had immediately been taken prisoner by the Russians and had been in Siberia until about 1920.

He was one of the few officers who went into the Czech army, or rather who was taken over into the Czech army. He struggled during his service to reach the rank of Staff Captain. He said it was the highest rank he could attain as a German. After he was taken over into the *Wehrmacht* he became a *Major*. Because of his excellent command of Russian he was used with the Russian volunteer units, the so-called *Vlassow-Armee*. In the context of that service he was made commandant of the group of Lofoten Islands off the Norwegian mainland. He was a small, white-haired man, a 'wiry' character with an expressive face and a lively temperament. He liked chatting with me and could tell riveting stories.

The officers' mess of our infantry barracks was, as is usual in barrack buildings, a separate building with several large lounges. Naturally, you only went to table when the commander had arrived, and only began to dine when he had picked up his spoon. The German army at that time was the first army in the world that made no distinction between the portions of officers and men. But the advantage of the food in the officers' mess was that a good cook ran the kitchen and she was able to use the rations that were assigned more economically and to cook more appetisingly. So the food cooked there for perhaps 20 to 50 officers was much better and of greater variety than the food provided for the 1000 or more members of the *Ersatz* battalion and the training unit.

In the kitchen of the officers' mess I got to know the famous *Schlesische Himmelreich* that until then I had only known from soldiers' tales. It consisted of very soft, almost melting, yeast dumplings with stewed plums or mixed fruit. The unique point was the addition of finely diced smoked meat, through which the dish received a distinctively spicy flavour. After lunch I usually withdrew into one of the many armchairs, where you could stretch out your legs and doze undisturbed. To me the gentlemen's evenings were no longer as exciting as they had been in Mörchingen. The reason was that by then only a minimal amount of alcohol was dispensed. Only on 20 April 1944, for the *Führer's* birthday, was there a celebration dinner and unlimited drinks. I remember that, for me and my close comrades, it was an hilarious celebration. I played the piano, and it lasted well into the night. 'Enjoy the war, for the peace will be terrible', was the sarcastic refrain.

A celebration of a quite different kind followed. As I reported to *Hauptmann* Brandt, the battalion commander, a colonel by the name of Werner was also present. I knew the latter from the Hindenburg-Hof. He was head of the army film unit that had moved from Berlin and had for some time been stationed in Schweidnitz. He had his quarters, as befitted his rank, in Kammrau, the estate of Count Kayserling located about eight miles from Schweidnitz. Werner informed me that on the following Saturday a birthday celebration was taking place for his granddaughter. They were one gentleman short, so I was to take that place. I then learnt they had been keeping their eyes open for a socially skilled young officer and had lighted on me.

It was to be an interesting experience. Until then I had never been in a house of the nobility of the eastern Elbe. *Oberst* Werner took me with him on the Saturday afternoon in his service car. Kammrau was a little village within the estate. It consisted of several farm buildings and a small castle. The lord of the manor was, if I remember correctly, a nephew of the philosopher Kayserling. The family was from the Baltic nobility and the Count himself had been a Chamberlain of Kaiser Wilhelm II.

I remember a series of interconnecting rooms, the last of which was the Count's study. All the rooms were tastefully and in some cases opulently furnished. There were many pictures, paintings and photographs with dedications, especially portraits of his Majesty. The Count, to whom I was only briefly introduced, was somewhat small and had a bald patch. He had the air of a private scholar and not of the owner of an estate. The dominant personality in the house was perhaps the 70 years old Countess who involved me in a lengthy conversation. She radiated a natural nobility. Of the other guests, with the exception of *Oberst* Werner, I have no recollection, but I do recall the younger people.

First there was the birthday girl who had just reached the age of 25, Baroness Viola von Richtofen. Her brother was a *Leutnant* of Reserve in an infantry uniform. He had lost a kidney as a result of being wounded. The father of young Richtofen was Lothar von Richtofen, brother of the famous Manfred, the red fighter pilot. He too was a fighter pilot holding the *Pour Le Mérite*. He had met his death in about 1930 as a civilian pilot. He had married the daughter of the house in which the two grandchildren grew up. Viola was a Red Cross sister in a Breslau military hospital. Blonde and blue-eyed, she was friendly, natural and almost maternal.

It appeared that her friend was a *Fräulein* von Garnesse, from a Huguenot family. Reddish blonde, particularly slim and tall was a Bezigna von Rohr, an uncomplicated young lady from the country nobility and the opposite of the governess type of *Fräulein* von Garnesse. The youngest was a *Fräulein* von Karlowitz, full of life and very pretty. She soon told me that her brother was a *Panzer Oberleutnant* from the Sagan regiment and was by then in Baden near Vienna. Of the young men, in addition to the Richtofen grandson, there was a commoner school friend, who had had infantile paralysis and thus was not fit for military service. Nevertheless he wore his disabled sports badge with pride. Then there was also the signals unit *Oberleutnant*, 'Conny' von Falkenhausen. He was perhaps 25 years old, with long hair slicked down, which, together with his general appearance gave him the dashing air of a greyhound.

Of course it was part of the visit to have a look round the stables and the farm buildings and to walk through the nearby estate area. There was a little castle pond, with water-lilies floating on it. The conversation was free and easy and lively. It turned out that a room had been prepared for me to spend the night, provided with a toothbrush, naturally! In the absence of a special invitation, I had not brought one with me. Before dinner we gathered in the drawing rooms for an aperitif and when the gong sounded, we went in to dinner. To celebrate the birthday the ladies were escorted to the table. A gentleman had to bow to the nearest lady and offer her his arm. The table was round and big enough for 12 people to be seated round it fairly comfortably. The dishes were of wartime fare and thoroughly 'unaristocratic'. They were brought, by means of a lift, from the kitchen in the undercroft of the house, then placed on a revolving platform in the middle of the table. The revolving table meant that the need to pass dishes round was avoided.

For us young people it was a jolly evening which lasted far into the night. I could tolerate a great deal in those years of my youth. There was never any danger of losing my composure, and I don't recall ever having had the need to excuse myself. In that way I passed the evening with great pleasure. Next morning I was at my place at the proper time for breakfast. Breakfast was taken *en famille* at the round table and afterwards I made a move to get back again to Schweidnitz. Count Kayserling wanted to put a *Landau* at my disposal so that the coachman could take me to Schweidnitz. However, I politely declined, with thanks. I had a real need for physical activity and looked forward to the brisk walk along the quiet country road on that beautiful May Sunday. I arranged it so that I arrived at the officers' mess just in time for lunch. On the way, I went over the impressions of the previous day and looked forward to the coming week and also to seeing Gisela.

Several times after lunch in the officers' mess I had sought out a cafe in the town square. There I had noticed grammar school girls, so easily recognisable by their school bags and by the topics of the conversations they had. It was not yet three years since I myself had been going to grammar school, and it gave me pleasure to watch the gaggle of girls. One of them particularly appealed to me, and I soon fell for her. She was just 17, had brown hair and a lovely open face, merry yet serious. Of course I did not know who she was, nor how I should approach her. I often posted myself on my bicycle near to the school at times when I thought lessons were finishing and I actually succeeded in seeing her several times and to notice that she had also noticed me. She wore her thick hair over her forehead, eye and cheek and would fling it back as a foal shakes his mane in a gallop. The gesture pleased me more than I can say and at the same time imprinted itself unforgettably on my memory. Her eyes were a mixture of brown, grey and green, and had a dark black rim. To me they spoke of fathomless depths, undreamt of sweetness, and measureless goodness and warmth of heart.

It was on the evening of 9 May when, through a fortunate coincidence, I was able to speak to her under touchingly memorable circumstances. I had passed the *Friedenskirche*, which had once been built in thanksgiving for the end of the Thirty Years War. The extensive, spacious half-timbered building was surrounded by old limes, whose first green shoots were just coming out. There in a park-like forecourt and the adjacent cemetery I felt the mood of the evening, a wistfulness and longing that was especially strong. I entered the church, from which chords of a chorale were ringing out. In an effort not to disturb the congregation, I did not look for a seat, but leaned up against a pillar. In doing so my gaze turned to a girl whom I recognised as Gisela. She had bowed her head and folded her hands, and I was surprised to see her there. It turned out she had been at the grave of her mother, who had died a few days after she was born. While the service was still going on she left the church and I followed her at a respectful distance. I saw her stop at a grave, the grave of her mother, and only when she had walked on and neared the cemetery gate, did I walk up to her and speak to her. She turned her great eyes upon me. Out of them there spoke seriousness, surprise, and, as it seemed to me, a gentle reproach. But perhaps I only felt this because I felt like an interloper.

Afterwards we met as often as Gisela could manage it after school. We went for walks together over the 'Ring', the former fortress wall, which had surrounded the town and which was a promenade walk luxuriantly overgrown with trees and bushes. Sometimes we went on our bicycles in the late afternoon, out into the May evening. We soon found a favourite spot, a bench at the edge of the woods to the west of the town, where the highway climbs uphill towards Burkersdorf. It was where the park disappeared into the forest and hills beneath the Riesengebirge. At our feet there lay the soft picture of the town, our dear town of Schweidnitz, with its towers and roofs lit by the rays of the setting sun.

Meanwhile, things moved on and the time of my departure for the front approached. During the past months it had become clear to me that I probably would not be satisfied with a career as an officer. If I were to stay in my chosen profession I would at least have to follow the career of a general staff officer. But to do that I would first have to become a *Hauptmann*. All that would take a long time. For the time being I had to go out to the front line again. I had had enough of the barracks, its many shirkers, and its defeatists.

I wanted to go 'into the field, into freedom'. I was eager to experience again the camaraderie of the front, the unheard-of experience of community, for which every young man had an especial longing. Out there, and nowhere else, was where I had that experience. For better or for worse you belonged out there, together. Out there, things were right.

I had an additional determining factor. I had won the Iron Cross Second Class, the *Infanteriesturmabzeichen*, i.e. the infantry assault badge, in silver, and the *Verwundetenabzeichen*, i.e. the wound badge. But I did not have the coveted decoration of the Iron Cross First Class and a hoped for *Nahkampfspange*, i.e. the close combat clasp. Without those it appeared to me, you were not a 'proper' infantry officer. I had therefore voluntarily signed myself '*kv*', i.e. fit again, which the medical officer would not have done. Even the fact that Gisela had suddenly come into my life had not been able to alter my decision.

I travelled home once more on the short leave that we received once a month. In my case, since the garrison was over 300 kilometres from my home town, it amounted to four days. I had found a way of making the most of every minute of those four days. I travelled at midnight from Schweidnitz and went with the *Ostbahn* to Vienna. Then I returned with the *Nordwestbahn* from Stockerau through Bohemia to Gorlitz, from there I arrived back on the same train I got on in Schweidnitz. On the evening of my departure some comrades and I had been drinking in the Hindenburghof. So I was fairly well oiled as I got on the train. In Kamenz in Silesia I got on the leave train from the front coming from Breslau to Vienna. I was exhausted and tipsy.

In the compartment I fell asleep and wakened with a shock when I heard the guard crying 'Mittelwalde, Mittelwalde'. Thinking that I had got on the wrong train, I jumped out and asked for the train to Vienna. A *Feldgendarme* told me that I had just got off it. Back in the train at last I began to think of some way of overcoming my intoxication. I succeeded to a certain extent. When I arrived in Stockerau my school friend Walter Hackl welcomed me at the station. He had already been several days coming at home, on leave from the *Afrika Korps*. There was a great 'hello' and we looked up a few inns in succession and tippled heartily. Then exhaustion overcame me again and Walter finally delivered me home where Mother received me, laughing.

Once back in Schweidnitz I learnt that I was to go into the field with the next marching company. On 4 June, a Sunday, it was time to go. I had assembled the company and a general had inspected it. Purple and white lilac was in bloom, and I had given orders to plunder the bushes by the barracks hedge so that every man wore a flower on his chest. Led by the regimental band, we set off for the station. It was the only time in my entire career as a soldier that I was able to march with a full band. So we went through the *Peterstrasse* and across the town hall square to the station. I marched at the head of the company.

At a window of her apartment in the *Peterstrasse* stood Gisela. She came to the station. The company was already entrained, and we were able to speak for a while together. Not only for her but also for me, that farewell was hard. She gave me a book *Wer Gottes Fahrt gewagt*, 'Who dares God's journey'. It had pictures and histories from the house of Flex, at its centre Walter Flex, the poet of the *Jugendbewegung* or youth movement, who was killed in action in 1918. I stood with Gisela a little apart from the others. There was a fence between us. She was wearing a bright summer dress with a narrow waist. Gisela's eyes shone moist and we kissed tenderly. To the strains of *muss i denn* the train began to move. Gisela's face and figure became blurred to me. Soon I could only see the white speck of her dress and finally even that disappeared. The dedication that she had written in the book read: 'For lonely hours in the field - from my heart - your Gisela'.

On 6 June we were sitting in the goods station at Lodz, which at that time was called Litzmannstadt. News reached us of the landing of Allied troops in France. Even if we ordinary *Landser* did not know anything of the wider picture, it was still clear to everyone that by then the war had entered into a decisive stage. However, that it could end with a German defeat was far from anyone's thoughts. In the 'travelling community' of the goods wagon we were temporarily filled with a feeling of special belonging. Once we arrived out there the companionship of the train would be immediately torn apart and we would be assigned to many different units. But at that moment everyone felt the common experience of an unknown, even if distant, danger. After some excited commentary on the news it became quiet and one man hummed a tune. Then one became several and finally every one joined in the familiar old melody:

So take my hands and lead me,
To my blessed end and eternally!
I cannot go alone, not one step,
where you will go and stay, take me with you.

When the last verse rang out, the modest beginning had grown into a choir. It was impressive how many men knew the words for the second and third verses.

On 11 June we were at our destination. The journey had passed through Warsaw, Vilna, Dünaburg, Molodetschno and Polotzk, as far as a Vitebsk, and finished in Lowsha. The command post of the Division was located there. The allocation of men took place as expected. The *Majority* of the infantrymen joined the newly reformed third *Grenadierregiment* of the Division. By then it consisted of regiments 7, 461, and 472. I became Adjutant of the 2nd Battalion, which was commanded by *Hauptmann* Muller. 'Pi' Muller had been among the seven 'seveners' who had been convalescing in Freiwaldau. When he found out that I had come on that transport, he asked for me as adjutant. Our 252nd *Infanteriedivision,* the *Eichenlaub* or 'Oak leaf' Division, was the division located at the point of connection between army groups Centre and North. That meant particular danger, because a preferred target for attack was at those points of connection, where areas of command were separated.

The enemy knew that there it would be harder to re-establish connections once they had been broken than it would within a single area of command. The Russian summer offensive was imminent. We were greeted with that announcement. So for formation and training, for getting to know one's way about, there only remained days, or at most weeks. On 15 June the *Füsilier* battalion under *Major* von Garn, deployed in the main line of resistance, had succeeded in shooting down a Russian reconnaissance aircraft. Its passengers had been general staff officers, who wanted to view from as close as possible the terrain over which their troops would attack.

The battalion was welded together 'in a flash', so to speak. The work as adjutant was exciting and reconciled me with the fact that for the time being I could not be with my Regiment 7. I was responsible for the preparation of battalion orders, correspondence and personnel matters. But above all, the fact that I was leader of the battalion staff with the orderly officer, the signals staff and the runners, was a new experience for me.

On 18 June an exercise involving the whole battalion took place, in which *Hauptmann* Muller and I participated on our horses. My Army-issue horse, the white horse Hans, was a wilful chap. It was difficult to keep him within the prescribed distance of half a horse's length behind the commander's horse. He had also well and truly stripped me of a waist belt against a wall. In order not to get trapped by my left leg, I had to jump off at the last moment. With that battalion exercise, my life as a 'cavalryman', so to speak, came to an end. From then on there was no more opportunity for riding. On 20 June the battalion was moved up to the village of Lowsha along the Vitebsk-Polozk railway line. Then there was no more doubt that the Russians would begin their offensive on 22 June, the third anniversary of the beginning of that campaign. On the evening of the 21st the commander, *Hauptmann* Muller, invited all his officers to celebrate the start of their new posts. For many, it would at the same time be a farewell.

I quote from the history of *Grenadierregiment 7*, by Romuald Bergner: 'The most serious defeat ever inflicted on the German *Wehrmacht* in the Second World War began on 22 June 1944, as the Red Army began the battle in White Russia'. The fact that the beginning of the operation coincided with the third anniversary of *Barbarossa* was no coincidence. The date had been deliberately set by the Soviet high command. That reminder of Russia's darkest hour was intended to inflame the passions of the soldiers of the Red Army and to inspire all the soldiers of the Red Army to give of their utmost. According to the final plan, *Bagration*, the Red Army was to begin large-scale offensives, following rapidly in succession, in six different sectors. That almost simultaneous large-scale offensive, in six widely separated locations, was intended to split the German defences, to splinter their forces, and to deny them the opportunity of deploying all available troops in a concerted effort to repulse the Soviet attacks.

The historian Andreas Hillgruber has shown that a direct causal connection exists between the collapse of Army Group Centre and the downfall of the Third Reich. On 22 June 1944 the Soviet general attack began against the front of Army Group Centre. In pincer operations the *feste Platze* of Vitebsk, Orsha, Mogilew, and Bobruisk were encircled. The mass of the Soviet offensive forces, however, struck out further westwards. The catastrophe took its course. In purely numerical terms it had almost twice the impact as that of Stalingrad. The operational effects were a great deal worse.

To the north of Vitebsk, where we were, the Soviets began their offensive in the early morning of 22 June. On a front extending 64 kilometres, the IX Army Corps with Corps Detachment D and the 252nd Infantry Division were conducting the defence. There, eight divisions of the Soviet 43rd Army attacked. To those were soon added the first division of the 6th Guards Army. It was intended to achieve a breakthrough some 25 kilometres wide. Along with the offensive divisions of the Red Army there rolled two armoured brigades into the focal-point of the breakthrough area. The two offensive wedges encountered the right-hand and central sectors of the 252nd Infantry Division. In the course of the night of 21 June and in the early hours of 22 June, the Russians pushed up nearer and nearer to our position. At 4am the enemy's heavy barrage began and at 4.20am they attacked on a wide front. Breakthroughs were made in the sector of the 1st Battalion *Grenadierregiment 7* and the Division's *Füsilier* battalion.

As I recall, the hurricane broke at 3.05am, on the dot, just as it had in 1941. The fire was concentrated mainly on the main line of resistance. Only isolated heavy-calibre shells dropped in the village. We had long since left our quarters in houses, and were waiting in the cover trenches beside them. I had been woken by the crash of bursting shells after just an hour's sleep. That action began for me with a thundering within my skull, weakened by schnapps and tiredness. Towards 5am the battalion received orders to move into the second line, that is, the trench that was planned for that purpose. It was good news, because as soon as the enemy attacked up front, we could expect the fire to be moved to the rear. Then it would be mostly the firing positions, villages, and roads, the position of which had been long established by enemy reconnaissance, that would be under fire.

We moved forward, the bombardment ahead of us and the impacts of heavy-calibre shells behind us. In the event, the Division was divided into two halves. Under its command remained *Infanterieregiment* 7, the divisional *Füsilier* battalion, and our 2nd Battalion 472. But of these, the 5th Company deployed on the left, the 1st Battalion, the regimental staff and the whole of Regiment 461 were pushed north-westwards. Even on the next day there was no news whatsoever of the 5th Company. In the meantime the second line had become the main line of resistance and the gap that had opened on the left urgently needed to be blocked off.

Visiting our main line of resistance, *Hauptmann* Müller and I found an 8.8cm Army anti-tank gun, commanding the road to Lowsha from a clearing in the woods,, on which the Russians were bringing up tanks. A T-34 passed by; one shot, and it was in flames. The second followed straight behind it. The next shot hit it, it stopped and from the turret an oil-smeared figure twisted itself out. A third tank came up and drove slowly past its comrades. The number one gunner of our anti-tank gun watched with a tense expression and once again pressed the firing button. Once again the shot scored a direct hit and from the tank the whole turret blew into the air. High flames shot up.

After a short rest of only one hour on the night of the 22nd, and no sleep the next night, on the night of the 23rd and 24th I still did not get a wink of sleep. Our command post was located in a leafy shelter, probably the construction shelter of the *Stellungsbaumeister*, when the second trench was constructed. In the morning we were still holding on. Then towards noon, as ordered, we withdrew behind the Vitebsk-Polozk railway line. The enemy was pushing up behind us, the railway installations were under fire. Beside the station, where just 14 days before I had alighted from the train, the remaining part of the battalion crossed the line. At the Lowsha station a goods train was waiting with steam up to set off to Polozk. Like a magnet it attracted the *Landsers* to it. Müller and I, with a great deal of shouting, tried to counteract the signs of disintegration. We just about managed to hold together the remnants of our battalion.

However, many did not think, but saw an opportunity to get away and wanted to use it. They climbed up and bombarded the engine-driver with appeals to leave. When the train had at last drawn up, our battalion was already in order and had withdrawn behind the railway line. The train had not gone 100 metres when it came under fire from an enemy anti-tank gun. A direct hit in the locomotive's boiler abruptly ended the journey. The passengers leapt out again and rushed on along the tracks.

As dusk was falling I received orders to undertake a counter-attack. With the men of my staff I put the Russians to flight from the houses of the village of Werbali. Since there were not many of them and since we roared like mad, the operation was fairly easy for us. In the evening a 'V-man' from the Division was brought forward. He was an Armenian in Russian uniform. During the night he had to scout around in the enemy lines and then return. Meanwhile, it was announced that the gap to the left was becoming wider and wider. There were no German troops within miles.

On 25 June the remnants of the Division were to cross the Düna. Around the village of Ulla and its bridge over the Düna a bridgehead had been formed. One kilometre across, half of it was occupied by what remained of our battalion. The Russians were feeling their way forward without serious pressure, but throughout the entire morning there was lively individual fire. At 11.30am the order came that at 12 noon the bridge over the Düna would be blown up. By then the bridgehead would have to be evacuated. Our artillery was just in the process of changing position and was not therefore available to provide covering fire. There remained three assault guns. We preferred to keep them with us rather than to let them go into firing positions across the river. *Hauptmann* Müller had allowed the other unit still in the bridgehead to go first. He wanted to cross the bridge with the last assault gun. My proposal was that those men who could not swim should immediately withdraw. The rest would then cross the river with the swimmers, instead of gathering before noon on and around the endangered bridge.

Müller decided to follow his own idea, but he became more and more unsure the closer it came to 12 o'clock. Finally, at five minutes to 12, it only remained to climb on to the assault guns and to go back. With 15 *Landsers* Muller and I clambered on to the vehicle. It was far too high for us. Everyone would much rather have gone into cover behind another comrade. The Russians were firing all around, and bullets rattled on the assault gun. But we clung on there, one beside another. Only two men were slightly wounded. At exactly 12 o'clock we crossed the wide wooden bridge. On the other bank a pioneer officer was waiting, to whom we announced that we were the last men out of the bridgehead. A little later, after we got down from the assault gun, the pioneer activated the detonator. As we marched away we saw, as we looked round, the bridge blow apart with a mighty explosion. Its wreckage fell into the river and over the surrounding area.

Five kilometres upriver we took up a new position to the right of the *Füsilier* battalion in the little village of Labeiki. Our right-hand neighbour was Corps Detachment D. They were the cobbled-together remnants of a corps from which the Russians had taken the village of Labeiki on the very first night. The position would have been just ideal. The excellently constructed trench ran along the western bank of the Düna on the steep bank that on average was 10 metres high. A frontal attack across the 16 metre wide river was practically out of the question. The occupied village of Labeiki was already on our right flank.

In allocating sectors I had even found time to enjoy the beauty of the landscape. It resembled an English park with meadows, groups of trees and bushes. There was an open view across the river under the summer sun. No shot had yet been fired. I had found a civilian motorcycle that had apparently been left by men from the *Organisation Todt* working there. On a track across a meadow I rattled across the sector to establish links with our neighbours. As a substitute for the ignition key I had a little piece of wood and, lo and behold! the Dürrkopp 125 worked. However, the track was under enemy observation. The journey went well until a Russian anti-tank gun got me in its sights. The first shot was too wide, but at the second I was nearly brought down as I tried to avoid the first crater. I felt the sharp draught of the third shot and then gave up the journey.

At dusk Müller returned from the regimental command post that was behind us, in the Ulla valley running parallel to the Düna. While *Hauptmann* Miller was away, after five nights and four days without sleep from 21 June, I slept for just three hours, in deep exhaustion. The combat actions and frequent changes of position plus Müller's hectic pace, and also, at the beginning, a Pervitin tablet, had not let me rest for more than 100 hours. I had been uninterruptedly awake. So I slept like the dead in some soft green moss. Then I needed half an hour to become fully awake again.

Müller brought the order to retake the village of Labeiki. To me he did not seem to be in his right mind, he was speaking incoherently and was not steady on his legs. He must have drunk too much schnapps at the regiment or, more probably, a small quantity of it had overcome him, since he was just as exhausted as I. But, perhaps he had a premonition that the time of his death was near. 'We're off, Scheiderbauer', was the first thing he said. Then he gave the details. The entire battalion staff had to take part in the attack. Labeiki was to be attacked from the north and south along the Düna, and had to be taken. We had to do it without artillery, without assault guns, or any other heavy weapons to support us, without even adequate information concerning the strength of the enemy, but with only 'Hurrah' and the 'moral' support of the night.

When dusk had fallen we moved forward. The night was no use at all to us. When the Russians noticed that an attack was underway, they fired flares and deployed anti-tank guns and mortars that they had already brought across the Düna. In a small pine wood, at close range, the attack ground to a halt. It seemed impossible to overcome the enemy's wall of fire. Anti-tank shells exploded against the trees. Ricochets and explosive shells whizzed, crashed and exploded in between. It was a noise that could not be drowned out by men's voices. The darkness of the wood was lit briefly and spectrally by tracer ammunition. When the magnesium glow of flares had gone out, the blackness of the wood by night surrounded us all the more profoundly.

Müller did not seem to me to be in his right mind. Gesticulating with his pistol he cried 'Hurrah', but that did not get the attack any further. Finally he sent me to the left flank, where I looked for *Leutnant* Kistner, the commander of the 7th Company. Seeking cover behind pine trunks, I went forward step by step and so drew near to the main trenches on the bank of the Düna. Instead of *Leutnant* Kistner I found a couple of helpless men waiting for orders. The Russians were still firing with everything they had got. Suddenly there was calm and you could hear the 'Hurrah' from the direction of the enemy, coming closer and closer. Briefly we thought that it was the attack of the neighbouring unit to the east of us. Nothing had been heard of them until that moment.

But the attackers approached surprisingly quickly and by their throaty voices we could recognise that they were Russians. They counted on us being more afraid of our 'Hurrah' than of the Russian 'Urray'. Because they seemed to be making their assault along the trench, I ordered the men to get out of the trench and to take cover to the side of it. In that way we could have let the Russians charge past us into the trench and thrown hand-grenades after them. The men leapt to the right out of the trench. While the threatening 'Hurrah' shook me almost physically, I turned to the left out of the trench, crept quickly into a bush and lost the ground from under my feet. 'A steep bank' was my only thought. I could not feel the ground under me. I was slipping and rolling downwards. I fell and went head over heels, until my fall came to an end in the soft sand of the bank of the Düna. I must have slipped down almost 20 metres. I had not taken into account of the gradient of the bank in relation to the higher level of the village of Labeiki.

I found myself alone. It seemed, in the almost complete silence of a dawning summer morning, that there was nothing else for me to do but try somehow to get back to my men. For almost 200 metres I went downriver along the steep bank, until I found a place where I could clamber up. Everything was calm, but I did not know where or if I would find *Hauptmann* Müller and the other members of my staff. They would doubtless have withdrawn from the pine wood.

Giving a wide berth to the command post, where some wounded men were gathering, I went forward again. On the way I met one of the staff runners. He told me that Müller had been killed. Soon afterwards they brought him in. A complete anti-tank shell must have gone straight through his breast and killed him outright. But the attack had been beaten off. I ordered the battalion back into the exit position.

As soon as it was light I went to the regimental command post for further orders. I took with me the dead *Hauptmann*. We put him, half lying, in the sidecar. I climbed behind the seat, laid his head on my lap and closed his eyes. His usually lively, familiar face bore a great strangeness and an exhaustion beyond words. The journey was uphill, on a woodland road along the valley of the little river Ulla, to the wooden house in which the regimental command post was located. The command of the regiment, or what was left of it, had been taken over by *Major* Arnulf von Garn. Until then he had been commander of the Divisional *Füsilier* battalion. While I was giving my report, two runners of the regimental Staff dug a grave in the garden. Müller's body was laid in it. *Major* von Garn and some men were standing around the grave. Garn began to say the 'Our Father' and all joined in. Then we scattered earth on the tarpaulin in which the body had been wrapped and the grave was filled in by the silent men.

Our battalion was without a commander. It was taken over by *Oberleutnant* Mallwitz. He had been commander of the 6th Company from 6-9 August 1943, and had been seriously wounded in the upper thigh. But he had held the village of Ivanowo. I went with him in the motorcycle sidecar forward to our command post. The order was to attack Labeiki again. We would need to use a little more cunning after our experience of the previous night. There could no longer be any talk of companies. The plan was for half the battalion to go forward and round the pine wood to the right. The other half with Mallwitz and me had to move forward in the trench on top of the steep banking. I remembered to look at the place where I had fallen down. After the strong defence put up by the enemy during the night, we did not have the remotest expectation that the new attack would succeed.

When we entered the village of Labeikia, that second time, there was complete quiet. There was no shot, although the enemy must have long since seen our movements. At last, on the final leg, we shouted 'hurrah' as per orders and broke in to the position. Right up to the last moment we were still afraid that the enemy would let us approach, only to wipe us out all the more certainly with fire from everything they had got. But they put up no resistance. With their hands in the air, Red Army troops climbed out of trenches and bunkers and gave themselves up. Forty prisoners, three anti-tank guns, a German assault gun, mortars and machine-guns were captured. In addition, there were six wounded German comrades who had been set free. They had belonged to the troops who had earlier occupied the strong point. They had been severely wounded, not brought in, but had had their wounds dressed by Russian medics.

Our joy at the small victory of Labeiki did not last long. Further to the right a breakthrough was reported. The front therefore had to be drawn back. In the afternoon, when we had hardly had chance to establish ourselves in Labeiki, the situation appeared to become critical. Contact to the right had again been broken. On the Lepel-Ulla road, running along the valley of the Ulla to our rear, there was heavy vehicle traffic. Obviously everything that could travel was making for the little village of Ulla. Everyone wanted to cross the bridge there and to be able to reach further roads on which to retreat.

Meanwhile we waited, concerned, for the order to withdraw. When it was finally given by wireless it was, to all appearances, too late. As the battalion, widely separated, moved back into the Ulla valley, on the road there were already scenes of a wild flight. I saw baggage wagons with galloping horses, motorised vehicles of all kinds, and among them soldiers rushing on foot. The vehicles were loaded with men and material. Obviously behind them Russian tanks were coming. The rumbling reached our ears. Those who were fleeing were driven before them. The picture of the flight, the approaching enemy tanks, firing their cannons and machine-guns, swept the remnants of the battalion along in the panic.

No commander was able to hold his unit back any longer. *Oberleutnant* Mallwitz had suddenly disappeared. I ordered the men from my little staff group, who were still around me, to cross the Ulla somewhere and to assemble on the other side. It was obviously out of the question that we would be able to reach the bridge at Ulla. In the ditch by the side of the road I suddenly found myself alone again with two enemy T-34 tanks driving past me at full speed. Both were loaded up with infantrymen, riding on them. The fantastic situation surprised me so much that I never thought of firing after them. With no cover I just watched the scene. The next rational thought caused me to jump across the road in order to reach the riverbank.

Completely calm again, I looked for a lump of wood in order to make the crossing easier. I found a veritable beam. Then a medic joined me. It was the red-haired Beuleke from my staff. I knew him from the Asorowa cemetery the previous autumn. Beuleke had stripped off down to his vest and underpants and said that he was not a good swimmer. I carried the beam, about the size of a railway sleeper, to the water. Then I told Beuleke to sit down on it, in front of me, and it would carry us both safely. Beuleke clung frantically to the wood. It was better after I had told him to stretch out his arms sideways, flat along the surface of the water. I had sat down on the beam in full uniform behind Beuleke. It sank about half a metre under our weight, so that we were submerged half way up our chests.

The little river was getting on for 20 metres wide and should have been crossed easily and quickly. My hastily conceived plan, however, intended to make use of the current and to go down river. I intended to connect up to a larger group and also to get to the opposite bank. On the right hand bank soldiers of all ranks were discarding their weapons, equipment and clothing. I shouted as loud as I could that they should find themselves lumps of wood. But many had been seized by panic and swimmers and non-swimmers alike were throwing themselves into the river.

Meanwhile, I steered my beam with the help of my hands, taking care that my machine-pistol did not get wet. Before getting on the beam I had tied it round my neck on a quite short strap so that, in spite of our being half submerged, it was protected from the water. As we were moving round a bend of the almost rushing river, bursts of machine-gun fire lashed the surface of the water. I struggled to look round to see if the firing just chanced to hit the river or whether we were observed by the enemy. In moving I unwittingly lost my right rubber boot. It had filled up to the top with water. The water had simply dragged it off. Angrily, I let my left boot follow it. It slid off just as easily.

After a kilometre of that memorable journey on the water I found *Major* von Garn standing on the left bank putting on his boots. He had swum alone across the river and, careful man that he was, had taken his boots off before doing so. I steered towards him and we climbed on to the bank.

The Divisional history (page 205) records those events as follows:

> On 26 July the enemy crossed the Ulla in several places and there rolled up the weakly manned positions from the rear, mostly from two sides. The combat weary troops - they had been in combat without a break since 22 June - had had no sleep and only a little food. They were trying, after their ammunition had run out, to make a fighting withdrawal over the rushing Ulla. Without bridges, without boats, under fire from the enemy the few survivors were trying to reach the opposite bank. Men who could not swim were hanging like grapes on men who could and dragging them down into the depths. Swimmers were pulling wounded men across the river and trying that several times until their strength was exhausted. Watery death reaped a rich but cruel harvest. On the morning of the next day on the road there appeared individual naked men, who were carrying nothing but a weapon. Everything was done to get these men fresh clothes, if only so that they could join in the fighting again.

With *Major* von Garn, Beuleke and I went to the road leading southwards from Ulla, an unparalleled road of retreat. Beuleke, who the previous year had escaped with me at Asorowa, left us in order somehow to find the baggage-train and to get hold of a uniform again. He was not the only one. Down the road were coming *Landsers* of all ranks. They were still rushing, many without uniform or only dressed in their underwear, without weapons and without equipment. Running towards them with just bare feet I was almost fully dressed. Von Garn said that the regimental orderly officer, *Oberleutnant* Kruger, had stretched a cable across the river at the regimental command post, by means of which 15 non-swimmers were able to pull themselves across. *Oberfeldwebel* Miller, the man in our battalion who held the Knight's Cross, was a non-swimmer. He said he had got himself across the river in his vest, with his service cap on his head in which he had wrapped his Knight's Cross. To protect the congested traffic on the bridge, an anti-tank gun had been positioned there. Its clear-headed crew were shooting up, one after the other, the tanks that had broken through.

Still barefooted I supported the *Major* in assembling the returning men, inso-far as they belonged to our units. But a *Leutnant* from the *Panzerjäger*, like me without boots, was among them. The hot midday sun soon dried our clothing. The fact that I had no boots and was not responsible for losing them was to me of little consolation. But I had rescued weapons, ammunition, map case, and uniform. I was glad that the *Major* did not blame me for the loss, but I was tormented by the undignified picture that I presented as a barefoot officer! We quickly gathered to-gether the remnants of Regiment 7. The remnants of my battalion we used for top-ping-up.

In the small baggage-train at the regimental staff there was so-called 'light gas clothing'. Other reserves of uniform and footwear were with the baggage-train said to be 80 kilometres behind us. Until the *Hauptfeldwebel* of the regimental Staff could get hold of a pair of decent boots, perhaps from a wounded man, I had to content myself with the famous *Schuhwerk*. They consisted of a rigid sole and an as-bestos cover coming from the sole and reaching to the knees, normally tied over the boot under the knee. They were never used in the Second World War. With such a temporary arrangement, that did not allow you to walk properly, I began my duties as second orderly officer in the staff of Grenadier Regiment 7. With *Oberleutnant* Kruger from Berlin-Charlottenburg, the 01 (assistant to the 1st General Staff Offi-cer), I participated in really dangerous tasks that we covered in our motor vehicles along hazardous routes during the coming days.

8

Summer 1944: Bitter defensive battles

Continuing withdrawals and defensive actions; retreat into the Baltic states

For the IX *Armeekorps*, in which the 252nd *Infanteriedivision* was fighting, the six weeks that followed 22 June developed into a memorable race. It stretched over some 500 kilometres from the area of Vitebsk in a generally westerly direction almost as far as the western border of the Reich in East Prussia. The wedges that the Russians had driven into Army Group Centre to destroy it, caused the *Armeekorps* to lose its connection with its right hand neighbour. Principally, it caused a gap of varying widths of up to 70 kilometres to open up between the Division and Army Group North, to which a considerable number of the Divisional units had been attached. Under the command of the IX *Armeekorps* were the remnants of the 252nd Division and of Corps Detachment D. Into them had been gathered remnants of other divisions which themselves had been shattered. Our Division had Regiment 7, the *Füsilier* battalion, and the remnants of my battalion that had been absorbed into Regiment 7. After the Düna position had been surrendered the regiment had again been under the command of Corps Detachment D. Only on 30 June had it returned to the command of its own Division.

On 29 June *Major* von Garn had succeeded in getting hold of some Iron Crosses for the regiment. They were distributed almost unceremoniously to the few experienced men. It was done in front of the tent that held the regimental command post. When Garn pinned the Iron Cross First Class on my chest I had just returned from a journey on the tracked motorcycle. I already had orders for another journey. So there was no time for joy and pride over that much longed-for decoration. Still, it was lucky that on the previous day I had got new rubber boots from the baggage-train.

On the following night a rapid withdrawal took place. It lasted well into the morning. The regiment was supposed to move to rest at a location 20 kilometres behind the most forward security positions, of which we certainly had seen nothing. By a pond, which lay in a hollow, we found the spot. The exhausted men laid down their weapons and equipment and most of them immediately went into the warm marshy water. The entire regiment of several hundred men swam, splashed in the water, washed or shaved. Many of them did this quickly and then settled themselves under the shade of trees in order at last to get some sleep. Von Garn and I had first to concern ourselves with setting up security positions and to convince ourselves that we were in contact with the Division, before we could think of relaxing.

The rest had not lasted half an hour when the sound of engines was to be heard. It had to be from our own assault guns or tanks that were standing in front of us to provide security. But we wondered why they were already moving back, since it was only midday. Our wondering immediately turned out to be pointless. From behind the hill of yellow grain enclosing the hollow to the north and west, an enemy T-34 emerged. A second and third followed. The tanks pushed slowly up on to the ridge of the hill, their long gun barrels towering skywards. The appearance of the tanks panicked the men who were bathing and resting. Once again a panicky flight began. But after a few hundred metres the officers succeeded in stopping the men and bringing them back.

Oberleutnant Mallwitz, who had reported to Garn immediately beforehand, ordered me to take care of the tank with him. Through the corn and past bushes we crept up to the tanks. What Mallwitz intended to do was not clear. Neither of us had anything but pistols which were useless. We could do nothing unless the tank crew stuck their heads out of the hatch. We came to within 10 metres of the first tank, which had stopped near a line of bushes.

In order for bravery to succeed, the right weapon must be to hand at the right time. Such an advantage, in the shape of a *Panzerfaust*, an adhesive hollow charge, or a *T-mine*, was lacking for us. On the contrary, the crew of the first tank had spotted us. They fired on us with their machine-guns and Mallwitz was shot in the knee. Then even he realised that we had to beat it. Mallwitz hobbled painfully and we moved slowly back. To our surprise the tanks turned round. They had become suspicious.

The emergency line was held until evening. The urgently needed anti-tank gun had come. It was standing in a hedge, well camouflaged. Garn and I were beside it when a second tank attack came in the afternoon. We scored a direct hit on the upper part of its turret at 30 metres range, on the most forward of the three tanks. Flames were soon shooting up and two smoke-blackened figures climbed out, holding their hands high above their heads. Pointing his machine-pistol, the corporal of a group of infantrymen in positions beside the anti-tank gun took them in charge. Von Garn had them taken to the rear in a regimental vehicle. At 10pm the regiment withdrew. The rearguard had to remain until midnight. Only then did Von Garn and I withdraw.

The following night the regiment managed to put some distance between us and the enemy. The march went on during the day, one behind the other, *gelaufen* as our Silesians said. I appreciated the advantage of not having to run, but for the most part being able to travel on vehicles. To the west of the little town of Kublici the broad sandy road went through forest for many kilometres. The area had for a long time been the home of partisans.

However, in June, the Supreme Commander of our 3rd *Panzerarmee*, *Generaloberst* Reinhart, having in mind the possibility of a retreat, deployed all his available forces there to fight the partisans. But there had been no time to bury the bodies. That was why long stretches were overwhelmed by a ghastly stench. It was said that hundreds of dead were lying in the woods. The July heat strengthened the smell of putrefaction. You had to pinch your nose and breathe through your mouth. Some men even put on their gas masks.

On that road, 132 years before, the *Grande Armée* had moved on Moscow. Not far from there is the source of the Beresina with its other tributaries. On the advance in 1941 our regiment crossed the Beresina at Stujanka, the site of the historic battlefield. During entrenching work at that time a Napoleonic eagle had been found. They had immediately sent it to the *Fuhrer's* headquarters. The parallels with the Napoleonic retreat were borne in upon us in a shattering way.

On the way to Globokie, the old Polish border town, a pig jumped out of a farmyard in front of the *Kübelwagen*. The poor creature kept running in front of the vehicle. Then it was overtaken, run over, and lifted into the *Kübelwagen* with broken limbs. The fact that in the evening the field kitchen was once again issuing pork, caused von Garn to utter the apposite remark: 'Just get yourself a calf in front of the *Wagen*, and not just a pig!'

On 4 July, as our next stage, we reached Dunilovici. From there I had to branch off to the north-west to get to the village of Nowopajewa and to direct the 3rd Battalion to its lines. I had just got off the motorcycle when I heard the familiar roaring of a 'Stalin organ'. My driver threw the vehicle into the soft bushes and we lay down flat in the sandy road because there was not a scrap of cover. The 'organ' sounded like the swish of a mighty scythe as it swings through the air before it cuts. All the shells crashed on to houses, into the gardens and on to the streets. There were 42 explosions of 15.2cm calibre shells. It seemed a miracle that no one was hit. Those weapons no longer had any effect on *alte Hasen*, or old soldiers, like us. When the 'blessing' was over we stood up, shook the sand out of our uniforms and drove on to look for the battalion.

In our quarters that evening the regimental medical officer treated me. Several times I had had injections of Cebion i.e. Vitamin C, into my behind, so that I was almost unable to walk. At that time the staff medical officer Dr Hellweg had little to do. The regiment did not run its own dressing station and, because of the speed of the withdrawal, casualties remained few. The wounded were immediately sent to the rear by the battalion medical officers. Sometimes though it seemed that the doctor would rather be the regimental adjutant. When new maps, always in short supply, were issued, I had to fight him for them every time. It finally dawned on him that as orderly officer, I was more in need of a map than he.

On the 4 July we passed Postavy. It had been set on fire by shelling and was well ablaze. The day before, on another dispatch journey, I had passed through the town and found it intact. Wind was driving the flames. Fire from the many trim wooden houses gave off such heat that in the open *Kübelwagen*, after two attempts to drive through the town, we had to drive round it. The motorised vehicles had to leave the road. In order not to sacrifice our precious wireless *Kübelwagen*, we finally drove two kilometres over open country, right in front of the point units of the Russian tanks. Then we finally reached the road leading westwards. At the edge of the road, there were many rolls of expensive field telephone cable. They would almost certainly fall intact into enemy hands, just as had happened with the Army's supply dump located east of the town. The responsible paymaster, despite being threatened with court martial, had refused to give out the cable supplies right up to the moment when the first tank shells were bursting.

Wir machen Parjecheli was the catch-phrase of those summer weeks. Freely translated it meant 'we're beating it'. The tempo of the withdrawal alone saw to it that we did not get very much sleep. We just had to take advantage of every spare quarter of an hour to grab a doze. One afternoon I had lain down in the leather-upholstered back seat of the wireless *Kübelwagen*. When the driver, August Wörtz, a Tyrolean from Wörgl, came to use the vehicle, he failed to notice that I was lying on the back seat. Reversing in the farmyard he drove so close to the wall that my foot, which was hanging out of the car, was trapped. I woke with a shout and bellowed a *Donnerwetter* at him. In the late evening the same thing happened. Driving back with Garn on an assault gun, as part of the rearguard, I had dozed off. In the darkness of the night we overtook a refugee column of ethnic Germans accompanied by a *Landesschützen*. Half asleep as I was, I had not noticed that my foot was hanging over the edge of the assault gun. So it got between the gun and the horse and cart that we were overtaking. But once again things were all right. I was relieved to be spared from ending up in a military hospital in such a way.

We were sorry for the people in the refugee columns and we wondered if they would be able to maintain the pace. The further west we went the heavier the traffic and the more congested the roads. In the baggage-trains, it was often said that unruly scenes took place. Again and again senior ranking officers exploited unconditional obedience. They stopped commanders of lower rank from moving first, and claimed precedence for themselves.

There were also said to have been people at work misdirecting the traffic. We had been warned as early as the summer of 1943 about strange officers in the trenches. The Russians had placed men from the National Committee of Free Germany in the uniform of officers or military police at road junctions. They were said to have directed withdrawing troops towards a pocket. I was convinced that it would not have happened to us. The conscientiousness and composure of *Major* von Garn guaranteed that we did not go in the wrong direction nor lose our way. Sometimes when I was not with Garn in the rearguard, I was the leader of the nightly column in the regimental staff. While the others on the vehicles were dozing or sleeping I drove on ahead on my tracked motorcycle with the column's drivers. With my pocket torch showing a green light tied on my chest, I led the regimental vehicles behind me without us ever losing our way.

One night *Hauptmann* Kaupke, the commander of the heavy artillery battalion, announced through the field loudspeaker that the Russians were in their firing position. Through the loudspeaker we could hear rifle and machine-gun fire. That meant that the Russians had occupied the next village to the west of us. Kaupke was there with his guns. The Russians had also occupied the road along which we were retreating. How often during that retreat had the enemy tried to overtake us with an advance party and cut off our line of retreat. After a hard search we managed to lead the regimental column out of the encirclement through woodland roads.

The next day, 10 July, the *Major* was out and about with Kruger, his 01. I remained behind in the command post with *Hauptmann* Grabsche, who had replaced the wounded *Oberleutnant* Stolz as Regimental Adjutant. Suddenly there came an unconfirmed report that the Russians had broken through very close to us. The excitable Grabsche ordered a counter-attack in which all available members of the staff had to take part. We advanced almost a kilometre to the east, but found no Russians and came under no fire. Finally Grabsche shouted 'Hurra' and ran round in front of the others waving his map board over his head. In the event it was much ado about nothing.

On 11 July we passed through Labazoras. In peacetime it must have been an idyllic village among the Lithuanian lakes. On my dispatch journeys on my motorcycle I never forgot how lucky I was that I did not have to march on foot. Even the battalion commanders covered hundreds of kilometres on foot. During the night, when I drove past such a column marching exhaustedly, I felt guilty that I had it so good. *Hauptmann* Husenett, who since Lowsha had been commander of the 2nd Battalion, did not envy me my 'wheels'.

Husenett's downy blond boy's face, even when things got rough, did not lose its friendliness. He was the same even when he begged me to 'sort out an assault gun' for him for the evening, or when he begged the *Major* to say that he could hold out for another hour or two, or when he was in urgent need of ammunition. Friendship bound me to Husenett almost as soon as we met. He was always eager to hear something about our situation and our neighbours'. To the left the gap had certainly become wider and wider. From a width of 17 kilometres during the last days of July it had expanded to more than 70 kilometres. The Corps, even on the right, was fighting without units adjoining them. It was like a wandering 'pocket', often having to fight to keep open the roads of retreat leading westwards.

The retreat drove me on, too. I rushed madly to and fro on my motorbike to the units under our command. To the battalions, the assault guns, the anti-tank guns, and the pioneers I took orders that were only in my head and for which there were no written papers. I had to find them with the aid of a map and often just by my own intuition. Often I was in danger of dozing off. Then, when the driver had to brake sharply in order to avoid a crater or another kind of obstacle, I was in danger of being thrown out. Or sometimes a Russian *Rata* suddenly dived out of the sky or a couple of twin-engined Martin bombers, supplied by America, dropped their bombs on the road along which we were retreating. Then the two of us had to jump off almost while we were still driving, and take cover where we could.

When I returned in the evening to the regimental command post, a seriously wounded soldier of the Russian Guards was lying in front of the farmhouse. He had several orders on his chest. He was the escort to two colonels who had lost their way in a jeep, also of American origin. It had hurtled into our lines. A machine-gunner lying in the ditch at the side of the road had riddled the vehicle with holes at point blank range. As a result the officers had been killed.

At that time I thought how good it would be to take a holiday in that country. To live in one of the small, moss-roofed houses, to wander barefoot through the hot sand of the country roads in summer and to be able to bathe in the dark warm lakes, must be a pleasure which could scarcely be called earthly. When we had time and a favourable opportunity, von Garn and I would stop, throw off our uniforms and throw ourselves into one of the many lakes of the Lithuanian lowland. But even pleasure in bathing occasionally meant sacrifices. On one of those days the Corps Adjutant, *Oberstleutnant* Gyncz-Rekowski, an elderly gentleman, suffered a heart attack.

In Alanta, on 12 July, the good days with the regimental staff suddenly came to an end. I had to go up to the front to take over command of a company. That meant continuing the retreat *per pedes apostolorum* i.e. on foot like the Apostles. During the night we withdrew 25 kilometres. I was surprised how little the march tired me. Around the village of Alanta a barrier was to be formed. After the company had dug their trenches and I had established the machine-gun position, I climbed to the pointed wooden tower of the brick church in which a forward artillery observer had already settled himself. I looked out of the belfry window of the tower further and further eastwards and saw fields, meadows, roads, woods, lakes and a little river in the light of the morning sun. That tranquillity did not last long. Soon the artillery observer and I were driven out of the tower by an enemy anti-tank gun. The Russians would have been able easily to work out that the tower was occupied, and as the number of hits increased, we both climbed down.

The knowledge that I was back in the main frontline again gave me the old familiar feeling of security. Once again I knew that whoever came from the front could only be the enemy. The dangers there were at their greatest and were ongoing, the physical exertions always at the limit of what we could bear. But to compensate there was no more fear of surprise attacks. On my motorbike I was travelling long distances, as orderly officer, behind the main lines through the forest. Once a couple of Russians emerged from the wood. That was an unpleasant surprise that for a moment left me not knowing what to do. But on the other hand when the enemy attacked from the front, overran the positions or broke through during the night with an assault unit, those were events for which I was always braced.

Now and again an exception to the turbulence of the retreat confirmed my rule. For example, when scattered units broke through to the west and reached our lines. On 13 July we were in position along a line in which a railway embankment crossed the main line of resistance. A *Feldwebel* and three men came along the embankment. It turned out that they belonged to the troops guarding an Army supply dump and their paymaster had let them retreat without orders. The supply dump, of course, had not been evacuated, for which the men, happily returning from there, got an earful from my men.

During the march the next night there were two stops. The reason for the first was a ditch into which one of the 15-ton tractors of the heavy artillery had skidded. The huge vehicle, however, was able to pull itself out of the mud as there was a firm enough tree close by, round which the steel cable from the built-in windlass could be secured. The second halt occurred towards morning. A grenadier on the march keeled over and declared that he could not march any further. Since neither vehicles nor horses were available on which he could sit, it was hard to know what to do. After a five minutes breather, we divided his pack, including belt, steel helmet, and rifle, among ourselves. With the admonition 'think of your old woman, mate', two men grabbed him under the shoulders, and put him on his feet between them. Supported in that way, we continued the march. After a while he managed on his own again. When we arrived in the new main line of resistance he thanked us for not having left him behind. That too was without infantry!

Scarcely had I settled in, or rather 'run in', again as company commander than I had to go back to the regiment. I had been lucky. In those three days the enemy had not been pushing up behind us so strongly as to cause skirmishes. But replacement officers had arrived. The *Major* wanted me, whom he already knew, rather than a new *Leutnant* as orderly officer with the regiment. Scarcely was I there than the enemy attacked. One of the first to be brought back was *Herr* Husenett. I say *Herr*, because in the German *Wehrmacht* there was a regulation that officers basically were *per Sie* among themselves, i.e. the formal form of address, and within the different ranks addressed each other with *Herr* and their surname. To some one you did not know, say on the railway, you said '*Herr Kamerad*'.

Herr Husenett had been wounded in the lungs. The young man who had been so kind to me, was at most only two years older. His usually fresh face was pale and yellowish. But he easily survived the wound, one of many, and soon returned to the regiment. In October he received the Knight's Cross, and was also decorated with the *Goldener Nahkampfspange* i.e. the golden close-combat clasp, and the *Goldener Verwundetenabzeichen* i.e. the golden wound badge. In 1945 he was killed in action

During the evening we took up quarters in a country house of aristocratic design. The assault guns remained at the regimental command post. Their crews, who were not used to spending nights so far forward, dug foxholes for themselves, over which they placed their vehicles. In that way they could be doubly certain, so to speak, of being able to sleep.

The next day we stopped in the still fairly well preserved German positions from the First World War. We even found concreted cellars, although they were naturally fairly overgrown. The *Ostwall* was an excellently built and deeply ramified defensive position, by which the enemy offensive should be contained. But, like so many rumours, it proved to be bogus. The fact that that campaign in the East had been won by our fathers and had been concluded with a peace was a thought that forced itself upon us. In the First World War they had only penetrated a few hundred kilometres into enemy territory, whereas we had almost got as far as Moscow and there was still no question of peace.

It seemed rather that we would have to keep on retreating. Because our retreat rolled rapidly back, often the few connections between east and west were heavily congested. Sometimes it needed longer stops and furious disagreements to clear the way for one's own column. It was still only a question of combat units and smaller baggage-trains who argued over their relative rank. The large baggage-trains had arrived days ago in Marianpol close to the Reich border.

To try to relieve the pressure of the pursuing enemy, on 15 July aircraft were sent in. Despite the fact that we had laid out the orange coloured recognition cloths and red swastika banners, they hit our columns. Among the wounded was the VW *Kübelwagen* driver from the Staff. So *Leutnant* Kruger, the first orderly officer, whom the *Major* sent off to the large baggage-train drove the vehicle. It was not exactly a 'genteel' occupation for an orderly officer, but it was good to have the baggage- train led by an energetic officer. Garn said he could manage with me alone.

In the evening came the report that *Hauptmann* Gräbsch had been killed. He had only just taken over command of the 2nd Battalion after *Herr* Husenett had been wounded. When he took over command of the battalion I realised that within himself he had felt some reluctance for the job. I knew then that he must have had a premonition of his death. I regretted my unkind thoughts about him. He had been a master optician from Beuthen in Upper Silesia, a brave officer and he certainly possessed many good qualities. After his death came the news that for action at the Ulla bridge he had received the Knight's Cross. *De mortuis nil nisi bene.*

I add a touching detail from the time of the retreat. The foals of the draught horses on the march with us, clung to their mothers, suckling as they walked. It was a sad sight. On 17 July we were removed from the command of the Corps Detachment and returned to the command of our own Division. The Divisional Adjutant, *Major* Östreich, was waiting for us at the edge of the village of Swenzoniai like a father waiting for his lost sons.

Sitting on a garden seat outside a house, rather like Napoleon III with Bismarck at Donchéry, he told us of the situation. It was the intention of the divisional commander to reform the 2nd Battalion of *Grenadierregiment 472*, whose adjutant I was. If successful he said, the Division would again have command of more than one infantry regiment. We should no longer need to fear the 'bogey-man' of staffs, whose troops have been wiped out. We would not be used to top-up other troop units. To me personally *Major* Östreich made the remarkable announcement that I had been 'posted as killed'. I was not left speechless, as I happened to be in a cheerful mood. But I thought with some concern about Schweidnitz and my parents and the fact that the news could possibly have reached Gisela by some circuitous route.

The next day, 18 July, I drove with *Major* von Garn to receive our orders at the divisional command post. It was likely that, for 48 hours, it would be located in an unostentatious castle that had formerly been the summer residence of the Lithuanian State President. The white painted building, shining in the sun, was set quite formally in the quiet countryside by Lake Lenas. While Garn was with *General* Meltzer, I dropped into an oversized leather armchair, in the spacious hall, laid my head against the bulging back and stretched out my legs.

I was awakened from my doze by the Ia, the first general staff officer of the Division, *Oberstleutnant im Generalstab* Hugo Binder. He told me that my battalion, shattered at the Ulla, was to be reformed with immediate effect. The remnants of Regiment 7 that we had absorbed would be discarded again. In addition, he said there were newly arrived replacement *Unteroffiziere* and other ranks, and some officers who could be spared from elsewhere. For me it was a painful farewell, especially from the unflappable *Major* von Garn. Command of the battalion was to be taken over by a middle aged *Hauptmann* by the name of Schneider. He was an East Prussian and a former '12-Ender'. He had been awarded the *Kriegsverdienstkreuz I Klasse* i.e. the War Merit Cross First Class. It was a decoration given to lines of communication troops. But he had no experience of the Eastern Front.

The Ia outlined the task to be undertaken by the new Battalion. He said the deep flank of the Division was to be protected to the north. The entire Corps, or rather what remained of it, was to continue to fight back westwards, but without connections to either side. Above all, he said there was no connection to Army Group North. The gap at that time extended to 55 kilometres. To support us in that task he would assign us assault guns as the occasion demanded. We would have the motorised vehicles of the staff of Regiment 472, those from the baggage-train, and a *Panzerjäger* platoon from the 14th Company. After the business conversation there was a personal conversation. Binder was a Swabian. From 1938 he had been with the *Gebirgsjäger* in Innsbruck. He talked about the Tyrol after he found out that I was an Austrian. Binder, who had smooth black hair and brown eyes, was stocky in build and obviously of high intelligence. The fact that he possessed the latter quality matched the idea that I had of a general staff officer. He wore the crimson red colour of the General Staff with the double 4cm white stripes on his riding breeches.

Kawarskas was the next station on our route. The little town was on the left flank of the Divisional sector. I was once again the battalion adjutant. I set up the Battalion staff in the modest country house of a former Lithuanian minister. It had obviously only recently been abandoned by its inhabitants. In the library, as well as books in various languages, there were a number of visiting cards from ministers, diplomats, and businessmen from several countries. Evidently they were relics from the times when Lithuania was still an autonomous state and had not yet been annexed by the Soviet Union.

Since we had gained some ground on the Russians, there was time to have a look around the village. *Hauptmann* Schneider and I had a look around the Catholic Church, and found the priest, who invited us to lunch. The old gentleman asked us to a meal of beef, which was tough as old boots, and rock hard dumplings in a simple milk sauce. The meal was served by a friendly housekeeper, who was quite wizened with age. To the question as to whether he would flee, he answered with an astonished 'No'! He said that God would continue to help him and he would remain with his flock.

In the afternoon, in accordance with orders from the administration in the rear, all men in the village of military service age had to assemble to be transported away. That was to prevent them being immediately enlisted into the Red Army by the advancing Russians. With tears in his eyes the old priest, who had been our host for lunch, came to us accompanied by a young woman. He asked Schneider to release his 'organist' who had only just married the young woman. Although Schneider had no authority to do this, he looked at me questioningly and I nodded to him. The priest was allowed to take with him his 'organist' and therefore the woman her husband. In the deserted chemist's shop there were some useful things for the battalion medical officer to take away. Meanwhile, for me, a more important find was a piano in the chemist's house. Like a thirsty man coming to water, I sat down and played once again, for the first time in months.

The next morning the enemy had pushed up after us. Siberian Guards troops attacked. The minister's country house was lost then retaken with the support of assault guns. The following night the little town was evacuated. Many wooden houses were burning, set on fire by enemy artillery. Clouds of smoke hung over the place. The glowing yellow and red of the flames lifted up vividly against the dark night sky. When I left the town to go westwards on my motorcycle, I nevertheless felt the chill of frost in the warm evening air. I could not get the poor old priest out of my mind.

In Kawarskas the post had arrived for the first time in four weeks. Letters from Mother, Father and Gisela, who all followed the *Wehrmacht* reports, were full of concern about my welfare. Father hoped that I had not remained in Vitebsk. He had read about the fighting in and around Vitebsk. Because of his experience in the First World War he was able to decipher the *Wehrmacht* reports and other *communiqués* concerning the fighting.

The battalion was not directly under the command of the Division, but under the command of Regiment 7 and *Major* von Garn. On the 21 July we received orders to re-take the village of Pagiriai. It had been occupied by the enemy the previous day. *Major* von Garn had himself come to lead the attack. Three assault guns from our old comrades-in-arms, the Swabian 232nd *Sturmgeschütz-Abteilung*, were also taking part. I joined the *Major* and went with him to make preparations. Then the assault guns drove up, and the battalion left the wood, fanning out. Garn and I rode at the head on the first assault gun, until enemy tank and rifle fire forced to us to get down. The village was neatly retaken.

The Russian infantry had evidently lost the vim and vigour that they had shown in attacking. They fled. A Stalin tank collapsed through the bridge over a stream at the entrance to the village. The tank crew climbed out and disappeared. They took with them their optical equipment that they had hurriedly detached. To salvage the colossal capture from the stream was not possible with the means at our disposal. So our people placed explosive charges in the engine and the cannon in order to make them unusable.

For the battalion command post I assigned trenches that must have been used as a cellar by the inhabitants of a farm at the edge of the village. The men fitted them out with 'corn dollies'. The situation seemed to indicate the firm prospect of getting some sleep that night in the bed that had been made. In the event, the miracle happened. I was able to sleep during the night for five hours without interruption.

At 5am the Second General Staff Officer of the Division rang. He asked where the two men were who should have reported to him at 5am to go to Königsberg to fetch a caterpillar tractor. With no idea what he was talking about, I asked him in turn which men he meant and what they were supposed to be doing. The general staff officer, also called Binder, only with the Christian name George, exploded. 'Are you mad, *Leutnant*, I spoke with you last night and gave you the orders!' I very respectfully pointed out that he must be mistaken. For once I had been able to get to sleep and had spoken with no one. I said he must have telephoned the battalion commander. Furious, he hung up.

After a while the telephonist, *Gefreiter* Hermens, whom I called Hermes, reported to me. The Ib, he said, had telephoned and asked for me. Hermens connected us and I had reported in. Whereupon the Ib ordered me to have two men at the command post, for 5am. They had to go to Königsberg to fetch two RSOs, i.e. *Raupenschlepper Ost*, half-tracked trucks. He said that, drowsy with sleep, I had dealt with that order in a quite un-military fashion with several *Ja, ja*! That had caused the Ib to interrupt several times to ask 'Can you hear me Scheiderbauer? Can you hear, *Leutnant*?' To this I had repeatedly said *Ja, ja*! and finally put down the receiver. 'Hermes, lad, you dummy, you knew I was asleep and was not quite with it. So why didn't you wake me up properly?' I reproached him via the receiver. The brave lad answered 'Ah, but I thought that the *Herr Leutnant* should get a bit of sleep'.

Up at the Battalion staff we had a large open Madford *Kübelwagen* at our disposal. I had brought it up from the regimental baggage-train along with the driver. We drove in the afternoon to the Divisional command post to receive orders. I took the opportunity of making my apologies to *Major im Generalstab* 'Schorsch' Binder. On the journey from Parigiai, westwards through the gently climbing terrain that was largely visible to the enemy, we were spotted by a Stalin tank. It sent a few shells after us with its gu, but thank heaven did not hit us. The driver, who must have formally served in the Dutch police, drove off, with a shout of *Karacho*, in a zig-zag course over meadows and fields.

On the evening of 22 July it was announced that an assassination attempt had been made on the Führer on 20 July. Among us there was more surprise than fury. We had no time to comment on the event and scarcely had any time to reflect on it. I thought to myself, it was doubtless a kind of treachery that had taken place. But, I went on to think, men with names like Yorck, Stauffenberg, Witzleben, and Moltke would not be likely to betray Germany, nor would they be likely to betray what the German Fatherland meant to them. I wondered if perhaps they had acted for Germany and not against her.

The following day the battalion was assigned to occupy and hold a sector eight kilometres wide. The lack of forces only allowed us to defend the as strongpoints of three villages lying within the sector. The Battalion staff also had to go into the main line of resistance. So we established ourselves in the Dvariskai strongpoint. The retreat road unfortunately led southwards. Therefore I kept the motorised vehicles safe along the westward course of the road. I did it because it was a fact that I had to assess the situation on my own and make the required dispositions. It seemed to me that *Hauptmann* Schneider was not capable of commanding a battalion. He certainly did not seem to be up to the job. He had no idea of how to command an autonomous reinforced battalion and would simply say 'Get on with it Scheiderbauer', in his broad East Prussian dialect.

Dvariskai lay on a gentle rise. Neat gardens and yellow wheat waved round the thatched cottages whose cleanliness bespoke a modest standard of peasant prosperity. To sit again at a wooden table with a clean plate was a pleasure in itself. My batman Walter Hahnel set about whipping up a big plate of rolls spread with *Konservenwurst*, with local bacon and a lot of eggs. After the telephone connection had been re-established and our connection to the right had been secured, we sat down to table in the battalion command post, a farmhouse. The Russians were evidently only feeling their way hesitantly after us. We hoped that we would remain unscathed until the evening when we were to leave the position. That hope proved to be unfounded.

From the advanced security positions, rifle fire could soon be heard. Therefore I sent the motorbikes to the rear on the retreat road that was still open. To gamble with them and lose them would have put an end to our task of protecting the flank, where particular mobility was required. Scarcely was the rifle fire heard than the new commander 'disappeared'. I had already noticed he did that in critical situations. Then he did not need to make decisions and could not be called to the telephone. Probably he was observing the advancing Russians with his binoculars, from cover. The rifle fire continued and drew closer. I had to bring up supporting fire. While I was sitting at the field telephone I noticed wounded men were struggling past and to the rear. A little later non-wounded were also passing. To me that meant that they were fleeing. The commander was absent all that time and I was tied to the telephone. Of the whole sector I could see nothing more than a bit of a wheatfield.

At the regiment and the artillery they wanted to know how the situation was progressing. I had been able to direct the artillery fire well for a quarter of an hour by the use of a map. Then outside I saw large numbers of *Landsers* rushing to the rear. Walter had taken up position at the window and had cocked his weapon, while I, with the telephone cabinet in front of me, sat at the other window in telephone contact with *Hauptmann* Bundt, the Adjutant of the Divisional Artillery Regiment. Just as I was saying to him that according to what was going on outside we would only be able to stay there for a few more minutes, I saw Russian infantry wading through the cornfields towards the house. Walter fired. 'Get out!' I ordered and shouted into the telephone, 'Fire on our own strongpoint, the Ivans are outside the house'.

I tore the telephone from the wires, sprang after Walter and left the house by the backdoor, just as two Red Army soldiers entered by the front. As the last to leave, I dashed with long strides after my comrades. After half a kilometre I at last caught them up and was able to build a new security position to the south of the village. While I was still at the house I had seen a wounded man lying there shouting imploringly 'Take me with you'. But, as the last man to leave, how could I have managed it? Some hours later, in the afternoon, Dvariskai was retaken with the support of assault guns and quadruple flak guns. I entered the farmhouse and even found a couple of rolls still on the plate.

The most dashing officer in our battalion was the 20 years old *Leutnant* Blatschke. In June he had been orderly officer for only a short time. But since the battalion had been re-formed he had commanded the 6th Company. Within our group he was the right man for a company commander, with its task of covering the deep flank to the left. At that time Blatschke, with his little band of men, had to hold the village to the south of Ponewisch. When the village was finally evacuated Blatschke, not a second before he was ordered, sitting on a motorbike, was the last man to leave the village. Nobody knew how he had come about the motorbike, and Russians had broken into the village on several sides. While the driver bolted away shouting *Karacho*, i.e. step on it, Blatschke fired with his machine-pistol in every direction. He finally reached the wood, not far from the settlement, and thus reached cover.

On the 28 July we reached Gedainiai, also called Gedahnen. It was a friendly little provincial town through which there ran a little river. On the raised eastern bank of the river, from which you had a wide view westwards, was the grammar school. I set up our command post there. Straight away I found the *Direktor's* room, because in Lithuania too, I gathered, grammar school *Direktoren* sat enthroned in leather armchairs. So the venerable seats were, so to speak, desecrated for a few hours by our tired schoolboys' bodies. We former *Pennäler* enjoyed almost as much as ever the natural science room. It contained the same skeleton of *homo sapiens*, the stuffed birds, the induction machines, and the loo just like our school at home. In a burst of black humour I planted my steel helmet on the skull. It looked like the natural model for an anti-war poster. It also reminded me of the helmeted Russian skull, from the summer of 1941, on which I had stumbled the previous year in the minefields in the Jelnja sector.

Since the battalion had been re-formed, its orderly officer was a *Leutnant* Gegel, with whom I did not get on. He was getting on for 40 years old, came from southern Hesse and was a teacher by profession. However, in line with the old prejudice, he was a 'know-all'. At the same time he was 'professionally incapable of dealing with grown-ups'. It obviously did not suit him that because of his position he was subordinate to me and that *Hauptmann* Schneider gave me a free hand in the command of the battalion. One time he tried to get above himself, and I had to sharply remind him of his duty. If my relationship with him was cool and tense, all the more friendly and heartfelt was my friendship with *Leutnant* Helmut Christian.

Christian was the commander of the two guns from the regimental *Panzerjäger* company that belonged to our reinforced battalion. It went without saying that he was always with his guns and brought them with him into positions. He immediately grasped the situation and, unlike Gegel, did not need me to explain what was going on. He and his few men were skilful at 'organising'. They had petrol and ammunition in abundance and Helmut's Mercedes *Kübelwagen* always carried plenty of rations and drink with it. Since for the most part he was not tied to strict deadlines for evacuation, he could also occasionally leave early and sort out a detour for the retreat.

His family had hotels in Oppeln, Upper Silesia and in Heidelberg. As the son of an hotelier he had a nose for open ration dumps and always struck the right tone with the paymasters. Along with him one time I was presented with burgundy and champagne. That happened on the sandy road along which we were retreating in Lithuania in the hot summer of 1944. While drinking it we stood leaning against the *Kübelwagen* or sitting on the running boards. One day his men brought a wolfhound a few days old. From then on the little dog made the retreat with them in the *Kübelwagen*. With its awkwardness and as a living creature in need of love it touched the hearts of the soldiers who played with it and looked after it.

On the night of 30 July, once again after having become completely exhausted, I slept through a surprise attack. I had lain down in the back of the *Kübelwagen* to get some sleep during the withdrawal. During the journey through a wooded district, partisans or members of the Red Army who had already outflanked us, had thrown hand-grenades into the column and fired off shots. I must have been sleeping like the dead, because I had heard nothing of the whole 'business'. As my batman Walter told me, they could not get me to wake up. The *Hauptmann* was said to have been lost for what to do, and instead of giving a sensible order he had tried personally to shake me awake. However, he failed.

On 1 August we reached the little River Dubysa. Unfortunately we had not succeeded in making a halt along its course in a north-west to south-east direction. The enemy had already pushed back the Corps Detachment who were fighting further to the south. At noon we crossed the bridge and rearguards had to stay for a time on the far side of the bridge. I remained behind with them. Then, an hour after the greater part of the battalion, marched on alone, westwards. On the way the thought struck me that I was walking homewards and that since 22 June we had somehow all been on the homeward trek, by detours or by direct routes, whether our homeland was the temporal or the eternal one. Sunk in those reflections I was walking alone on the sandy road against regulations, that is, without runners. Along my march I met *Major* von Garn, my especial comrade in arms during that retreat. Our battalion was still under his command.

The regimental history wrote about him: 'The regimental commander *Major* von Garn could issue no orders in the confused changes in the situation. Mostly there was no time, as in many cases the Division was having to communicate orders verbally. 'Withdraw immediately,' was what was ordered.'

If what the Ia had said was correct, Garn told me, along the stretch from Ariogala to Raseinen we would have the last stage of the retreat before us. The news sounded hopeful. Even today, after almost 43 years, I can still see us marching along together, I at the side of my exemplary, revered superior officer. I eventually saw him again in 1955. I am bound to him in a strange way even now, just as he is to me.

We were coming from the south-east. Two roads, which remarkably ran parallel to each other, led to Raseinen. As late as midnight we were situated one kilometre east of the two roads and some five kilometres outside the town in the last line before Raseinen. General Meltzer himself had indicated the line to me by telephone. He had done that not in accordance with the requirements of the terrain, but by using the General Staff map, i.e. 'from the bend in this or that stream or road over the 'U' from the place-name Nadukiai', etc, connecting on the right to what remained of the Corps Detachment. For reasons relating to the terrain, however, I disregarded the strict order not to deviate an inch from the line which had been indicated and thus had been ordered. But our main line of resistance would, in following the General's direction, have run in to a valley, behind which some 500 metres away there rose a gently sloping incline. But to withdraw up that incline under fire during or after an enemy attack would have meant sacrifices that I did not want to risk.

Hauptmann Schneider was afraid to take responsibility for not following that order, when I told him what I intended to do. He shrugged his shoulders and would come to no decision. So then, at my own risk, I gave the order to construct the main line of resistance up on the hill 50 metres in front of the edge of woodland. The nearby woodland would if necessary soon be able to take us under its cover. When the General rang back some hours later, Schneider disclaimed responsibility and I had to go to the field telephone. In the hope that he had not learnt from the neighbouring Corps section what the actual course of our main line of resistance was, I lied boldly and directly. Instead of the actual course of our line, I described what I would imagine the course of our line to have been if we had followed his orders. It happened, after it had already been reported, that enemy infantry were working their way up in small groups to our positions and we were already under artillery fire. On the two roads we could see enemy T-34s advancing unhindered. They were only stopped outside the town through the anti-tank barrier that had been set up there.

At about noon on 3 August we reached the little town of Raseinen. Its oldest building was a huge convent several hundred years old. I had a fleeting desire to have a look at the inside and, so to speak, *furore teutonico*, to inspect the enclosure of the nuns, the abbess's room and things like that, which could be interesting. Instead of that I politely asked at the dining room counter for a couple of scrambled eggs. The young woman, not a nun, a little while later pushed the plate to me through the hatch with one single tiny egg on it. In doing so, she treated me as if I were begging for the daily ration of soup which was handed out to the poor. Before her eyes and those of the nun in charge of the kitchen I had Walter eat up the snack and said to the women that they should keep their supplies well up for the Russians, because they would show appropriate reverence to the holy women.

I quote from the Divisional history concerning the fighting around Raseinen:

> The enemy pushed into the town of Raseinen with tanks. By a counter-attack carried out by the 252nd *Infanteriedivision* Raseinen was snatched back from the enemy again. Despite sending in the 7th *Panzerdivision* and *Gruppe* von Werthern, on 9 August Raseinen was lost once again. But the enemy contented

themselves with their success and did not push any further forward. Deployed along the slope and at the edges of the town were: Divisional *Fusilierbataillon* 252, *Grenadierregiment* 7, *Grenadierregiment* 472, supported by *Artillerieregiment* 252, *Panzer-Jägerabteilung* 252 and *Pionierbataillon* 252. With the deployment of all the available forces of our Division and the 7th *Panzerdivision*, in exemplary co-operation, the town of Raseinen and the old positions were taken again on 15 August. In heavy fighting that lasted for several days, the positions were held.

In that fighting in the sector of the 252nd *Infanteriedivision*, in addition to the units already mentioned, there were also involved a reconnaissance battalion, the SS *Fallschirmjäger* Battalion 500, 2 assault gun brigades, army artillery units, and several 8.8 cm self-propelled guns. The Division was mentioned on 15 August in the *Wehrmacht* report. In July/August the enemy had sent in against the 9th *Armeekorps*, and thereby also the 252nd *Infanteriedivision*, their 5th Guards Tank Army with the 3rd Guard Tank Corps and the 29th Tank Corps. Their forces too seemed to be exhausted. The Lithuanian people were particularly friendly and ready to help the German troops. The time in positions that then began was used to reorganise the troops and to re-fill the command posts.

Finally the remnants, or rather the ruins, of *Grenadierregiment* 461, the 3rd Battalion, *Artillerieabteilung* 252 and the 2nd *Pionierkompanie* arrived back with the Division. With the newly arrived replacements came *Oberst* Dorn, recovered again from his wounds, who took over the command of *Grenadierregiment* 7. *Major* von Garn took over command of *Grenadierregiment* 461 and *Major* Herzog took over command of *Grenadierregiment* 472. In magnificent summer weather the unit was welded together again. By combing through all units to the rear, by lightening the load on vehicles, and reducing the amount the men carried, the unit was made mobile.

On 5 August the Russians, with strong infantry and tank forces, took possession of half the town, including the raised *Osthügel* with the hospital, visible from afar, and the convent. They also commanded the low ground adjoining it to the south and the high ground beyond it. From my command post there was played out before my eyes the enemy tank attack across the lower ground. The tanks approached the firing positions of our artillery on the western edge of the low ground, where, well camouflaged in bushes, the howitzers stood in position. From my window I observed how seven tanks were destroyed by the gunners' direct fire. They were firing with impact fuses. The last tank had approached to within 50 metres of them.

With my Battalion staff I had struck lucky again. The battalion was at first held in reserve. Later one company after another was taken away and placed under the command of the battalions of the old regiment. In the absence of our own battalion sector my activity was confined therefore to passing on as quickly as possible the orders assigning units to other commands. I had to ensure that the companies in question got quickly and surely to the appropriate battalions.

Meanwhile, the town was under heavy fire. I had immediately reported the repulse of the tank attack to *Major* von Garn whose regimental command post was in a house in the town from which the plain could not be seen. We on the other hand were in a sawmill on the western edge of the town, where the street to Vidukle crossed a stream. The gate to the sawmill was still and deserted. The inhabitants and workers had disappeared. In the smoke-room of the house there was hanging a row of massive sides of bacon. The men of my staff immediately tucked in to them. Fathers of families took advantage of the forced break and made up packages to send home. The one-storey building of the sawmill was partly covered with trees and from several windows allowed an uninterrupted view across the low ground to the heights beyond.

My friend Helmut Kristen had taken up quarters with his company 100 metres to the south of the sawmill in a little farm. In the blazing midday sun I took a walk to his farmyard. He too was enjoying the enforced rest. In the shadow of a nut tree we drank a bottle of Bordeaux which came from the army supply dump at Globokie. His little dog was hanging his head. He was obviously sick and apathetic, while we were enjoying life. The little dog died a few days later of distemper. Loving care and even a consultation with the artillery vet had not been able to help him.

Our command post in the sawmill proved no longer to be ideal. Again and again individual artillery shells were exploding in the vicinity. Finally eight tank or anti-tank shells smashed through two walls of the room above my head. So the transfer of the command post 300 metres further westwards to a little house on the road to Vidukle was indicated. But even there we were not secure. For the first time since the previous June, we received getting on for 100 replacements for the battalion. They were 18 and 19 years old *Kölsche Jungs*. During the time in which they were being allocated the Russians dropped some shells on the road in front of that house. Most of the poor young lads did not even take cover they were so shocked. Three of them were killed instantly. Two others were wounded. The others were shivering with shock for a long time, while we old and experienced men, as if by nature, it seemed to me, got up unscathed.

During the night the Russians had dropped leaflets over the town, most likely from a slow-flying biplane, one of which I had found on my way to the regimental command post. It was a safe transit for deserters and concerned itself with the events of the 20 July. 'Hitler called on the hangman Himmler and ordered him to ruthlessly annihilate the German generals and officers who spoke out against Hitler. Hitler is also pushing experienced generals to one side and putting in their place crooks and adventurers from the *SS*, with no talent. Leave the front, get back to Germany, and you, too, take part in the fight against Hitler and his bloody clique! Up and to it!' Then came a personal note, 'To our comrades in Regiment 7', with a description of the casualties of the 11th Company which mentioned the names of men killed and wounded. 'Why do you want to be killed or to be shot up and crippled at the last minute? Just to prolong the existence of the doomed adventurers like Hitler and his clique?' The situation was not as simple as the leaflet made out. Nobody thought that it was simply a matter of the survival of 'Hitler's clique'.

On 14 August the counter-attack began to re-take Raseinen. Regiment 7 and the units under its command, with the addition of a Tiger and Panther *Abteilung*, two mortar regiments, and two Army artillery units supported the attack. *Oberst* Garn was back in command. His Adjutant was *Hauptmann* Nicolai, my friend from the spring in Schweidnitz. *Major* von Garn, promoted to *Oberstleutnant*, had to hand over the command and temporarily lead the *Panzergrenadier* regiment in a counter-attack on Schaulen. I was sorry that he was not allowed to command the attack on Raseinen. It would have been a worthy conclusion to his career as a regimental commander in the '7th'.

The supporting units had been brought up the previous night into the most forward trenches. The Tigers and Panthers, those excellent tanks, were assembling behind houses and ruins close to the main line of resistance. It is true that my confidence in the assault and fighting ability and versatility of the tanks was lessened when I saw that their crews consisted of young men. Thin little chaps with children's faces, in the midst of it all, they looked lost. They had not yet grown up together and not yet grown together with their vehicles and cannons. That was the impression given by the men of our old escort, the Swabian assault gun *Abteilung*.

The attack went according to plan and was successful. The Russians were thrown out of the town with heavy casualties and moderate casualties on our side. Only the convent could not be taken. The 23 years old *Hauptmann* Ahlers from the *Fusilierbataillon* was indeed able to get into the church with a few men, but came under fire from the chancel and from behind the altar and had to get out again. Several T-34s were standing in the convent courtyard, protected by thick walls. All the same they were encircled and cut off.

On 15 August several enemy deserters were brought back. They were elderly men who came from Tschernovitz and the Bukovina that had been annexed to Russia in 1940. They had all taken part in the Great War and served in the Austrian Army. In itself, that was shocking.

In accordance with the situation in the town we were able to move the command post forward again. It was in a modern villa built in the *Bauhaus* style and made a strange contrast to the mostly simple neighbouring wooden houses. Since the Russians were continuing to fire on the town, we took up our quarters in the cellar of the villa. I then spent a few days mainly lying on one of the tubular metal bedsteads brought down from the house. Since all the units under the command of the regiment were connected to the telephone in sequence, it rang without ceasing. You had to count every ring so as not to miss the call that was intended for you. But in doing so you could listen in to every conversation and thus gain an overall view of the up-to-date situation. I sat, or rather lay, at the telephone, while *Hauptmann* Schneider either slept or stretched his legs outside.

So for me there was no question of sleeping and, with the receiver at my ear, I dozed away the night hours, listening in to everything that the individual callers had to say. The reconnaissance training battalion, normally stationed in Krampnitz near Potsdam at the weapons school for armoured troops, was posted to Army Group Centre because of the disastrous situation. It had come to Raseinen where it was placed under the command of the homespun *Grenadierregiment 7*. Its commander, *Major Graf* Krockow, spoke there with *Hauptsturmführer* Mylius. The latter was 'snappish', with a sharp voice. However, *Graf* Krockow inimitably talked through his nose like a Prussian *Graf* Bobby. They consoled each other by assuring themselves that they had not been in such *Scheisse* for a long time.

Mylius was the commander of a unit also under the command of Regiment 7, the *SS Bataillon z.b.V.* 500. It was composed of men who had 'all done something wrong'. In order to get to know the *SS* sector, I had spent the afternoon with

Hauptmann Schneider in their position. It was obviously the worst in the Raseinen hot spot. It was hopelessly unprotected. From the flank, on the other side of the plain, enemy anti-tank guns fired on every movement in the trenches. The *SS*, as they ran through them, suffered casualties. The officers and men whom I saw in that command post were fine specimens of manhood, the typical *élite* that was found in the *SS*. I thought to myself that the Vandals of King Geiserich, or King Teja's last Ostrogoths, must have looked like them at Vesuvius.

When *Hauptmann* Schneider and I made a move to go, *Oberst* Dorn appeared, giving a friendly greeting to me, the only person he knew. He was wearing a white summer tunic, radiated calm and rest. I could tell that he had just come back from convalescent leave. His greeting was interrupted by one of the two battalion medical officers of the *SS*. They had two medical officers in contrast to comparable army units with only one. He reported to his commander that a *SS-Unterscharführer* had carelessly shot off his arm with a *Panzerfaust*. The heat of the gas escaping backwards, he said, had immediately sealed the blood vessels. The man was still standing and in possession of all his faculties. He had gone on foot to the dressing station, the arm that he had shot off clamped under his healthy one!

The deployment of the *SS* battalion in our unit evidently demonstrated the military senselessness of setting up such a *praetorian* guard. Every one of those fine *SS* men was a NCO lost to the Army. Even more stupid seemed the formation of the *Luftwaffe* field divisions. With those 100,000 or more soldiers of the *Luftwaffe* the burned-out divisions and regiments of the army could have been sensibly topped up.

The Russians still occupied the convent. In order to put an end to that situation a 28cm mortar had been requested and brought into position overnight. At noon on 20 August it fired 24 shells on to the convent. Almost all of them had delayed fuses. They had exploded on the target that was by then only a heap of ruins. Four survivors were taken prisoner, all completely terrified.

All the rest, I did not know the exact number, were dead. Where the nuns had gone I could not find out. The prisoners also revealed the reason for the tough enemy defence of the convent. A general with his staff had carelessly ventured that far forward, obviously confident of the progress of the offensive. He had, however, slipped out in the night before the mortar bombardment. Since he was not caught, he must have got unchallenged through our lines.

After the modern *Bauhaus* villa had been occupied by my staff, the battalion, subdivided into companies, had once again been sent into action. It went as a complete unit and in conjunction with the *SS* battalion. But on the evening of 21 August we had orders to occupy a sector north of the town. The left-hand third of it reached the Dubysa and there connected to a *Volksgrenadier* division. That was the name given to the divisions of the last wave that had been assembled after all lines of communication and the so-called home front had been combed through for men. We could be sorry for any one stuck in such a unit. I considered myself fortunate to be with my old mob, at least in the 252nd *Infanteriedivision*.

The remnants of the Regiment were then driven back on 22 June to Army Group North. They had returned from Dünaburg with their staff and the regimental commander, *Major* Herzog. My welcome from him in June had not been pleasant but it was then frosty. He found no word of recognition for the fact that we had brought back the few survivors of our 2nd Battalion safely through the long retreat. From one remark, I thought I heard that *Leutnant* Gegel, the hypocrite, must have landed me in it. Certainly he had not forgiven me for the fact that he occasionally had had to obey my orders. I had unwittingly remarked to him that I did not like 'this joint'. The commander, he said, was collecting together scattered men in Dünaburg. The adjutant was making the retreat with the baggage-train. In addition the undamaged 13th Company, the infantry gun company, was similarly with the baggage-train. Through *Major* von Garn and the Ia of the Division, I had brought up a detachment of light infantry guns and two vehicles and thereby run the risk of losing them, but success had proved me right. What a difference between that unjust and unpleasant person and *Major* von Garn with his achievements.

I quote from the regimental history: 'On 2 September *Major* von Garn was awarded the Knight's Cross for outstanding tactical command of *Grenadierregiment* 7 in the heavy fighting and withdrawal during the period from 27 June to 1 July'.

The enemy seemed to leave us alone for a long time, and the battalion established itself in the new sector. The companies worked industriously on constructing the position. The battalion command post was located in a small ravine running north-south, the eastern slope of which was ideally suited for the construction of the bunker.

Life together in the Battalion staff was, so to speak, harmonious. *Hauptmann* Schneider remained passive as far as command of the battalion was concerned. The orderly officer, since Gegel's departure, was a *Leutnant* Martin Degering, the son of a ship's doctor from Bremen. For a very long time he had been in the French lines of communication. It was then his first time in front line action. The battalion medical officer was a Dr Franz Josef Mies from Rheine in Westphalia. He did a good job, in that he reliably completed the change of position of his dressing station. I well remember the operations clerk, *Unteroffizier* Dressner. He was a teacher about 35 years old. He could judge what weight of responsibility I had to carry in commanding the battalion. Once he very kindly expressed his admiration for that. Apart from the signals man, Hermens, of whom I have already spoken, I vividly recall the wireless operator *Obergefreiter* Guth. In all the noise of the fighting he would listen in extreme concentration through his headphones to his wireless set.

A person of a special kind was Walter, my batman. He regularly piled up my plate high, and when I said to him that it seemed that he would never become a fine man, he was honestly troubled. His hair was oiled and curled over his round face, from which he peered with a squint. He also wore a small Menjou beard. He had been unemployed for a long time and said that he had felt quite well during that period. From time to time he had knocked about in the backyards of Breslau as a 'busker', an occupation which must have been quite lucrative, until he was put to working on the autobahn. When Walter gave the best examples of his art, the whole Battalion staff enjoyed it. In one of his heartrending songs of an invalid there was the verse: 'With both legs shot off and also my right hand, still I live on unresenting in my dear Fatherland'. No one could keep a straight face in the face of this. To me as his *Leutnant* he was loyally devoted. He asked me for my wristwatch, which had stopped, so I had to have a *Wehrmacht* watch brought from the baggage-train. I gave my old one to him not remembering that it was a confirmation present from my godfather, Erich Scheiderbauer, who was killed in action by Lake Ilmen in 1942.

In the Raseinen position there was regular post once again. On the 20 July I had written to Mother that, 'after four weeks now our link home through the post has been re-established'. At the same time I asked for photos, since after my involuntary water journey in the Ulla my pictures 'had been completely stuck together and had become unrecognisable'. On the 30 July I had written to her that I was not able to give any news, we were 'just at war'. I said that our Division had been mentioned in the *Wehrmacht* reports on 21 July. She then looked through the local newspapers to find relevant news about it. I had time again for letters that were not simply 'quite short'. I had to write to Mother, to Father, to Rudi, and of course, to Schweidnitz to Gisela, to whom my heart belonged. Father wrote that he was very eager for news from me, but that the main thing was that my mother should often hear from me. The only thing, he said, was that I should not be careless, because you can be as brave as you like, but still be prudent and careful. 'Our prayers surround you. God will preserve you just as he has until now! So all the best and God protect you'!

If we had not realised what legendary good fortune had been granted us to have been able to fight the withdrawal from Vitebsk to Raseinen as an intact unit, we were reminded of it by the individual scattered men who reached our lines during those days. Many had been on the way for almost four weeks. An *Oberst* and his batman came through 'in robbers' clothes'. An artillery *Unteroffizier*, a native of Klagenfurt, wore full uniform together with his Iron Cross First Class. He had a full beard and badly inflamed swollen eyes. He had been lying for three days and nights behind the Russian trenches until he had got through on the fourth night.

In the light of such events, and the overall situation in the east, it was no wonder that an order, issued as a result of the events of 20 July, had not come through. According to it the *Wehrmacht* was from then on to salute with the *deutscher Gruss,* i.e. the Hitler salute. 'The *Reichsmarschall* as the highest ranking soldier of the German *Wehrmacht* had asked that favour of the *Fuhrer*.' The favour made us equal with the *SS*, the Party, and the State. Even today, however, it seems to me unheard of that we should be reminded of an order that we felt to be ominous, even as we received it.

Leutnant Blatschke had complained about an enemy *Ratschbum* that was giving him a hard time in his sector. I spoke about it with Helmut Kristen, who offered help with the following result. After hours of intensive observation, Helmut had discovered the well-camouflaged gun near to a solitary house about 300 metres behind the enemy lines. During the night he brought up two of his 5cm anti-tank guns into a good firing position. Nearby there waited under cover the company vehicles. As dawn was breaking the gunners aimed their guns and, just as the enemy anti-tank guns became visible in the light, for a full minute fired shot after shot on to the target. We watched it excitedly through our binoculars. The flames shot in the air, ammunition exploded, and the *Ratschbum* was silent from then on. Helmut Kristen and his men, however, packed up their anti-tank guns and drove away as if the devil was after them in order to escape the appropriate 'blessing' that the enraged Russians would bring down upon us, as indeed did happen.

Towards the end of August it had at last become quiet and we had made ourselves at home in the position. General Meltzer had just received the Oak Leaves to his Knight's Cross for his achievements in commanding the retreat. One day he visited the battalion sector and was satisfied with it. Afterwards he sat with *Oberleutnant* Hrabowsky, his orderly officer, in the greenery that the staff runners had set up next to the bunker. He was cheerful and chatted in a friendly way. In general he directed his remarks to me, something that I felt to be a deliberate mark of distinction.

Then the adjutant's clerical work claimed my attention again. All sorts of other decisions were piling up. *Hauptfeldwebel* Bierlein of the 5th Company came up with a letter from a neighbour telling him that Bierlein's wife was 'two-timing' him. Bierlein got a week's special leave to sort things out at home.

Oberleutnant Merkle, who for a short time had commanded the 5th Company, and had been killed in action, on the plain in the first Russian attack on Raseinen. His parents wrote asking about their son's personal effects. The dead man who I had myself seen lying on the ground, was unable to be recovered. His body had been exposed for a week to the heat of the sun, but had been found after the town had been retaken. It had been stripped by the Russians. I would indeed have been unable to report to the parents that he was buried, but had had to say nothing about what became of his things and why his burial was delayed.

As had happened the previous summer in the Nemers positions, a fresh order warned of explosive 'toys'. It said that the Russians had dropped fountain pens and lighters whose explosive charge would explode in the hand of the finder the first time they were used. It was a further development of the explosive shells that were known in the First World War under the name of *Dum-Dums*. They had been banned under the Geneva Convention. But what did a treaty mean in a war of ideologies, in that war against Bolshevism? In any case we did not even know if the Soviet Union had signed the treaty.

As the unit commander of the Battalion staff I also had to become involved with the task of the Divisional court martial. It had to punish a staff runner because he had contracted a venereal disease and thereby had weakened the armed forces. The *Obergefreiter*, so he told me, had been released one evening three weeks previously from the military hospital in Tilsit. He found that there were no more trains going to the front. Instead of spending the night on straw at the front control point, he preferred the soft bed of a woman of easy virtue. The result had been gonorrhoea. He then had to go back into hospital. Since he was a capable and reliable runner, I decided to put the matter on the back burner, because to judge by the overall situation, the case would perhaps resolve itself. Otherwise I would have had to send him to the penal company.

At that time, under the direction of pioneers, it was engaged in laying mines in the combat area in front of our main lines. The penal company was an Army unit. The 'small sinners' were sent there to do several days' construction. Essentially, however, the penal units consisted of *Luftwaffe* and Navy soldiers who had been sentenced to longer terms of imprisonment for more serious crimes. The sentence had been commuted to one of proving themselves at the front. The crimes that had led to their sentences had in most cases been committed in the occupied districts in the West. The unit commander had an unenviable task.

In front of the sector of our neighbour to the left on the Dubysa, the Corps had ordered an assault unit to be prepared. It was to be carried out by our battalion, since they did not to have confidence in the *Volksgrenadiere* to achieve success. The officer selected for that duty, *Leutnant* Blatschke, was furious that, as he said, he had to snatch foreign chestnuts out of the fire. We went across to our neighbour and had a look round the sector.

On the way Blatschke told me that in a house directly behind the frontline of his company's sector there was a *Blüthner* grand piano. The house was visible to the enemy and stood empty. To judge by the way it was furnished its owners must have been educated people. After Blatschke left, I went with Walter into the darkness. The windows had been shattered by fire. Because it was visible to the enemy, we were not able to use a light, but the moonlight gave light enough. From time to time flares blazed up and you could hear rifle bullets chirping as they whizzed by. In the glimmer of the moonlight ('thou fillest again bush and valley...' as Goethe wrote) I sat down at the grand piano and played and sang, even though I could not do it perfectly, from Schumann's *Mondnacht*. For a while I actually had the illusion that the heavens were kissing the earth to sleep. Then I went on, because I knew it better, to Matthias Claudius' 'The Moon is risen...'

On the way back to the command post I reflected on the great good fortune which I had encountered since 22 June. Thinking about what had happened to those who returned from behind the Soviet lines, and other scattered troops who came back over the lines near us and elsewhere, I wondered what I myself would do in similar circumstances. After my experience in swimming the Ulla, I would try to get through by night as far as the Memel, that is about 80 kilometres further southwards. Then I would let myself be floated down river on a piece of wood to the Baltic. It would then have still been warm enough to do it.

9

Autumn/Winter 1944: The Narev bridgehead, a training course and special leave for bravery

Transfer to the Narev bridgehead; attacks and counter-attacks; training course at Döberitz; 20 days' special leave for bravery

On 24 September it was announced that the Division would be withdrawn from its positions and relieved by the 95th Infantry Division. An advance party set off. By rail, the first part of the Division travelled on 29 September through Tilsit and Insterburg to Zichenau (Cziechanow), where they were unloaded. The Division was then out of the command area of the 3rd *Panzerarmee* and the IX *Armeekorps*, under whose command it had been for more than two years. Henceforth it was joined to the 2nd Army (*Generaloberst* Weiss) under the command of the XX *Armeekorps* (*General der Artillerie* von Roman). The troop units which then arrived were allocated quarters in the area to the south of Zichenau.

At the end of September the units of the Division went into assembly areas to the south-east of Nasielsk. The task of the Division was to eliminate a larger bridge-head that Soviet troops had formed across the Narev between Serock and Pultusk (Ostenburg). In the 2nd Army sector the enemy had formed several bridgeheads over the Narev. They could be considered as jumping-off points for a large-scale enemy attack, especially as they could be expected to expand them at any time. *Hauptmann* Schneider and I learned of the position at the regimental command post. It was clear to us that we were to come into a new future hotspot. We consoled ourselves with the assumption that sooner or later the 'old magic' would work again, even in Raseinen.

In the evening, in my capacity as battalion adjutant, I drove out to the baggage-train in order to be at the Vidukle railway station early in the morning. Since the whole Division was to be unloaded within two days, even with the danger of air-raids, day time had also to be used. This required not only the greatest possible haste but also familiarity with the local conditions. I arrived at the baggage-train, and enjoyed the advantage of being able to sleep alone in a room, in a good barracks bed on a straw mattress. The soldiers of the baggage-train had unhesitatingly placed the room at my disposal as their chief. They had quickly cleared the bed in the empty room on the side facing the enemy, but that did not trouble me just for the one night.

On 26 September the battalion was unloaded in Zichenau. A look at the map showed that we were behind the most southerly of the two bridgeheads on the Narev. The short journey through German East Prussia had, depressingly, made clear to us the extent to which we were already fighting 'along the inner line'. For parts of the way we travelled attached to a regular passenger train. Civilians got into the staff compartment, even a *Hoheitsträger* from the Party in his brown uniform. He did all the talking and expressed really confidently the simple message that 'the *Führer* will soon sort things out'.

In Deutsch-Eylau where the branch line led southward into Polish territory, there was a longer stop. In the orderly surroundings of that German railway station, that looked clean swept, the transports with our 'mob' presented a really strange picture. The companies were loaded by platoons into cattle trucks. Other wagons were loaded with horses and old vehicles from the baggage-train. Among it all straw was everywhere, there was baggage-train equipment, and even live cattle and pigs. There were also Russian women with their headscarves, who worked as washerwomen and on other jobs for the baggage-train. We were there too in our shabby uniforms. I wore a pair of deep yellowish-brown Lithuanian riding breeches that Walter had found for me on the way, together with boots. The boots fitted well and saved my rubber boots. Yellow lice had first to be removed from the trousers before I could wear them. Then there was the disciplined yet free atmosphere. I addressed as *du* the staff runners, telephonists, and wireless operators of whom I had become fond. At the beginning of the sixth year of the war, it seemed that in our frontline units, all human relationships had been reduced to a certain essential core.

After the unloading, *Hauptmann* Schneider and *Leutnant* Degering remained behind in Zichenau. They wanted to find a cafe and 'to be able to talk once again with German women', as Schneider said. Meanwhile, the battalion set off on the march towards the village that had been assigned as our destination. As we marched through the village, in ranks of three, we sang lightheartedly, in a way we had not had the opportunity for in a long time. It ended on the popular 'Honolulu' song: *Ich ging einmal spazieren, um mich zu amüsieren...* 'I once went a-walking to have a bit of fun'. The simple content of the song is that a soldier follows a girl who then rebuffs him with the answer: 'I'm married, I've been married a long time, and what you can do, young man, my husband can do too'.

I drove out from the end of the village on the motorbike and sidecar. After branching off from the highway there was not much more chance of driving. The region of Polish sand was beginning. The motorbike, the driver and I, pushing the bike sank to our knees. The sand and the pines stirred up memories in me of the *Hasenheide* in Döberitz, on which two hundred years ago, *der Alte Fritz* had exercised his Grenadiers. Just two years previously on the company commander's course, I had *lang gemacht* i.e. 'served my time' there, as the phrase went, *bei Preussens* or 'in Prussian times'.

There followed a few days of complete quiet. In order to keep our forthcoming attack as secret as possible, no exercises of any kind were staged. The men tried to catch up on the sleep they had lost in the summer. They lay on their backs for days on end and when it was dark visited the front-line cinema that had been established in a neighbouring village. *Wien 1910* was showing there and it would have interested me because of the young Otto Wilhelm Fischer whom I liked very much. But I remained in my quarters in order to get a little peace and quiet. I was afraid too that I would be seized by homesickness for Vienna. But what I once more thoroughly enjoyed again in those days was riding. It was one last opportunity for it and only then was my life as a cavalryman to come to an end.

On the other hand, I denied myself another kind of pleasure. My batman Walter, always very concerned about my physical welfare, told me that Marja, a pretty and buxom washerwoman from the staff baggage-train, had fallen for me, and he offered to arrange a rendezvous. He could not understand and was almost hurt when I told him that I was not interested in anything like that. The fact that he had made the offer made further explanation seem superfluous.

On the night of 2 October the battalion was brought up to a point four kilometres behind the frontline. We were placed in houses that were still standing there. The order went out that, during the day, no movement must take place on account of enemy aerial reconnaissance. The attack was supposed to be a complete surprise. It was therefore impossible to take a walk. We could only leave the hovels to answer calls of nature.

In the afternoon came the regimental order for the next day. The Division had been given the task, together with the 3rd and 25th *Panzer* Divisions, of eliminating the bridgehead at Serock. After a concerted preparatory artillery barrage lasting 30 minutes, our Division was to move up between the two *Panzer* divisions. Within our Division it had been ordered that Regiment 461 would advance on the right, and Regiment 7 on the left, while Regiment 472 had to follow in the second wave. Most importantly, participating in the attack too were an assault gun brigade, two *Nebelwerfer* brigades, one heavy *SS Panzerabteilung* (Tiger), one *Heeresartillerieabteilung*, two mortar battalions and one flak regiment. The fact that we were to run up in reserve behind the two other regiments was almost a source of relief to me, since it showed me how highly General Meltzer valued the capability of the regiment and its commander. But it strengthened my resolve to return as soon as possible to my Regiment 7.

We spent the night of 3 October on straw in a hovel. We were lying pressed closely together, waking, dozing or sleeping. In the straw I found a small crucifix that I kept since it did not belong to anyone there. One of the people who had slept there before me or an inhabitant of the house must have lost it. I do not know what became of the crucifix. However, I lost it later when I was a prisoner. But there came to me the cheering promise of the *in hoc signo*, and I knew full well what victory that meant.

At 5am the half-hour heavy barrage began. We moved slowly forward between batteries of howling mortars and barking cannons. We had never before seen that kind of concentration of our own heavy weapons. We still had ammunition, we could still fire it, we could still attack and hopefully we could still gain the victory. Regiment 7 had already reached its target for the day at 10.30am. The attack had gone off smoothly and the enemy had fled. They had left behind few prisoners, but a lot of material. *Oberleutnant* Husenett and his company had taken an enemy mortar battery.

Half an hour after the attack began we had crossed the trenches. We looked with amazement at the American war matériel that had been left behind, from tinned meat to a motorcycle and sidecar and heavy Studebaker lorry. Some Russian trenches smelled of perfume. By this and by the articles of clothing that had been left behind, it could be seen that women, perhaps women soldiers, had been there.

The Russians had not built bunkers, they simply had dugouts, each for two men, over which short thick tree trunks had been laid. They were an example of the admirable Russian capability of combining improvisation with the greatest usefulness. Since the entrances to these small bunkers opened, from our point of view, on the side facing the enemy, for myself I preferred to spend the night in a simple one-man foxhole without a roof. I remembered *Major* Brauer and *Leutnant* Buksch who had met their deaths a year before, at Nevel, in such a dugout that faced towards the enemy.

On 5 October, the second day of the attack, the Division was once more successful and Regiment 7 had reached the Narev at 2.30pm. We, in 472, moved up behind them as reserve and at the same time as spectators. The high ground facing the river was shelled by our mortars and artillery and then stormed. I was able to observe it through the field glasses. On the way I saw a human torso that had been torn apart by massive force. It was lying beside a destroyed SS *Panzer* reconnaissance vehicle, burnt out, a relic of the heavy fighting at the time that the bridgehead was being formed. From that sight even the hardened among us turned away in horror.

After the southern half of the bridgehead had been pushed back and was again in German hands, on 8 October the attack on the northern half was to take place. On 6 October we were moved 10 kilometres to the north, into a village that on the map looked like a star made up of roads. At the centre was a crossing from which seven roads or lanes stretched out exactly following the points of the compass. The only problem was that there was no road leading south-westward. As such, the crossing formed an ideal target for heavy weapons and was constantly under fire. In spite of that the cellars of the surrounding houses were fitted out with command posts from all possible units. The frontline was not a kilometre away towards the east.

As the orders had said, quite generally, that units should take over the command posts of the units to be relieved, *Hauptmann* Schneider had insisted on moving into the cellar at the crossing. He remained impervious to my suggestions for us to take up position in a cellar away from the crossing, especially since the cellar roof, only some 10 centimetres thick, did not provide adequate protection. The constant impact of shells very close by was gruelling even before the attack. In addition, runners and all who wanted to get to us were exposed to the most serious danger. When finally the leader of the signal section and two men had been wounded, I went on my own initiative to look for a suitable command post. I found it 300 metres along the road leading westwards, in a considerably deeper and better-covered cellar. Without Schneider's approval, I asked the regiment whether we could move. It was approved and *Hauptmann* Schneider himself was afterwards pleased that we were away from the main impact area.

There were no good omens for the second part of the attack on the bridgeheads. With the rain, mist and badly softened ground it presented a very difficult task, to which situation the confused terrain was also a contributory factor. We had advanced only one kilometre. During previous days the Russians had laid many mines, so that numerous tanks drove over them and were lost. In addition the preparatory fire was weaker than it had been on 4 October and we had not succeeded in destroying the underwater nets over the Narev. As they had done in Stalingrad over the Volga, the Russians this time too laid nets under the surface of the water across the river, over which, with columns of carriers, they brought ammunition and above all mines.

The units had to dig in just where they were. The battalion command post was in the open behind a small rise in the ground that did not deserve the name of hill. Foxholes were lined with straw. The nights were already cold and we were freezing pitiably. Since 3 October no one had been able to wash. To add to that it began to rain continuously and the tarpaulins, after 24 hours, were almost completely porous. The Russians were preparing a counter-attack. Every hour, low flying aircraft flew over our positions and fired on the roads, luckily mostly behind us. But an unmistakable sign that an attack was being prepared were the shells exploding in the air by means of which the enemy artillery registered their fire.

On 14 October the expected counter-attack took place. There was surprisingly little Russian artillery preparation. Instead, there was a large-scale deployment of aircraft. With machine-guns, cannon and shrapnel bombs, the *Ratas* and IL 2s attacked everything that they thought to be German positions. Up to 20 aircraft circled in our immediate vicinity. We knew better than to stick our heads out of the ground. Whether casualties were too great or the men had been worn down by the air-raids, in any event they climbed out of their foxholes and came back. As they were struggling to get back to the rear across the wide field, I stood desperately on the battalion's hill, waited and shouted to them until they had got up to me. But my cries of *Stellung, Stellung* were in vain. They limped, rushed, and ran on, 50 or 100 metres ahead of the Russians who were charging after them.

Finally I saw that I was alone, facing the brown wave of the attackers. To stay so long had been idiotic, but I had been gripped by resignation. Then, not 40 metres ahead of the Russians, who were moving more slowly, I turned and ran. My map case under my arm, clearly recognisable as an officer, I ran on, weaving, in front of the Russians. I am convinced that the only thing that saved me was that the fact that the Russians were advancing at the run. Some were running ahead and their wave was fairly thick, but none of them wanted to stop and aim at me or the others. I ran and ran and after 200 metres I had reached the retreating line of our men. We reached the firing position of a battery that was ready to fire directly on the Russians. I succeeded in bringing to a halt a handful of men, by which action a small amount of infantry cover would at least remain for the guns.

The enemy infantry assault halted facing the battery position. However, we were exposed there to the latest attacks of the enemy aircraft. In one such attack Walter, my batman, was wounded. He was able to limp and reported to me with tears in his eyes. He asked me to write to him and take him back when he was recovered.

The heavy air raids had continued throughout the entire day. Nevertheless the main line of resistance was stable again and I could go looking for our company. I gave my situation report in at the regimental command post. On the way forwards to the 5th company I had to take cover in a right-angled trench from the attack of a low-flying aircraft. It was only by leaping round the edge of the trench that I was able to avoid an exploding shrapnel bomb, but a tiny fragment of iron caught me on the left hand side. When I mentioned the incident in the course of conversation in the Regimental bunker, the 'Old Man' made a snide remark. It simply sounded stupid and hurtful. He was becoming more and more repugnant to me.

The following incident took place in the sector of Regiment 461 and, when things had calmed down, word of it quickly got round. A Russian sergeant had driven forward with the ration vehicle for his company on the road that crossed the lines of both sides exactly at the so-called 'Close-quarters Corner' in Budy-Obrebsky. There the trenches were only 30 metres apart. One might have assumed that alertness on both sides, there of all places, should have been greater than usual. But that was not the case. The vehicle passed undisturbed along the road, which was not interrupted by trenches, and drove getting on for two kilometres further into the area behind our lines. Finally the driver became suspicious and turned round. When he had almost reached our most forward line again, he was at last nabbed. The rations, and especially the vodka that he had loaded up for the following attack, were distributed among the regiment.

On 18 October the enemy attacked once again. In one of the repeated air-raids *Oberfeldwebel* Scheidig, the leader of my runners, was seriously wounded. A hole in his back, the size of a large coin, pointed to considerable internal injuries. Scheidig, a tried and tested combat soldier, had been a platoon leader with the 6th Company and I had brought him in to the Battalion staff so that it might be easier for him. However, things looked bad for him. Scheidig died while he was being transported to the dressing station. Meanwhile the air-raids went on. Every now and then we managed to shoot down an aircraft. Pilots suspended from their parachutes, for the embittered *Landsers*, became a gruesome form of target practice. Not far from our command post a twin-engined Martin, of American manufacture, had crashed and, unusually, had not exploded on impact.

In the evening we caught scraps of a speech on the radio by Himmler, the *Reichsführer* of the *SS*. After the assassination attempt on Hitler on 20 July 1944 he had been appointed *Oberbefehlshaber der Reservearmee* and also *Oberbefehlshaber Heeresgruppe Mitte*. For a man who had never been a recruit, never mind an officer it was a memorable career. From the speech I only noted that *Volksartilleriekorps* were being formed, part of the *Volkssturm* as the last, 'secret weapon'.

On 1 September I had written in a letter to Rudi that the sixth year of the war had begun, and that this would certainly be the last. Then, on 20 October, I received a letter from Father, dated 10 October, which read as follows:

At last some news from you in your letters of the 19 and 23 August, which certainly are pretty out of date. On the afternoon of the 1 September we moved out of Cambrai in a rush, and the same evening the British were said to have moved in. After a lengthy odyssey I have ended up here on the left bank of the Rhine – it is called Dormagen. There have been, and still are, many heavy air-raids, but up to now not directly where we are. You asked about the *Kriegsverdienstkreuz*; nothing at all is happening on that front, and besides I've got other things to worry about. No prospect of leave… I would be very glad to hear from you directly again. Yes, I heard from Mother that recently things seemed to have gone well for you, considering the circumstances. Now a lot seems to have happened again where you are. May God continue to protect you, as he has until now. As for the battle on the 'home front' you will hear direct from Mother how things stand. I mean their cruelty in wanting to take away our flat, or rather your rooms. Your Mother is in complete despair. I fear that she is going to be driven into another nervous breakdown, and I can do nothing about it, there is no possibility of getting home. I also don't know what will happen if we suddenly come home and find that there is no longer room for us in our own house. Well, hopefully God will allow justice and reason to triumph, even at the last minute. My one hope is that soon it will all be over, it can't go on for much longer. Please write to me really soon, accept my most heartfelt best wishes and be guided by my prayers.

Hope that the war would soon be at an end was something that I did not cherish even in secret. I also did not believe that a single one of my comrades shared it, because the alternative, namely what would become of Germany if the dams of the Eastern Front broke, was plainly unimaginable. In that sense, and not for the sake of Hitler and the Party, we had our duty to do and did it diligently, even if it was soon to be with the last strength we had.

Father's concern for Mother was something I shared, as much as I could, at 20 years old. She was by then 45 years old. As a result of the war she had been separated for four years from our father, to whom she was happily married. Even today I can remember how she suffered from the fact that she, facing the menopause, was separated from Father. She had neither relatives nor female friends nearby and there was no community life. She had never been particularly well able to manage, and had always relied on the help of servants or friendly neighbours. She was just not up to the adversities of life in the fifth and sixth years of the war. It is true that she also had the worry about the welfare of Father and of us, her sons. Father, until then had not been in physical danger. Rudi had only been so recently. She still trembled for me whom she knew to be in constant danger whenever I was at the Eastern Front.

She and Father always had an idea where I was. With the help of the *Wehrmacht* reports, together with the scanty news concerning the situations in which I found myself, and from the tone of my letters, they could build a picture of how things were going for me. In August 1944, she went for a few weeks to her sisters in Dresden with little Liesl. She thought of staying there longer and told us what she intended to do. In exchanging letters Father, Rudi and I had trouble talking her out of the idea. I understood the reasons, namely the 'total war effort' that had just been announced in a spectacular way by Josef Goebbels. I said that our flat should not remain empty under any circumstances. Someone else would simply be put in there instead. The block on leave, which was in force again just at that time, would soon, I said, come to an end, and then we would have no proper home to return to. I said that she should write to me as often as she could, that the post was our only connection with home, and that without it I would get no news at all from Stockerau. From Schweidnitz, on the other hand, from Gisela, I received post regularly.

In the event, it was advisable that Mother went back home again. She failed to get through the official medical examination and was not drafted in to war work. But a part of the flat, two closets, was requisitioned, which she had to clear. 'Like a lioness' she fought to keep our lads' room. On 2 October I had written to her that she should just ask the gentlemen in the offices whether we, who were laying our heads on the block at the front, were actually 'homeless'. Was our room to be taken away from us for the reason that we were 'always at the front and there is no leave'. Then I tried to console her, because there was 'no point in cursing', I said. 'Be patient for just a few more months, then the war will be over, for a little while longer you must just bite on the bullet, then we will all be coming home in person'.

It was fortunate that Father was able to get special leave and it was also fortunate that Rudi, too, after 13 months, had got leave in September. He wrote to me on the last day of his leave and quoted in his letter 'it is all so deeply sad', words whose source I can no longer remember. In my letter of 9 October, from right in the midst of the action on the Narev, I asked Mother to excuse the fact that I had not managed to get round to writing. 'Really, I had no spare time and had no time to collect my thoughts. But in spite of this I am more than ever with you in my thoughts, dear old Mother, and I hope, at least in spirit, to be able to make the difficulties of the time somewhat easier for you. How much I would want to help you, if only I could. But then we are all hoping that very soon there will be a fundamental change in fortune that must come. My nerves are again a bit 'below par'. But I always very much enjoy your dear letters and those of my dear girl from Schweidnitz'.

In a letter of 11 October to Father I wrote: 'I am on the lower Narev in a quite lousy district. The little book *Im Streite zur Seite*, 'In the conflict at your side', which you sent to me, is very good and has really been of value to me. It's true that it cannot be disputed, at least I cannot, that often it is not possible to go on by your own strength and your own consolation. So I pray, and hope, that we will all happily meet together soon'.

At the Narev bridgehead around 20 October, the battalion was pushed back some kilometres to the south. We had set up the command post in one of the separately built cellar vaults usual in that district. It was high enough for you to be able to stand up and to walk around. It was getting on for eight metres long and three metres wide. By our standards, then, an apartment. Incidentally, in that billet there were also rats. One of the runners almost caused a disaster by firing his rifle in fury and shock at a gigantic specimen that emerged in full daylight. There was a crack as if we had received a direct hit. The bullet ricocheted, shattering the chimney of the petroleum lamp that stood in front of me on the table. Then it struck the wooden door that a fraction of a second later was opened by a wireless operator coming in.

On 24 October *Hauptmann* Schneider was transferred. He was to go first to the *Feldersatzbataillon*, the training unit with the 'large' baggage-train of the Division. It was somewhere to which he was better suited than he was to a combat unit. He was a good-natured man of stolid stature and it was not easy for him to say farewell. He thanked me for the help that I had been to him during the time in which he had commanded the battalion. So it was he, at least, in this regiment who found a word of recognition for me. As he did so I remembered Raseinen. When, to my objection that the *Hauptmann* was not there and that I could not transfer him, *Major* von Garn had answered, 'Then you'll just have to lead the battalion'. A few days before Schneider left, something happened to us that made his farewell easier.

One day towards noon we had wanted to have a look around the positions of *Leutnant* Christen's anti-tank guns. The crew of a *Ratschbum* must have seen us. They had us in their sights, but fortunately we were in a field whose flat furrows offered us some slight cover. Nevertheless, the fellow shot so precisely that I felt the suction and pressure of the shell that hurtled only centimetres above me. With great clarity I felt my hair actually stand on end. After a very long two or three minutes, during which the enemy gunner had fired off about 10 shots at us, I managed to leap into another furrow. It seemed to be deeper. A little bit further on, Schneider also lay there. After the Russians had fired about 50 shells at us they finally stopped. Nevertheless we continued to lie still for a while longer, so that the enemy would just think that we were dead. Then we jumped up and ran to some bushes about 50 metres away and that at least offered us some cover. When we got there we saw that the sweat of fear was running down our faces. As men used to say, 'yea'!

Until the new commander arrived, the battalion was taken over by my old company commander from 1942, Beyer, who in the meantime had become a *Major*. The command post was then moved into a single house that had a view of the frontline and thus also lay in the direction of fire of the *Ratschbum*. No light, and no smoke was therefore to become visible. I found that Beyer was telephoned at night by his wife, who was serving as a signals auxiliary in the *Oberkommando des Heeres*. It reminded me of the wood at Shabino, when Beyer sang to the encamped company the well known and popular Berlin song of the *krumme Lanke*, on which a lover sat with his *Emma uff der Banke,* 'Emma on the bench'. Beyer sat in stoical calm at the table playing patience. While he was doing so he whistled with gusto the best-known melody from the *Millionen-des-Harlekins, da capo,* over and over again.

On 4 November the new commander arrived. He was a *Major* Walter Premrou from Steyr in Upper Austria, who had previously commanded the so-called assault battalion of the 78th *Infanteriedivision*. Their insignia was the iron fist of Götz von Berlichingen. As fellow-countrymen we immediately liked each other and I was pleased with my new superior officer. Like *Major* Beyer, however, Premrou too was killed in action in February 1945.

On 10 November, to my great surprise, I received orders to attend a course at the Infantry School in Döberitz from 20 November to 10 December. I immediately saw the opportunity of jumping ship, i.e. of returning to Regiment 7. I made farewell calls to people in the battalion and celebrated my departure with Helmut Christen, my especial comrade, from the retreat we had just made. We were in agreement and cursed about the unfair treatment in the '472nd'. The regimental adjutant, *Leutnant* Wix, junior in length of service, who had made the retreat with the baggage-train, had just become an *Oberleutnant*. At five minutes to 10pm we heard once again 'Lili Marlene', the song that was broadcast every day at the same time from the soldiers outside Belgrade. It had long since become a legend. Even I, who had at first disliked the song as I had disliked other hits, had to surrender my resistance. The voice of the singer Lale Andersen and the simple text, the contents of which every soldier had already experienced for himself, had won me over. Even irreverent parodies - I recall one cruel one concerning the first Russian winter of 1941/42 - could not take away the magic from the melody.

Major Premrou had spoken with the regimental commander and asked that before the beginning of the course I might be allowed a few days' leave. I was lucky and I could scarcely believe that in a short time I would be at home. In the last hours before I left I was overcome with such a state of nerves that I felt I was physically shivering. I was afraid that at the last moment orders would be given for a total block on leave and travel, or that the notorious direct hit would strike.

Arrived at the baggage-train, I got into a wooden washtub and took a purifying bath. Then the driver, Alois Wörz, a Tyrolean, took me to the station at Nasielsk. There I waited for the regular train to Thorn. I felt like a man in a dream. In the compartment were sitting two German girls who came from a farmstead near to the front. Their parents had sent them back to relatives in western Germany. Everything was so wonderful and, after this exciting summer, so incomprehensible. The burden of all responsibility was lifted from me and tiredness overcame me. Leaning against the older of the two girls, I fell asleep. In Thorn our ways parted.

Of my journey home and my arrival there I no longer have any recollection. I gather, from a later letter from Mother, that she was startled by the doorbell at 9pm, and there I was standing at the door. She and little Liesl were quite well, but completely surprised. My week's special leave flew by, but none of my classmates was at home. They were all scattered at the fronts in distant garrisons and even my girls, with whom I had been friendly - Herta Henk and the Skorpil-Mädi - had been drafted in to war work. That too was also what had happened to Gisela. She was somewhere in Saxony where I could not reach her, because she herself would certainly have not been allowed out. Only Hermi Eckart had been temporarily spared from work service because of diphtheria. She was in an isolation hospital.

I had a vague friendship with her brother Hans. At that time he was an *Untersturmführer* in the *SS*. Hans, whom I met again later during my studies, at that time said to me that he was 'working for the Americans'. In 1949 he was kidnapped in Stockerau by the Soviet secret police. He had to spend six long years, until the treaty, in captivity, among other places in Vorkuta.

So my only company was classmates of Rudi's, namely Ernst Vogl and Egon Papritz, who went by the name of 'Kitty'. Papritz was an officer cadet *Unteroffizier* in the *Infanterieregiment Grossdeutschland*, and was on leave. Vogl was a gifted pianist, the son of a factory owner. As a Hitler Youth leader he had his military service deferred. Vogl later took over his father's pump factory and in addition became a well-known contemporary composer. Papritz on the other hand was, like so many others from Rudi's class, killed in action in 1945. So with those two I'd got together a few times in the 'Vogl-Villa' and one evening joined a game of poker. Being no poker player, and as such not favoured by luck, I was the evening's loser and at the end had gambled away my entire monthly salary of a *Leutnant*, 300 Marks. The next day I had to go to the bank and withdraw money from my savings to pay my debt of honour. In the meantime my savings had grown to about 4000 Marks.

On 18 November the plan was that I should travel to Berlin. Allied terror air-raids on the 17th and the 18th on Vienna had caused railway disruptions. The Northern Railway Bridge was damaged so that my departure was delayed until 19 November. I wrote of it in a letter of the 18th to Rudi in which I also told him that 'Kitty' and I had naturally paid honour to the Rubik Asylum with the daughter Gerlinde Rubik. I said I had met my schoolmate Herbert Weyr, whose mother continued to be 'the centre of discontent'. Julius Zimmerl, I said, had been taken prisoner in Italy in August, and the previous day had written from America, to the great joy of his relatives.

Arrived in Döberitz, I wrote to Mother and Rudi that the train had only departed at 2am from Floridsdorf. Hopefully, I wrote, Mother had got used to solitude again, but for me, on the other hand, it was fairly difficult. We could console ourselves, I said, that all unnatural circumstances and also the present conditions would all come to an end someday.

The course on which I had been sent was evidently intended to provide, not only leave, but some sort of winding-down period. It was for people like myself who had survived the heavy defensive fighting in the East, the West, but also in Italy and in the Balkans. As always, here too I was one of the youngest, but we had all commanded companies and there was nothing in the way of theory that they could have taught us. We had all experienced things for real without theory. Differently from the beginning of the previous year, we had our quarters not in poor barracks, but in the 'Olympic Village'. There were individual rooms for each of us.

I lived in the 'Weimar house'. The second apartment was occupied by a *Fallschirmjäger Leutnant*, whose right arm was decorated by two *Panzervernichtungsstreifen*, i.e. tank destruction badges, and who had just become, for the second time, father of a little girl. From my Division *Leutnant* Edion from Regiment 461 was there. He held the silver *Nahkampfspange*. Later, in January 1945, he was killed in action. Another comrade on the course for company commanders of all frontline units was *Oberleutnant* von Rohr, the owner of a *Klitsche* in Pomerania and, as it turned out, a cousin of the Benigna von Rohr whom I had got to know in the house of *Graf* Keyserling. Of the training officers I can still well remember *Oberleutnant* Brucker, a fellow Viennese, the Knight's Cross holder *Hauptmann* Johanssen and *Major* von Dewitz. To *Major* von Dewitz I must have looked particularly young, because he repeatedly asked me 'how old are you, Scheiderbauer?' And my answer, 'Twenty', amazed him every time.

At that time a large part of Berlin had already been destroyed by bombs. One night, not far from the Olympic Village, a land mine went off with a massive explosion. But the air-raid sirens did not prevent us from going as often as we could into the town and, as far as possible, having a bit of fun. I recall two pretty Latvian girls from Riga whom *Leutnant* Edion had turned up. One of them had known the fighter pilot Novotny, who, a fairly long time ago, after 251 victories, was himself shot down. As a Viennese, he had been given a hero's grave in the City of Vienna, in the Vienna central cemetery.

In Döberitz at the entrance to the buildings of the infantry school I found that three-verse poem, the last verse of which will move me as long as I live. It is also the motto under which the last years of my youth were set:

Plain and brave, early or late,
unshrinking in the assault,
unassuming infantry,
may God protect you.

During the infantry course, to Mother's great delight, Father got a period of special leave to sort out the problems 'on his home front'. While I was pleased for Mother, yet I was sorry that I had not been able to see him. I had not seen him since the spring of 1942, nor Rudi since April 1943. Anyway, on 30 November *Leutnant* Edion and I had a great surprise. A telegram from our Division told us that we had been given 20 days' special leave 'for bravery'. That happened in accordance with an order which permitted a unit to send not more than two per cent of its current establishment on leave 'for bravery', irrespective of any block on leave which was then in force.

Mother was very pleased, as she wrote to me on 5 December. 'So at least at Christmas we shall not be completely alone... Yesterday Father went away again - I am dreadfully upset and have no idea what to write to you'. To Rudi, too, I sent the happy news and wrote to him that he should see whether, on his way to war school, which was imminent, he could not arrange to meet me at home. In my Christmas letter to him of 18 December I complained that this time nobody was here.

Around the 15th Mother had gone with Liesl, who was still only attending school irregularly and very seldom, to Aunt Lisa Scheiderbauer in Aisting near Schwertberg to get supplies for Christmas and to 'really treat me' to the *Geselchte* (salted and smoked meat) she had promised me. In my letter of the 18th I also wrote that in the *OKW* report the sober announcement had just been made that in the West a German offensive was under way. 'I think this is the dress rehearsal. God willing!' Even today I can remember how, while that announcement was being read out, the tears sprang to my eyes, so much was I hoping, one last time, for a change in fortune. But it was in vain, and after only three days all hope was gone. But the fact that we did hope for a change in fortune, will show the present day reader what irrational feelings guided us, in assessing a strategic situation long since become hopeless.

Everyone who knew me envied me my leave. 'In any event', I wrote, 'it's stirred up all kinds of dust, from those who are happy about it and from those who envy me!' Unfortunately I arrived eight days too late to be able to see Father. I would set off again on New Year's Eve or New Year's Day. He then wrote to me under the field post number of my old regiment 08953. I was looking forward to that, because with the help of the Regimental Adjutant, my friend from Schweidnitz, Klaus Nicolai, I had managed to arrange that I got back into the '7th'.

The really great happiness of my leave, however, was that Rudi arrived home quite unexpectedly for two or three days. If as children we had quarrelled from time to time, from my sixteenth year truly brotherly harmony had reigned between us, even if each of us had his own friends. Since he had joined up in August 1943, contact between us had dropped off, but the ties of feeling had become even stronger.

At the bridgehead of Nettuno near Naples he had an experience that left its mark on him. It also made a great impression on me, almost as if I had gone through it myself. He had been at night with seven comrades in a barn and had been asleep when the impact of an incendiary bomb at point blank range left the hut in flames. Rudi was the only one who had the courage to dash through the flames out into the open. While his comrades horrifically burned to death, he had only singed his face and his hair. After a short spell in hospital he had new pink fresh skin. He was home, again as good as new. We walked proudly side by side through our home town. In his smart black *Panzer* uniform of the *élite* unit *Hermann Göring*, with its white collar tabs, tall and slim, he was the very image of a fine young man.

I had no idea that I was never to see him again. He on the other hand, as I later realised, had a premonition of his early death. In March 1945 he once again passed through Stockerau and said farewell to the people who knew him with the remark, 'Now they're scratching around for heroes and then we'll be sent out to the slaughter'. In his papers we found Josef Weinheber's ode *Den Gefallenen*, 'To the Fallen'. It was handwritten on a loose sheet of paper. For one last time, after Christmas 1944, he had taken photographs of us both. I remember Mother's admonition from the proverbs of Solomon, which she had often quoted to us and which had now become reality: 'O, how good and joyful a thing it is, when brothers dwell together in unity'.

His look on that photograph, his last, became my favourite. Later his portrait was painted from it. He seems to be looking into the camera lens, but far beyond it, right through the observer and out into the unknown.

10

January 1945: The Russian Vistula Offensive

Return to the Eastern Front; the Russian Vistula offensive - aged 21 years

However bleak I found the difficulties of everyday life at home, and however much I actually longed to be back at the front and with my comrades, it was still hard for me to say goodbye. As always at the end of the leave, Mother had not come with me to the station. I could not bear our feelings, especially those of my dear mother, to be watched by strangers. Mother knew that. She always swallowed her tears and stayed behind at home. With a bag of freshly washed clothes in my hand, I left the house. Mother waved to me from the window for a long time. In Vienna I struggled to get from the North West Railway Station to the Northern Railway Station. The platform, as I was used to by then, was full of soldiers, women and children, all saying goodbye. Throughout the entire journey from Stockerau, I had an anxious New Year's Eve feeling. Vienna's formerly peaceful appearance, where only blackout precautions reminded you of war and danger from the air, had been lost. It had become a city behind the lines. The front ran through Gran and by Lake Balaton. As the leave train slowly moved out from the platform, I was depressed by the tears, and the pain of farewells, that I saw around me.

In the dark New Year's night my thoughts raced ahead into the New Year and what it might bring. The Reich was gripped by its enemies on its Eastern and Western borders. In East Prussia the Russians had touched the soil of the Reich and committed unimaginable atrocities. During my leave, almost daily, hundreds of American bombers had flown over our small town, down the Danube, towards Vienna. Standing at the doors of their houses, many inhabitants had watched the great aircraft taking their course, unopposed, with imposing equanimity. Father, in his Christmas letter to Mother, had told her if the worst came to the worst to stay where she was. Rudi and I had pressed her to flee in any event if the Russians came. We had even put together, for her and for little Liesl, some light baggage for that eventuality. A stroke of good fortune let our Father return home just at the right time. That removed from her the responsibility for taking a decision, and both parents did the right thing in not fleeing.

In Thorn I left the leave train. It was going on to Königsberg. I changed to the passenger train to Sichelberg (Sierpc). There, *Leutnant* Brinkel the first orderly officer of the Regiment got on. By profession he was a Protestant pastor in Silesia. At midnight he had heard the Führer's address promising 'victory to our armed forces'. It was full of optimism.

The railway ended in Nasielsk, six kilometres behind the front. Brinkel and I marched together to the Divisional command post. It was a gleaming white winter's day. The sun illuminated the Sunday peace and the war, for once, was still. At the Divisional Staff everybody apart from the guard was still asleep. They had been celebrating New Year, and the Divisional Adjutant, *Major* Östreich, had to get out of bed on our account. He said we could have stayed at home to see in the New Year. That was easily said, my leave ended on New Year's Eve, and that was when I had to begin the journey. Quite apart from that, I could not have celebrated knowing that the next day I would have to travel to the Eastern Front, for the fourth time. The nearer the front I came, the more I had the familiar feeling of 'butterflies'.

But there was some compensation in the fact that I was back with the '7th'. I looked up Klaus Nicolai. We had a quick welcome nip and went to the bunker of the regimental commander. *Oberst* Dorn, the *Grand Seigneur* from the Rhineland, welcomed me to the regiment and informed me that I was to get the 1st Company. The company was at the moment in reserve in the so-called second trench of the extended trench system. The next day it would move back into the frontline. At the 1st Battalion, *Hauptmann* Fitz and *Oberleutnant* Küllenberg, the *Hauptmann* and the Adjutant, welcomed me with a loud 'hello'. I knew them from the previous summer. Then a runner took me forward and at the Company I was welcomed by *Leutnant* Martin Lechner who was to take over command of the battalion's heavy weapons company.

I had become friends with Lechner in spring 1944 in Schweidnitz. At that time he had come from the war school to which he had been sent as an active *Unteroffizier* with above average potential. He had good manners and you could not see the '12-Ender' in him, even if at the *Ersatz* battalion he had not had any comrades. I had put myself out a bit for him for which, I noticed, he had been grateful. But we celebrated our reunion with the appropriate drop of the hard stuff. Before that of course we had done another tour of the bunker. I had to see and greet the men. They should get a look at their new 'boss' straight away. After that we sturdily went on to have a few jars, because that was still the best tried-and-tested way of getting things off to a good start. Finally Lechner got up and made a speech on the theme that the 1st Company must be the 'first' not only in name but also in achievement, something it was now and also must remain in the future. Not quite so awkwardly and seriously as Lechner, I also said a few words to him and to the men of the company. I stressed my pride at now being commander of the 1st Company of our old regiment, and that was the truth.

The next night we moved into position in the *Nase von Poweilin*. It was extremely unfavourable, because the main line of resistance ran at a right angle, one arm pointed in a westerly and the other arm in a southerly direction. The Russians could come from two sides, in the intersection of the angle enemy fire was possible from three sides. Our neighbour on the right was the 2nd Company, on the left was the Divisional *Füsilierbataillon*. Only a hundred metres of the trench had been dug out to knee depth, so that during the daytime you could only move through it by crawling.

Because of the way the trenches ran in the entire *Nase*, the men of the company regarded themselves, in the event of the expected large-scale enemy offensive, as 'written off'. With almost complete certainty, those in the *Nase* could expect to be overrun or cut off. As far as anyone could see, there was no way of escape. Fire could come from three sides, attacks from two sides, and to the rear in front of the second line were our own minefields only passable in narrow channels. Whoever survived the heavy barrage before the attack had to face the attack itself. Scarcely anybody would be able to survive that. Because of the minefields and the completely open, gently rising terrain, to retreat did not offer the slightest prospect of getting through in one piece. Thoughts like this I had to keep to myself, and particularly the thought that, if the worst came to the worst, I had only my own pistol to keep me out of the Russian captivity that I viewed with such fear and horror.

During those days, or rather nights, I was continually moving around the trench from post to post and bunker to bunker, in order to get to know every one of the men under my charge. Many knew me by sight, many by name. Actions like Upolosy, Nemers and Raseinen and many others, bound us together. Also I spoke the language of the Silesians, who still formed the majority of the regiment. I was able to converse with them in their local dialect, so that none of them felt that I was a stranger. Soon after I joined the regiment I had learned to speak Lower Silesian and Upper Silesian. Once, on an exercise march in the vicinity of the garrison, an old dear had said to me that I was certainly a Schweidnitzer. Telling her that I was not, I had laughed at her, and she had got angry.

My company troop leader was the young Berlin *Unteroffizier* Ulrich Lamprecht. He was a student of Protestant theology with the Iron Cross First Class on his narrow chest. Every day he read the book of proverbs of the *Herrenhut* Brethren. In the days that remained until the offensive, I read the proverbs with him and also the corresponding references from the New Testament, which I had in my pack. Among the runners Walter Buck stood out, He was a 35 year old businessman from Hamburg. He matched the type of the intelligent soldier, who has long since passed normal military age, and who lacked the ambition of youth. He was reliable and did his duty well, as did the other runner Reinalter, a farmer from Swabia.

As in all the earlier trenches, in this trench too some branch trenches led to the separate *Donnerbalken* or 'Thunderbox'. It was the one little place where you could be alone at the front. In that quiet hermitage, you could, if it suited the enemy, actually spend the quietest minutes of the day or night. In summer as in winter there was the smell of the chlorine. Then, in the icy cold of winter, strange towers, frozen stiff, stood up in the pit as in a dripstone cave. It was then that I decided, if I was granted a happy return home and had the opportunity, I would somehow sing the praises of the latrines, which I have now done here!

The company command post lay on slightly rising ground, in the middle of the bridge of the *Nase*. The linking stretch leading to the main trench could be seen by the enemy, during the daytime. Therefore, if at all possible, we had to remain in the bunker. In that way, during the long days up to 14 January, I learned how to play *Skat*. I never had any interest in card games. Many a time comrades or superiors had asked: 'Can you play *Skat* or can you play *Doppelkopf?*' When I said 'no' it usually prompted the surprised and amused question, 'Eh lad, how did you get to be an officer then?' On 6 January I had the great surprise of seeing a schoolmate from Stockerau, *Leutnant der Reserve* Otto Holzer. In the autumn he had passed out of war school, and came as a platoon leader into the heavy weapons company. It was a huge pleasure for me, even if our time together during the evenings did not last long. Subsequently, after Otto was wounded in February, we did not see each other again.

A 'visit' of another kind was the assignment of a 'trench dog'. Not the designation for a new weapon or machine, it was an actual guard dog. It had been selected to alert us to 'alien elements in the trench'. It was a smallish, wolf-like mongrel, and despite my love for dogs I had no confidence in its military value as an additional defence against the ever-active Russian commando units.

On 9 January I received orders to prepare an assault unit to bring in prisoners. It was to be led by me because I was the most experienced of the company commanders. The order, and above all the fact that I was to lead the assault unit, did not comfort me at all. I still did not feel myself to be sufficiently familiar with the terrain. I would also be responsible for the operation. There were others who had not yet had the opportunity to win a decoration. I spoke about it openly with Martin Lechner, who agreed with me entirely. But the assault unit was called off, on 12 January, after it had been announced that the Russians had begun their large-scale offensive. With 3,000 tanks they moved up from the Vistula bridgeheads of Baranov and Warka.

Those were the omens as I faced my 21st birthday the next day. I celebrated it, therefore, on the evening of the 12th in the expectation that from 12 midnight on the 13th a special feeling of 'consecration' would set in, befitting the significance of the fact that I had attained my 'coming-of-age' as a citizen.

On 13 January the enemy's major offensive in East Prussia began. It was still quiet where we were. There was harassing fire of varying strength and noise, and from time to time snatches of songs from the enemy trenches. With the field kitchen came 'best wishes' and the usual bottles as presents. The General, the Divisional Adjutant, the commander and the commanders of the Artillery regiment whom I knew, *Oberst* Dorn and the battalion commanders all sent their congratulations. I was touched by the expressions in them of the respect and esteem in which my achievements were held. In the light of what faced us, the wishes were of particular warmth and sincerity. Unfortunately, the mail that I used to send them all home was lost. Unexpressed, but certainly honourably meant, was the wish that *Leutnant* Roberts had expressed to me in the summer in Raseinen. When we were saying goodbye to each other, as we were changing positions, he squeezed my hand and, smiling sadly, no doubt with the premonition that he was to die soon, said 'stay alive'. He had been killed in action in October on the Narev.

At 6pm the company commanders received their orders at the Battalion. Since *Hauptmann* Fitz had left in the night after he had been wounded, *Oberleutnant* Husénett, wearing the Knight's Cross, had taken over command of the battalion. I had gone off with the runner, Buck, and the dog. At the battalion command post we had learned more about the serious situation in the Vistula bridgeheads and in East Prussia. There was no longer any doubt about the fate that awaited us.

On the way back, I went with the runner into the completely destroyed village church of Powielin. It had been a quite simple little old wooden church, but the tower had been shot off during the recent fighting. One single token remained to remind you of its religious purpose, namely a large cross on the side of the altar. 'Thy will be done', I could have no better prayer. When I got back to the company

I strode once again from bunker to bunker, and went from post to post, to give everyone one more word of confidence.

On the morning of 14 January, as we had since the morning of the 12th, we were expecting from hour to hour the beginning of the heavy barrage. According to the custom of the Russians recently, the thunderclap was to be expected on the hour, i.e. at 6am, 7am or 8am. After we had been spared the unavoidable event on the 12th and the 13th, the beginning had to be today, because the long-observed preparations of the enemy allowed for no other possibility. They would have to get as far as possible in daylight after the effect of their devastating fire. It would last several hours and would land on our positions. Their attack would necessarily have to be as early as possible. Thus the preparatory fire would also have to begin very early in the morning.

I was with the men of my company in the bunker. We were lying or sitting on bunkers or at small tables, weapons and steel helmets ready to hand. An all-consuming nervousness, that no one let show, dominated us. A cold feeling crept over me, that trembling in the stomach that used to affect me in school before exams. But when at 7am the fire did not erupt, I hoped that the Russians would today be sparing us once again. The feeling was reinforced because even on the dot of 8am, by my service watch, nothing happened.

But just as I was about to say what I was thinking, there began the dreadful crashing, the familiar noise of 'Stalin organs' firing. Several of them must have been firing in sequence, because the crashing went on for what seemed an eternity. Only within the detonations of the organ shells did the barking reports of cannons and those of howitzers, mortars, and the *Ratschbum* sound out. The earth was literally shaking and the air was thudding. An uninterrupted grumbling thunder descended upon the German lines. Obviously the enemy were trying to destroy the minefields of our trench system, extended fourfold, and to flatten trenches and shatter bunkers.

The only things dangerous to us in the company bunker were the shells dropping very close by, of which there were not a few. The whistling, rushing and crashing of shells round about indeed almost drugged the senses. But we were lucky and along the whole 'bridge of the nose' we only received a few direct hits in the trench and none on the bunker. I got the impression that the Russians were sparing the *Nase*. Even the advanced observers of the artillery and our heavy weapons company beside my command post remained untouched.

After exactly two hours the bombardment suddenly broke off. A paralysing calm fell over the front. It meant that the Russians were moving their fire forward, in order not to endanger their attacking infantry. *Raus*, I ordered, and that meant going into position in the small trench system around the company command post. All nervousness had fallen away from me. The patient waiting in the bunker was at an end, we could see and deal with the enemy. Outside there was fog, but it was the powder smoke from the massive amount of exploded shells that had dropped on our positions. I thought that I could not believe my eyes when on the right I saw that the second company had already retreated a long way. I then saw the enemy rapidly advancing in battalion strength on to the second trench. The Russians went round my company and cut us off. But from the left, charging at the company command post, there came the left wing of a confused brown wave, approaching unstoppably with cries of *Urrah.*

But the most shattering thing about the picture was the fact that individual German soldiers were running away in front of the assaulting Red Army troops. They were wobbling with exhaustion, without weapons and equipment, plainly at the end of their strength. But we had to fire, even at the risk of our comrades thinking that we were firing at them. So I carefully took aim at the Russians storming up behind them. They had in the meantime approached to within 100 metres of us. In the feeling of desperation that there was no way that we could escape from that dire position, other than dead or as prisoners, an uncanny calm came over me.

As I had learned as a recruit in our much vilified drill, I took aim and fired, disappeared behind the parapet after firing, then quick as a flash popped up again a little to one side and got the next enemy in the sights of my *Sturmgewehr.* I succeeded in hitting enemy officers and machine-gunners. They were clearly recognisable, especially the officers, by the arm movements with which they accompanied their already audible orders. Thus, as one after the other fell, hit by my bullets, I was seized by a triumphant savage pleasure and by the hope of escaping once more. I watched one of the men I shot, stepping on persistently with his head lowered. Then, he was hit by my bullet. Slowly he struck his chest with his hand and finally fell forward. That picture will never leave me as long as I live.

The miracle happened. The targeted fire from my rifle, and those of the runners, brought the attack to a standstill. The Red Army troops went to ground. Then, pursued by our bullets, they drew back far to the rear and sought to connect up again to the forces on their right. We had lost our connections both to the right and to the left because the Russians had already pushed forward a long way, Meanwhile, my platoons had left the trench. They gathered in a line, one man behind another, in the secondary trench leading to the command post. I gave orders immediately to go back into position. There was no more immediate danger just then, for the very reason that the enemy was not at all concerned about us. However, the longer-term situation seemed hopeless. Sooner or later we would certainly fall into enemy hands.

I was still considering how we could get out of that wretched situation when, on the right from the sector of the 3rd Battalion infantry fire could be heard. It could mean nothing other than that our battalion had held its position. It must therefore be possible to connect up to the 3rd Battalion via the abandoned sector of the 2nd Company. There was no longer any wireless contact with our own battalion. Even the advanced observers had evidently been able to withdraw in time. So I had to make the decision to remain in the position or to connect up on the right to the 3rd Battalion.

I decided on the latter course because it seemed to me to be unlikely that the position could be held. It could also be assumed that orders would be given during the night to evacuate the main line of resistance, insofar as it was still occupied by our people. In the light of that it seemed unimportant from which point the company should begin its withdrawal. Since the waves of the enemy had rolled past us on the right and on the left, I gave orders to withdraw along the main trench to the right towards the 3rd Battalion. The *Oberfähnrich* took the lead and I myself remained at the rear. Like the captain of a sinking ship, I was the last to leave my company sector.

An enemy reserve company spotted our withdrawal, changed its direction and made moves to attack us. A particularly dashing group was storming up at a run outside the trenches while my company was withdrawing hurriedly along the trench to the right. To make the withdrawal easier, I formed a rearguard with a machine-gun and the two runners. With care I picked out again the nearest of the attackers. When they felt our resistance, they left off their pursuit. It was doubtless not part of their immediate task.

Eventually there only remained a short length of trench to overcome, in which there were Russians. We managed it with a few shouts and a short *Huura*! It was easy because for the most part they were wounded and the group had no leader. We even took prisoner some slightly wounded troops and chased others away. Those who were seriously wounded we left alone. Soon we had connected up with the 3rd Battalion. The men took a breath, and I went to the battalion command post. The commander, *Hauptmann* Dolansky, greeted me with words of recognition for our achievement. He immediately reported our arrival to the Regiment through the still intact telephone line. All that remained of my strength deserted me and I could almost have fallen asleep. I really had to 'pull myself together' so as not to give in to exhaustion.

Towards dusk a captive Russian captain was brought into the bunker. An active officer, about 25 years old, he said he had never been in action before. He had only arrived a few days previously with an entire division from Siberia. Through this and other information we slowly formed a proper idea of the inexhaustible reserves of the enemy.

The third line of trenches, to which we had had to withdraw during the night, ran along the back of a slope. In front of us was some woodland. On the right of it about 600 metres away there was a single farmhouse surrounded by fruit trees. As we could see from their movements, the Russians had already reached the edge of the woodland. Our trench was continuous and well constructed and excellently camouflaged with snow. We ourselves, as we moved into it from the edge of the woodland, had only noticed it when it was a few metres away.

We must have only settled down in it for an hour, when out of the woodland came two Russians who briskly and unconcernedly walked towards our trench. They had machine-pistols slung around their necks and were walking comfortably side by side almost as if they were whistling a little song. They came to within 200 metres, to within 100 metres and even nearer, without having noticed our trench in front of them. I quietly gave the order to let them approach and to take them prisoner. Fifty metres away from us they slowed their steps. Twenty German voices shouted *Stoi*! Whereupon they turned round and ran back, weaving as they went. In the hail of bullets they collapsed. I had not anticipated that. They must have been riddled with bullets.

Some time after that period of cruelty and bitterness there was movement at the farm. As a result of it the enemy artillery opened up and obediently dropped shells on us. I scanned the farm with my binoculars and discovered the advanced observers. There were two men with wireless sets, whose heads, shoulders and equipment could be seen behind low cover. I asked to be handed a rifle with a telescopic sight and for a runner to observe through the binoculars. Then I pushed my-self carefully over the parapet of the trench and calmly took aim. There was a soft pressure as I fired. The observer's head sank on to the cover and that of the second man disappeared. My runner saw through the binoculars the dead man being dragged back into cover. An hour later came the order to evacuate the position. In the meantime another Russian artillery observer had taken over directing the fire, which unfortunately was so accurate that we had some casualties.

A position as well constructed as the fourth line, in which we spent the night of 17 January, I had never seen. The bunkers were as much as three metres below ground level. The trench had been dug out to the height of a man. It was provided with secondary trenches, and in places with rails. The rifle positions and machine-gun nests were tactically in the correct places. It could not have been better in the trench warfare of the First World War. So this was the so-called *Gauleiterstellung*, which led over 1,000 kilometres along the eastern border of the *Reich*. It had been built in autumn 1944 by women and girls who were either volunteers or on war ser-vice, under the direction of officers who had been injured in the war. On the Oder, even Gisela had participated with pickaxe and shovel in that massive project.

From my perspective in the trenches, the position, apart from some buildings that should have been blown up, was an ideal one in which to spend the winter. Not a spadeful more could be dug out of the frozen ground. The Powielin position, with its trenches in places only knee deep, bore no comparison to this one. But I had no feeling of confidence. Even though I had no overview of the wider situa-tion, I did not reckon on staying there long.

My feeling had not deceived me. After sleeping for a few hours in deep exhaus-tion I had woken up. At dawn I emerged from the bunker. The houses in front of the position, 50 metres away, made me nervous. As it came light, movement could be seen. It turned out that there were some individual Russians in the houses and that more were moving in. In ones and twos they came running over the bridge which led over a stream on the other side of the farmyard. I had the machine-gun spray the bridge, whereupon in the background a movement to the left, along the stream, could be seen. After quite a long time, individual rifle fire sounded from the neighbouring sector to our left. The direction of it moved more and more obliquely to the rear in our direction of retreat. While it was gradually becoming light, the enemy were also advancing on the right about one kilometre away. We were threatened with encirclement. Our neighbours on both sides crumbled. They left their trenches and withdrew, widely separated.

The battalion commander, *Hauptmann* Wild, could not decide to evacuate that magnificent position without orders. There was neither telephone nor wireless connection to our Regiment. In view of the threatened encirclement it seemed crazy to stay in the position. Behind it stretched several kilometres of open plain, offering no kind of protection. To withdraw across it in daylight would involve heavy casualties. No runner came from the Regiment who might have brought the order we were waiting for. The pale day brightened and the rifle fire behind us to the left became more concentrated.

Hauptmann Wild waited and brooded. To surrender the position without the enemy attacking was a decision with far-reaching consequences. Even apart from the possibility of court martial proceedings, the order to evacuate meant giving up trenches and bunkers of such good quality as we had never had before. Even if the enemy had dug in on the other slope of the bank only 100 or 150 metres away, this would still not have been any 'close-quarters corner' such as we had in October in the Budy-Obrebski position. At the company commanders' meeting I pressed for the order to withdraw to be given. I pointed out that otherwise, if there were any further delay, the battalion of nearly 150 men would be lost. *Hauptmann* Wild came to his decision. We climbed out of the trenches and moved off over the wide, snow-covered field.

While the battalion was retreating in open order, suddenly bursts of fire from machine-guns and machine-pistols hit the right flank. There were Russians in a small trench system, not 30 metres away from me. Men hit by the bullets were collapsing all around. One cried out that we should take him with us. Who could have done that? Everybody was running, and in long jumping strides I ran along with them. Then suddenly there was a blow against my head. As I was running, I was spun round. I fell, and pulled myself together again. My head was thumping, but I felt that I was not wounded. Stumbling, I ran on, zig-zagging across the expanse when there was no cover.

After some 100 metres the commanders were able to bring their units under control and to change the running flight into an orderly retreat. At the end of the fields lay the next settlement. A machine-pistol barked out from there and a voice, going haywire, was shouting out. Both weapon and voice belonged to *Oberst* Dorn, who was firing in the air over our heads in order to halt the retreating troops and bring them into their positions. 'You *Schweinehunde*, will you stand still!' he roared, although this was not necessary. I had never seen the *Oberst*, this quiet and kindly man, so excited. Clearly he had not seen and did not know anything of the retreat of our neighbouring units and nothing of the enemy machine-gun fire that had hit us from the flank as we were retreating. But the *Oberst* was fair and experienced enough to immediately grasp the situation and not to hold us responsible for it. He knew that in the sixth year of the war the troops were already too worn out to be able to make anything of a situation such as this.

Lengthy retreats demoralise any troops, as had been seen in the summer of 1944. There on the Russian front was added a massive momentum not present on the other fronts, apart perhaps from the partisan war in the Balkans. It was the fear of being taken prisoner, the fear of falling into the hands of an inhuman enemy. Goebbels' propaganda had a boomerang effect. The bitterness with which the war was waged against Bolshevik Russia marked it out as a struggle between personal deadly enemies. The disregard of the Red Cross, the news of the atrocities carried out by the advancing Red Army, all this had long since extinguished the chivalry practised in earlier wars. However, it seemed to be still present on the other fronts in the West and South. Two ideologies were battling it out. The protagonists knew that the conflict would only end with the destruction of one or the other. In the East it had never been a decent war.

One notable thing was that on the evening of 17 January 1945, quite against my usual careless custom, I had put on my steel helmet instead of my field service cap. An indeterminate but compelling feeling had made me do it. When I was at last able to take off my steel helmet I saw the reason for it. The bludgeoning blow, that had thrown me to the ground, came from an infantry gun. It had very nearly penetrated the helmet, but the inserts of sheet steel and leather had stopped it from going right through.

From the beginning of the large-scale offensive on the 14th until the 20th January we had carried out a fighting withdrawal of almost 70 kilometres. We had to take up positions in front of the little town of Bielsk. Since only the commander, *Hauptmann* Wild, had a map, the process of directing us in to our positions was a very long-winded affair. Also, the allocation of sectors did not seem to be quite right. Wild drove for a long time in a regimental vehicle around the district in order to find the right sector. We had to shift sideways. He had already directed away half the battalion, then went to find it and did not come back.

The Adjutant, *Oberleutnant* Küllenberg, and I remained behind, as the only officers, with the other half of the battalion. It was a bright and sunny winter's day with good visibility over a long distance. We were standing on the top of a gentle rise, parallel to which, and some 700 metres to the left, to the south, ran the road to Bielsk, 4 kilometres away. To the right of it, one to two kilometres further on, at a right angle to the first road, another road led to the town. Two small areas of woodland lay between. On the latter road, which could not easily be observed, enemy tanks were advancing, to judge by the noise they were making, But on the left, one brown lorry after another, carrying anti-tank guns or infantry, rolled in the direction of Bielsk.

Küllenberg and I considered our position. As it later turned out, a battalion runner sent by *Hauptmann* Wild had not got through. In the meantime it had got to 3pm. Getting on for 30 lorries had already driven past us and on the right, to judge by the noise, at least as many tanks. So our only option was to withdraw, to lie up in the nearest woodland and to wait for the approaching darkness. In two hours it would be dusk and after that it would quickly become dark. To the woodland it was one kilometre, in between there was a village. We moved through it in column, widely separated. The few inhabitants, mostly old people, observed us with indifferent faces. They may have felt pleased that we were retreating, but also uncertain as to what was going to happen. Not far behind the village we reached the protection of the woodland. Russians travelling to Bielsk on the road to the left of us seemed to have a definite destination. Although they must have been able to see us, they left us alone. Possibly they thought that we were their own people. That gave me an idea.

When we arrived in the woodland, sentries were posted at its edges and then we began to get changed. The winter clothing that we were wearing over our uniform was white on one side and covered on the other with brownish-green camouflage patterns. At a distance it could not be distinguished from the brown cloth of the Russian uniforms. So we turned our uniforms inside out. Brown on the outside, we had a better chance of being taken for Russians and not being recognised. Till darkness fell we remained undisturbed.

Then a tense operation began. Everyone stuck closely to his neighbour as we stepped through the snow. We could touch no village, no farm. The aim was to push through the most forward enemy lines in a wide arc around Bielsk, and thus reach our own lines. A critical point would be the road on which the tanks had been advancing. Now and again we could still hear the sound of engines from there. Before we set off, Küllenberg and I had looked at each other. The question as to who would be able to keep it up remained unsaid.

After an hour of wading through the snow we reached the road. Firelight shone from farmhouses. They were already occupied by the enemy. While the men, distributed in the nearest hollows, were under cover, Küllenberg and I stalked our way forward to the road. The broad tracks of the enemy T-34 tanks had left deep tracks in the snow. On the road there was no traffic. The opportunity was favourable, we brought up the men and our crossing was successful.

On the other side of the road we began afresh the process of creeping up between the farms. We approached to within only 50 metres of one of them. In the light of a fire Russians were making themselves comfortable. They were cooking and roasting, making a noise and felt quite safe. We, on the other hand, refrained from doing anything that would give us away, in order not to endanger our goal of reaching the German lines.

Almost two hours later we found ourselves to the south-west of the town. We had almost described a semicircle around it when a village came into sight. According to the distance and the noise of the fighting during the day, the Russians could have only got this far. We halted once again, and Küllenberg and I crept alone into the village. In a ditch at the side of the road we took cover and waited until we saw people, friend or foe. We waited a while and consulted in whispers.

Suddenly two chaps came along the road, in fur caps and snow jackets with telephone equipment round their neck, evidently Russians. Since they had to pass quite close to us and would anyway see us in the light of the snowy evening, there was only one thing left for us to do, namely to let them come to within a few metres of us and then take care of them. Walking side by side they approached us, suspecting nothing and without a care in the world. When they were quite close we jumped up, our assault rifles at the ready, and shouted *Ruki wjerch!* The two of them were completely taken by surprise and raised their hands in the air. Then one of them, when he had recovered from the shock, said, 'Oh God, *Herr Leutnant,* you didn't half give me a fright!'

So we relaxed a bit! The two of them were *Strippenhengste,* i.e. signals troops from our artillery regiment. They had to check the telephone lines to an advanced observer, who was supposed to be somewhere further forward, that is, where we had come from. That meant that without noticing it we had successfully crossed the lines with our 80 men. Both sides had, in view of the darkness evidently 'called it a day' with the occupation of farms and houses. *Hauptmann* Wild and the other half of the battalion were soon found.

After such adventures it was the greatest pleasure to put the first cigarette in your mouth. Inhale the first pull at it, then to the able to breathe out again. I had begun to smoke when I was at grammar school, and Father, who was a non-smoker, had had no objection to it. On the contrary, and this reinforced my habit, he had spoken of comrades in the First World War who were smokers and who in critical situations kept or found their calm with the help of tobacco.

That night there were still a few hours' rest to be had on a German estate. I was sitting with some men in the library of the house and found there Stefan Zweig's *Sternstunden der Menschheit.* I read for a little while, sitting in an armchair, until my eyelids closed and my head sank backwards.

In order to relieve the strain of the winter retreat, we received orders to requisition farm vehicles. Affected by this were the Polish farmers who had remained on their farmsteads, while the Germans with their heavily loaded carts had already fled. The farmer from whom I had taken two nags together with his light vehicles complained a lot. The unit commander, in accordance with the Hague Convention on land warfare, had to issue a written receipt for the requisitioned goods. But it was no use to the poor farmer. Nor was it of any help to him that the interpreter told him that the whole of Poland, when the Russians occupied that country, would long to be back with the Germans. We, however, if we were not actually in combat, could load machine-guns and boxes of ammunition on the vehicles and now and again one of us could rest his weary body.

On 23 January *Oberleutnant* Küllenberg was shot in the stomach. Apart from the commander, I was then the last officer in the battalion. As we were withdrawing during the day in open order I had fallen through the ice while crossing a frozen stream. The water had got into the felt lining of my boots. I either marched along in wet boots, with my feet to a certain extent warm, or if I was not moving they got cold and threatened to freeze to the soles.

The following night brought me the craziest experience of that winter retreat. I had received orders to take over command of the rearguard. Who else could have done this, since there was no other officer there anyway. I had bent over the *Hauptmann's* map, the only one in the battalion, and with clammy fingers had dug out of the map case a pencil and a little slip of paper. Out loud to myself I had spelled out the unpronounceable Polish place names and written them on the slip of paper. A few lines, an arrow pointing north, and the sketch was ready. The runner Buck had similarly had to look at the sketch and then I reported my departure. '*Auf Wiedersehen, Herr Hauptmann, Leutnant* Scheiderbauer reporting his departure', I had said, in a fairly unmilitary fashion, and Wild had replied 'Go with God, my boy, go!'

The company of only 14 remaining men, sat in the overheated room of a farmhouse warming themselves before the 20 kilometre night march, or rather, journey. The 14 chaps comfortably fitted on the vehicles, so that it was clear that their feet could be protected. The entire battalion was 'motorised' in this way with the help of 10 such 'combat vehicles'. The head of the column set off, and I remained behind with two vehicles as rearguard. It was a dark, almost mild night, and we were not freezing to any great extent. No wonder that the men dozed and dropped off, and seemingly the horses did too.

Then suddenly the penultimate vehicle had driven into a ditch and the men on it, woken up with a shock, were only just able to jump down from the vehicle as it tipped over. 'Dopey sod!' they cursed the driver, and 'wretched nag' was how he cursed his horse. Of course the men pushed the vehicle back out of the ditch again, loaded the ammunition boxes back on to it, pulled up their hoods and sat back on it. They were annoyed about the 10 minutes the accident had lost, and the fact that by then they had lost touch with the battalion.

We drove on and the men dozed on. But I stayed awake, lit up my sketch with the glowing tip of my cigarette, took compass bearings, and waited for the left-hand fork in the road leading westwards. But it didn't come. We drove past a brightly-lit farmhouse in front of which a lorry was standing. 'So we're not last', said one of the men. The situation slowly began to seem suspicious to me, because we had already gone too far northwards. But suddenly we heard vehicles in front of us that must come from the battalion. Out of the darkness the outlines of houses emerged. It was doubtless a village in which the battalion was waiting for its rear-guard. The distance became less and less, and the outlines of buildings, trees and vehicles became clearer and clearer. These must also come from other units. We overtook some, until an obstacle brought us to a halt. I jumped down in order to look with the runner for *Hauptmann* Wild.

We passed figures shrouded in white and were suddenly asked, in Russian, 'Well, who are you?' I assumed that the man asking the question was a Russian *Hilfswilliger*, many of whom served with our baggage-train, and had paid no more attention to him. But then the chap had moved his hand in a suspicious way and was holding a weapon in it. My runner, the medic, suddenly planted one on his chin. Bellowing loudly and falling backwards he shouted '*Germanski, Germanski!*' Shots cracked out and shouts rang out.

There was complete confusion in the Russian baggage-train into which we had stumbled. No one could recognise anyone else in the darkness. I shouted 'Out! Into the fields!' We had to get away from the village street and the vehicles. The only option open to us was the field to the left of the road, because on the right the road was blocked. Franz stuck close to me. The other men were swallowed up in the snow and the night. After an hour of strenuous searching and muffled shouting we had only found seven of the fourteen. Then we set off, without vehicles and without machine-guns. I could not hold up any longer if I wanted to avoid being seen when it got light.

It was the only time during my time as a soldier that I lost my bearings at night. The sky was cloudy and the Pole Star could not be seen, and my sense of direction let me down. I was convinced that the west was in the east, but my compass showed the opposite. I wavered between which I should trust, my instinct that had never yet let me down, or the compass. Then reason and drill, which were the stronger, won through and trust in the compass saved us. We were stamping through the snow in the direction my compass showed as west. From time to time we had to wade up to our knees through the snow. At last a farmstead came in sight. There we had to ask the way. Fortunately I had written down the place names along our retreat. I could not send any of the men still shocked by the experience to the farm, so I went again with Franz.

While the rest of the group waited near a tree that we hoped to be able to find later, Franz and I, with the safety catches off our weapons, crept closer. A dog set off barking, but from the house there was neither light nor any sound to be heard. We knocked on the window and on the door until an anxious farmer opened up. Were there any Russians here yet, the Upper Silesian Franz asked him in Russian, to which the Pole replied: 'No, you are the first'. Smiling to ourselves we got him to tell us the way to the road and the names of the next villages.

Soon we had found the road again. Just as it was becoming light, we at last found the battalion in the third village. With the help of *Hauptmann* Wild's map I had to establish that we had missed the fork in the road by five kilometres. At the regiment and at the Division they were agitated when they found out, on the basis of my report, that enemy baggage-trains were already in the village where we had had our adventure.

On 25 January we had come to within 10 kilometres of the Vistula to the south of the town of Graudenz. From midnight there was a two-hour halt. After that we were to march on again. Since the enemy was not pushing up behind, we only had to take normal security precautions. There was enough time to knock up a decent stew for the men. The farmhouse, in which we were, had been deserted by its inhabitants. They had fled. But the stock was still there. Two men who knew how to do it hurriedly slaughtered a pig. The portions we needed were cut out, the rest was left. The Ivans could make a good meal of it if it had not become inedible by that time. In a massive pan that the farmer's wife must have used at harvest time and at celebrations, the pieces of meat simmered in such a way as to make our mouths water. Outside it remained quiet and we were lucky enough to be able to eat our fill until we left.

After three hours' slow night march we crossed the frozen Vistula. Pioneers had reinforced it to form an ice bridge so that tanks and heavy artillery could also get across it. At 5am in the area of Deutsch-Westfalen, I set my foot on the western bank. The positions ran along the riverbank on the Vistula embankment. On the western bank a strip of meadows about one to three kilometres wide then ran along the river, ending in a steeply climbing hill. About 10 kilometres north-eastwards was the town of Graudenz with the visible silhouette of its fortress. Called after the Prussian General, Courbiere, it stood high above the Vistula.

11

February/March 1945: The last days

Continual close-quarters combat; badly wounded; emergency operation in field hospital; moved to Danzig; hospital surrenders to Russians; prisoner-of-war

The Vistula embankment was occupied by alarm units that had been pooled together at the nearest frontline control point. We had the presence of such a unit to thank for a last day of rest. The German inhabitants of the prosperous town had not all yet fled. They hoped that the enemy could be brought to a standstill at the riverbank. Despite the ample evening meal, everyone ate his fill of the plentiful supply of food. While the men were cooking chickens I scoffed a full ten scrambled eggs that Walter had rustled up for me by way of a change of diet. When the field kitchen arrived in the morning, most of the men made short work of another pot full of bacon and beans. The joker Franz said, tongue-in-cheek, that as far as he was concerned the *Führer* could do away with the card system. After the meal we stretched out to sleep. Someone had found a gramophone and got it working. Of the two records only one was chosen. Adolf Hitler's speech, 'Give me four years', was not requested. Instead we had an old song, the melody of which I know to this day. It rang out from the tinny sounding gramophone: *So liebt man in Lissabon, in Tokio, Wien und Rom; die Sprache der Liebe ist überall gleich* ('Thus people love in Lisbon, in Tokyo, Vienna and Rome; the language of love is the same everywhere').

On the afternoon of 27 January we moved into the positions on the bank of the Vistula. My company's sector was the village of Jungensand, to the south of Deutsch-Westfalen. On the snowy riverbank there were willows. Adjoining it was an embankment, some five metres high and sloping on both sides. To the east of the embankment ran the village street. On the other edge were clean, for the most part smallish farmsteads all planted out with gardens. Since there were no trenches, we dug foxholes in the embankment. In the farm that I took as my command post I met a *Leutnant* with a few troops on leave from many different units. As they got out of the train in Deutsch-Kone they had been gathered together into an alarm unit. The *Herr Kamerad* had let his men sleep in the outhouse while he had spent the night with mother and daughter in the farmer's bedroom. Grinning offensively he suggested to me that I should do the same. Without saying anything I looked at him, not understanding and full of contempt.

Since the enemy obviously had need of a break, as we did, we were granted two days of rest. As our physical exhaustion abated, the oppression of our minds and spirits proportionately increased. The deserted dwellings, farms and settlements created a thoroughly sad atmosphere. There were columns of German refugees, old men, women and children with belongings they had had to snatch together as best they could in the emergency. We had already overtaken some of them on the way.

Everything reinforced those sad impressions. The realisation hit me that the area, German for more than half a millennium, would be irretrievably lost.

In the stables there was still some warmth. Many farmers had not even been able to take all their stock with them. Gates and doors were standing open, as if the houses were still inhabited by their owners and they had just gone out into the fields. The cellars and barns were full. The shelves of the dining rooms were stocked. In addition to the large amount of meat daily, we even had stewed fruit. We would have done without it only we were still standing at Smolensk. We, the infantrymen, were to be the last to set foot over the threshold of those countless homes about to be given over to the enemy. 'Oh Germany, poor Fatherland', I thought at the time. I happened to find in the First Letter to the Corinthians, chapter four, verse seven, the text that essentially 'hit the nail on the head' in describing what was happening to us. 'Even unto this present hour we both hunger and thirst, are naked and are buffeted, and have no certain dwelling place'.

Meanwhile, it had become known that we were in a pocket of huge proportions. The Russians in Pomerania had reached the sea. So we would see whether the troops, encircled and cut off, were still capable of breaking through to the West. This was what many hoped. Others feared that Danzig would be declared a *Festung*. As such it would have to be defended, as usual, 'to the last drop of blood'. The fighters wore grey, not brown, tunics. The pause for breath granted us by the enemy seemed to be ending. The Russians again began firing registration fire. Streets, embankment and houses were under not very heavy, but regular, fire from heavy weapons.

As I was standing outside the door of the house, a *Ratschbum* shell hit the lintel. Apart from a tiny splinter that hit me in the mouth, nothing else happened. But it was puzzling where the shell had come from. The house was covered by the embankment in such a way that it could not be hit by direct fire. So the firing must be coming not from the bank immediately opposite, but from further up or down river. That too seemed to indicate that the Russians were up to something in our sector. In fact, during the night of 29 January the enemy had crossed the Vistula in the sector of our neighbouring battalion in Deutsch-Westfalen. They were then in the village with at least one company. Reserves, which could still have thrown them out again during the night, were of course not available.

The Division decided to take our battalion out of the line. Then, next day, it would be possible to carry out a local attack, with the aim of driving the enemy back on to the right hand bank of the Vistula. A meeting and the issue of orders took place in the regimental command post in the Schwenten forester's house. A crowd of senior people was present, as befitted the occasion. *Vater* Dorn outlined what he described as a 'shitty' situation. That was to be expected from the conditions of the terrain. Since the plain in the glacial valley of the Vistula offered no cover, consideration had only been given to an attack from the north and south, along the street, moving from house to house. Two assault units were to work their way forward through the bushes on the bank on the far side, that is the enemy side, of the embankment directly on the riverbank. I was ordered to take command of the group advancing from the south. So this was the *Himmelfahrts-Kommando*, that, evidently, I was not to escape (translator's note: *Himmelfahrt* in German means 'Ascension' in the sense of Christ's ascension into heaven. Its ironic use here is echoed by the term *Himmelfahrts-Strasse* ['Ascension Street'] used in Auschwitz for the road leading to the gas chambers.) I said *Jawohl* and did not show any fear.

As we were taking our leave, I thought that I could sense different looks and different handshakes from usual. I could feel that none of them wanted to be in my shoes and were happy that the lot had not fallen to them. The esteem of the artillery commander, the visible respect of the *Panzerjäger* officer and the fatherly kindness of *Oberst* Dorn made me inwardly happy. Then I was truly glad about *Freimuth* Husenett. In the meantime he had relieved Klaus Nicolai as Regimental Adjutant. At 22 he was only one year older than I. He wore the Knight's Cross and the *Goldene Nahkampfspange*, was clean, modest and cheerful. In his soft voice, in a heartfelt and brotherly way, he said, 'Look after yourself'.

How seriously and importantly the operation was regarded by those higher up was indicated by the fact that the battalion was to spend the night in peace in *Schloss* Sartowitz. Sartowitz, some five kilometres behind the frontline, was a trim manor house in the German *Ostland*. The great house was situated in a select spot high over the Vistula valley, on what was once the bank of the glacial valley. The view from the terrace offered a tormentingly beautiful picture across the ice-covered river. There were little villages in the foreground and out to the horizon, was the town of Graudenz, embedded into the fortress above it. But because the great house could be observed by the enemy, and there had been instances of shells hitting the house, for the sake of peace and quiet we preferred the gentleman's residence. It was in a deeper location than the main house and was covered by the trees of the park. In some of its 99 rooms we settled ourselves down.

Before we all went to sleep I gave precise instructions to the NCOs. Then I had to tell the men what awaited them the next day. However, I had to give them confidence. That had never been harder for me to do than it was then. I could not conceal from them the fact that there was only a slim prospect of our survival. But, I said that they should nevertheless reflect that we were always, every one of us, in the hands of God. He would be with us every day, as always. Therefore He would be with us 'tomorrow'. Nothing would happen to us without His willing it, I said. God was 'with us', as it said on the belt buckles we wore next to our bodies.

At 3am, after I had lain for four hours in the deepest sleep, I was woken up. It was a battalion runner. Drowsy with sleep, I tripped over my boots. We had been permitted to allow ourselves the luxury of sleeping in the beds with our boots off. What was the matter, I asked *Hauptmann* Wild. He looked at me and said quietly: 'Don't worry, it's been called off, we're going on with the retreat'.

The enemy had extended their bridgehead and the village of Schwenten had been lost. Our battalion had to retake it. The first target of the attack was a four-sided complex of farm buildings. It was a commanding position on a hill to the south-west of the village, surrounded by woodland 100 metres away from it. Two assault guns were coming up to our support. With my company of only 20 men I had to attack at a right angle to the other battalion. The assault guns remained with them. I had to push forward and draw the attention of the enemy on to me. The battalion with the assault guns would then advance.

The enemy had seen the movement associated with our preparations and let us know of it with fire from an anti-tank gun in the farmyard. The shells exploded on the trees over our heads. But the oaks and beeches were strong and gave us some protection. Our attack began after several salvoes from our artillery and mortars. We came out of the protection of the woodland and immediately came under fire from the anti-tank guns. We went to ground, but the assault guns could be heard. There was consternation among the gun crew who could be clearly seen in the corner of the farmyard. I leapt up and cried *Hurra! Hurra!*

Once we were on the go I did not need to give any more orders. The men were behind me. Walter overtook me because he wanted to be first in the position. The Russians too, perhaps a platoon of them, were running away on the other side of the farm and the anti-tank gun was standing there abandoned. We charged after them and into the farmyard. There were no longer any Russians. Only the gun, the limber and two pathetic Russian horses remained behind. In the limber box the men discovered what the Russians had plundered, namely a whole pile of quarter-kilo pieces of German dairy butter.

As I came out of the farm gate I saw the battalion advancing with the two assault guns. I waved to the approaching platoon and turned round towards the enemy. Some of the men had already turned towards the valley in which the roadside village of Schwenten lay. Along the village street, fleeing in confusion, were a good two companies of Russians. They doubtless felt that they were threatened from the flank. 'Off, down, in there', I shouted and once again the *Hurra!* rang out from the few of us. The enemy, far superior in number, were running away.

In the forester's house, in which a few days before *Oberst* Dorn had been based and where the orders had been given for the counter-attack which had been called off, I set up my command post. It is true that we were in the cellar, whereas the *Oberst* had been on the ground floor. I looked at the room in which the meeting had taken place. A hole, one metre wide, was gaping in the wall. When it hit, it had caught the *Oberst* in the head and shoulder. In the cellar a Russian command post had already been operating. Telephone equipment and half-empty American meat conserves with Cyrillic labels were lying about. And then the room was permeated by the almost indescribable smell of the Russian common soldier, which I can still smell today, but do not think I could begin to analyse. It could be a mixture of damp leather, horse shit, but also possibly the smell of the unwashed.

The main line of resistance had been maintained for two or three days in front of Schwenten. After the departure of *General* Meltzer, the Divisional commander was *Generalleutnant* Drekmann. At noon he visited my command post. In broad daylight he came driving up to the forester's house, along the road, in full view of the enemy, with the red flashes on his overcoat. Outside the house he stopped. It was only with difficulty that he could be persuaded to come down into the cellar. At first I thought, because of the grand way in which he had arrived, that he was over-excited. But the reason for his behaviour soon became clear. He had obviously been knocking back too much cognac. His initial briskness soon passed over into joviality. Then he adopted a patronising and encouraging tone as far as the situation was concerned. When the opportunity presented itself, I mentioned that I was the Regiment's 'last horse in the stable', namely the last *Schützenkompanie* commander to have survived from 14 January. That made no impression on him and he soon drove off again.

Walter shouted loudly after him the wish that a *Ratschbum* would get him. That would teach him the meaning of fear. But luckily for all of us that did not happen. On the contrary, the same afternoon a similarly careless attitude had the result that little *Hauptmann* Hein was not so lucky. He had been called *Freund Hein*, in 1943, by *Oberst* von Eisenhart. Like many others he had also been a friend to me. It was said that, in the school of the neighbouring village, the Divisional commander had held a large officers' meeting. The Russians must have noticed. They radioed to their firing position with the result that there were several dead and wounded including *Hauptmann* Hein. The careless General, however, had remained uninjured.

On 7 February the Russians had pushed us out of the village. I had given up the command post in the forester's house and withdrawn 500 metres up the road to the Maierhof. There a man from the 14th *Panzerabwehrkompanie*, had put paid to a 'Stalin' tank with a Panzerschreck. The main line of resistance then ran along the front of a brick-red so-called *Insthaus*. At the rear were the entrances to the living quarters of the estate workers, the *Instleute*. I lived in the kitchen of that squalid dwelling. Facing the doors to those dwellings was a ramp a metre high, to which I owed my life.

To get some air I stepped through the door on to the ramp, leaving the door open. Every now and then a mortar shell exploded close by. But the ramp was in the blind corner of the building. It seemed to give cover against shell splinters that came from above and also against the dangerous splinters from mortar shells that flew out horizontally. Then, suddenly, a shell exploded very close by. A blow on my chest flung me through the open door back into the room. The men leapt up and surrounded me, helped me up and asked if I was wounded. At first I did not know. Then I saw and could feel that my limbs were in one piece, I could move them and I was not bleeding anywhere.

What had happened? A shell splinter, just the size of a fingernail, had gone through my winter overcoat. It then bored through the 32 page map, which had been folded 16 times, stuck between my winter clothing and my field tunic. The paper of the map, folded many times, had so reduced the momentum of the shell splinter that it had been slowed down before it went through my field tunic. The shell, as it fell, had passed within 20 centimetres of me and the slope of the ramp. The ramp had caught all the shrapnel flying in my direction apart from the one shell splinter that I pulled out of my coat. However, my intention to send home, as war mementoes, the shell splinter and the map that saved my life was fruitless. At that time the post was no longer functioning properly.

The following night I was ordered to lead an attack in order to move the main line of resistance forward a little. Nobody knew where the enemy was. A Russian Maxim machine-gun was popping at us from the rising ground to the east of the forester's house. However, there was to be no preparatory barrage. We were to report and then to drive out the enemy with a shout of *Hurra*. It was a well-known fact that the Russians avoided fighting at night. But the high-ups had evidently forgotten that we too were no longer the heroes of the first years of the war. In spite of everything we went forward.

There was impenetrable darkness. Soon it took all our efforts to keep the leading man in sight. We were shadows and outlines creeping over the snow-covered terrain towards the chattering machine-gun. Every one of the soldiers no doubt felt, as I did, the pounding of his own heart. After a while the enemy machine-gun ceased firing. We got as far as the forester's house, but it too had been abandoned. The enemy had evidently withdrawn of their own accord. We had by then reached the southern edge of the *Tucheler Heide*. With differing degrees of intensity, the enemy went about driving us out of the wooded terrain.

By 11 February we had spent three days and three nights in the woodland and in the snow. We had been without a roof over our heads and without sleep. On the first day the Russians were still trying to advance into the woodland, but then had given up. I had not heard for quite some time the rattling and twittering of infantry weapons in the woodland. Sometimes, when a ricochet whistled into a certain corner of the woodland, it sounded just like singing. 'The little birds in the wood, they sing so wonder-wonderfully' was the line that occurred to me, in romantic longing. But it was not at all romantic just very serious when one of the 'singing' bullets slashed open the flapping leg of my winter trousers. In snowy hollows we tried to snatch a quarter or half an hour of sleep. We did not manage to sleep for longer because, as time passed, the cold, 10 degrees below zero, penetrated our ragged uniforms. In my case there was the added misery that my feet, which had otherwise been warm with walking, threatened to freeze to the soles of my boots. They had turned to ice.

On the evening of 12 February we crept into the Mischke forester's house. It was the only house for miles around. At night it was packed full of soldiers from various units. Following *Hauptmann* Wild's orders I tried to get my people, insofar as they were not outside on sentry duty, together in one room alone. My attempt failed. So I had to go round trying to free up at least a few corners of rooms for us. It was important, because the forester's house was on the front line in our sector. At any moment an enemy assault unit could attack. To be able to repulse it, the unit commander had to have his people together at all times ready for combat at the shortest notice. That, however, was not guaranteed if the members of a large number of different units were lying about, mixed up in the numerous rooms.

In the very first room I met resistance from a *Feldwebel*. The men around him, apparently his people, made room to a certain extent willingly, but he on the other hand remained lying down. I spoke to him sharply and gave him 'as an officer the direct order' to get up immediately and to leave the room with his people. He remained unaffected. 'I will give you two minutes. If you have not obeyed my order by then I shall shoot you!' I did not wait to see the effect of my words, but went to *Hauptmann* Wild, to report the incident to him. Wild sat in the light of my tallow candle, not looking up, and said drily: 'Do what you want'. '*Herr Hauptmann*, I just can't simply shoot the man!' I exclaimed. But *Hauptmann* Wild, the brave man, the fatherly comrade and the pastor, seemed to be at the end of his strength. He did not express an opinion and he took no part in what was agitating me. He shifted on to my shoulders the responsibility for deciding and acting, and once again replied tonelessly and apathetically, 'Do what you want'.

Irresolute and uncertain I turned back, fearing that the chap would still be lying in his corner. That was in fact the case. I could no longer restrain myself. Stirred up to the highest degree, I shouted at him: 'Get up immediately and leave this room, or I shall shoot you on the spot!' Inwardly I was trembling. I wondered whether the chap would obey this order. While my trembling fingers were reaching for my holster, another *Feldwebel*, one of his comrades, intervened to calm and to placate me. Even his words, that the man who was refusing to obey my orders was a tried and tested and excellent soldier, I turned against him, saying that in that case he should know all the better that he had to carry out my orders like any others. But even as I was saying this, and as the *Feldwebel* had pointed out to me, I felt that the behaviour of the man refusing to obey my order could not have any rational cause. He was completely exhausted and at the end of his strength.

What would have happened, if I had shot the man? Nothing would have happened. As in earlier retreats and crisis situations, it had become the duty of senior officers to use weapons in cases of refusals to obey orders. They could shoot the offender immediately and without a court martial. I was therefore, formally, completely within my rights. The facts of the case clearly attested to a refusal to obey orders. Moreover, my commander had expressly given me a free hand. The order was in fact completely well founded. But what were those men doing in our sector? Were they men who had been scattered or were they deserters? To establish which it was, I was much too agitated and did not have the time. I had only time for the shot that would re-establish discipline and order.

But I did not fire! The man was almost as exhausted as I. Probably, just like me, he had not slept during the previous days and nights. He had most likely been overwhelmed by a physical, mental, and spiritual exhaustion that left him no longer in control of his actions. It would have been the same for me, if I had not been an officer, if I had not had to be a leader and if the enormous agitation about the inconceivability of this refusal to obey orders had not then overwhelmed me. A remnant of common sense within me restored my sense of proportion. I gained enough control over myself to be able to ponder whether the insignificance of the case was worth his death. Was it right that my order should be carried out by that man? So I came to the conclusion that I should not allow myself to be guilty of his death, even if I was in every respect justified in doing so, even if it was my duty to do so.

I walked out into the dark of the February night. I was oppressed by the dichotomy of feelings of defeat that my formalistic spirit had suffered. But I was also glad of my victory over that spirit. For one trembling moment, I had held the life of that man in my hand and nearly destroyed it. Outside, the *Feldwebel* comrade of the mutineer joined me and said that I was 'a fine man'. He seemed suddenly to trust me, because he had recognised me as a fellow countryman. Then, in all seriousness, he proposed that I should travel to Vienna with him. He had, he said, a motorcycle and sidecar, his unit had been wiped out and he had had 'enough'. With me as an officer, he said, we would easily get through the *Feldgendarmerie* checkpoint and through the *Heldenklaus*. I was speechless. Should I now have this man arrested, taken away, and shot? I shook my head, uncomprehendingly, without saying a word. He disappeared.

15 February is the date of my last letter to Mother that actually reached her, in which it says:

> The past four weeks have made inhuman demands on us. We continue to be in the hardest action on a Soviet bridgehead south-west of Graudenz. Enormous physical exertions through snow, rain, cold, marches, all combined with the most intense moral stress, have almost completely 'done for' us few, who are still left from 14 January. But the good God in heaven has been so clearly protecting

me. In the meantime I have been wounded for the fifth time, apart from that wound in 1943 which was only slight. Daily events have been a strain, the like of which did not even happen in the summer of 1944. It was in Döberitz that I last had my hair cut. Since 14 January I have not cleaned my teeth. I have not had a shave for a long time. You will be able to imagine how attractive I look. But we want to keep on holding out, if it leads to everything being better in the end, and then it means that we can all meet again happily in our homeland. Hopefully Rudi will get out of East Prussia in one piece! On the way I met people from his *Ersatz* unit from Rippin, including an officer cadet colleague from Hilversum... I am writing this letter in gloves... Yesterday, with the first post since New Year, I received a letter from Father and two from Rudi. Tell Liesl thanks very much for her good wishes on my birthday.

On 16 February we were marching in a northerly direction towards Dubelno. Clouds of shrapnel had indicated that the enemy attack was going to continue. It was always the same. A couple of hours, perhaps a night, perhaps two days without pressure from the enemy. Then the Russians attacked again, pressing and pushing us back. Meanwhile, we had been driven on to the Tucheler Heide. For more than four weeks we had had 'no abiding city'. Around noon I had a splinter from a mortar shell in my right upper arm. It came through the open window of a farmhouse in which we were resting. It was of course too small a wound for a military hospital. But, for all that, the feeling of nerves that had gripped me since morning fell away from me. I then knew why.

You could see that on the other side of the Vistula a captive balloon was sitting enthroned in the sky, untouched. There were no German fighter aircraft in its vicinity. Our *Luftwaffe* had long since vanished into thin air. Only on the next morning did a German fighter aircraft attempt to approach the balloon. But it was driven away by hundreds of Russian flak and other guns.

Meanwhile the cold had broken. On 17 February we were lying in fresh trenches in front of the Graudenz-Könitz railway line, on a tongue of land a kilometre wide, in the midst of woodland. It was a typical stretch of countryside for the Tucheler Heide. The Russians had pushed forward through the woods. To the north and to the south they had reached the railway line. Until then we had stood firm. But we were then shelled by a series of salvos from German *Nebelwerfer* that the enemy had captured. The enormous detonations of their heavy calibre guns made the still, frozen earth shake.

We pressed ourselves against the walls of our trenches and wished that the attack were over, so that such hellish music might come to an end. Despite the mortar fire, which had had a very demoralising effect, the enemy only advanced hesitantly. It was easy to keep them at a distance with targeted rifle fire. Once again my *Sturmgewehr* with its U-shaped back sight and the flat pin was proving its worth.

The next day the railway line in our sector was given up. We withdrew over a bridge that had been prepared for blowing. It led over an artificial ravine. Nobody knew who was supposed to be blowing up the bridge, or when and from where it was to be done. So it was a matter of climbing down 25 metres into the ravine and clambering up again on the other side. Actually I saved myself the trouble and ran across the bridge, feeling foolhardy. Certainly, once across, I became aware of how careless I had been.

In the next village there was a short halt. The halt was rudely interrupted when out of a haystack a Russian machine-pistol sprayed fire and two of our people fell, hit by the bullets. From a little distance away I saw an *Unteroffizier* having a go with the *Sturmgewehr*, whereupon a Russian came crawling out. Evidently he was making a move to flee. The corporal fired once more, and the treacherous deed was atoned for.

Some days later *Hauptmann* Wild assigned me to his staff, if you could still call it that. But he doubtless wanted to do me a good turn or to protect me a little, because in fact I was the last officer who was still there from 14 January. In any event it did not matter to me, I simply moved about here and there on foot. Whether I commanded the 10 men of my company or supported the *Hauptmann* in commanding the 50 men of the battalion, there was no essential difference. We pulled back further. On a narrow country road that ran through the heath in the middle of splendid woodland, we were still about 20 kilometres south of Preussisch-Stargard and 60 kilometres away from the Baltic at Danzig.

On 24 February *Hauptmann* Wild celebrated his 35th birthday. The kitchen *Unteroffizier* had not forgotten him. He brought a cake into the forester's house in which we were resting. It had been part-baked during the retreat. But he only produced it after he had fed us with roast pork and no one could eat any more. Sitting in the deserted house, in a velvet-covered grandfather's chair belonging to the forester, I stretched my legs out on to the leather armchair opposite. Exhaustion overwhelmed me. I was wakened by the explosion of an anti-personnel mine. It was two o'clock in the morning. An enemy patrol must have trodden on it. 'What the hell', I thought, 'the enemy never attacks in the dark at night'. Besides, I could not care less. I wanted to sleep. 'You can all go hang!' Drowsy with sleep, those were my thoughts.

At the northern edge of the Tucheler Heide, a little beyond the wood, the battalion had moved in to a wide sector. We could only hold on at key points. On the morning of 26 February we had repulsed an enemy patrol. Since then the enemy had not pushed on after us. They were obviously exhausted and needed a breather. They stayed in the wood, preparing for another assault. Because of that, we hoped that a few days' rest would be granted to us. Almost overnight the snow had disappeared. The warm March sun had sucked it up, and a mild wind was blowing over the fields, all newly brown. In the open meadow, tiny shoots of green seemed to be sprouting. My imagination seized on to an illusion of reawakening life. Our winter clothing was handed back to the baggage-train.

The railway station at Gross-Wollental was the battalion key point. It lay furthest to the left. It was occupied by the remnants of 'my' 1st Company. There were still 15 of them, commanded by a *Leutnant* who had just come from Germany. They had installed themselves in the railway buildings and had a good field of fire. Within the solid, thick walls they felt themselves to be protected, for the time being. It was the typical brick station of a smaller town, such as could be found in a good 1,000 stations in northern Germany. A little while before it had still been in operation. The air still smelled just like a railway station.

The small farmhouse that housed the command post had thin walls. The only room was on the southern side facing the enemy. Since we had already grown apathetic as a result of our exertions, comfort had won the day over the regulation efforts to provide security. Instead of taking up our quarters in the stable on the southern side of the house, we used the room facing the enemy. There were two beds. Men and officers slept in them, in shifts, of course without being able to take off their boots or clothes. We had not been used to such peace for a long time. I could count on my fingers the days and nights that I had not slept without my boots. That continued during the war of movement, the trench warfare, or whenever else, in that campaign.

In my dreams I heard the hiss of a hand-grenade and the nasty quiet fizzing of the fuse before it exploded. I was dreaming that an enemy assault unit was in the process of digging us out, and had thrown a hand-grenade into the room. Still half asleep I jumped out of bed and the laughter of my comrades brought me fully awake. But there was an element of truth in the dream. An infantry gun shell had come through the wall over my head and the headboard of the bed. It had stuck into the opposite wall of the room. Mortar was still crumbling down from the wall.

On 4 March 1945 at 8.05am, a forward observer reported heavy enemy movements from Gross-Wollental moving northwards. At 8.15am, accompanied by intense aircraft activity, there began a heavy enemy preparatory barrage, particularly on the sector of our left-hand neighbour, Grenadier Regiment 7. Following that, the enemy, supported by strong armoured forces, attacked from the direction of Gross-Wollental and Neubuchen towards the railway line.

That was how the regimental history described the start of the day. As I recall, the neighbouring sector on the left was under heavy fire. The commanding high ground to the north of Gross-Wollental lay behind us to the left, and fell into enemy hands. The battalion, that is, our 15 men, received orders to re-take the high ground. First we had to pull back a little to strike. Then we moved up to where the artillery positions were, in order to be able to move in a semi-circle round the high ground that had been lost. In the meantime the enemy were giving the terrain a vigorous pounding with heavy weapons. In particular they fired on the farmhouses that lay on their own. They rightly suspected firing positions to be there. They had also spotted our movement while we were approaching the open heights. At the last farm at the foot of the heights there were field howitzers under trees that were firing on them.

From the enemy positions came the thumping of the mortars. All round we could hear shells whistling towards us and exploding. From early morning I had felt, 'in my water', a sense of apprehension. So I was almost relieved when what I had dreaded actually happened. I had thrown myself to the ground. But I jumped up too soon, in order to move towards the house, thinking there might be better cover there. I must obviously not have heard the mortars fire because of the sound of the explosions. The severe pain of a considerable flesh wound in my left buttock forced me to the ground. I painfully crawled towards the house. I felt a lack of air that worried me. I knew I must have been shot through the lungs. One of my runners dragged me into the house where I was laid down on a bundle of straw. A medic from the artillery bandaged me up. I was taking shallow breaths, gasping and struggling for air.

The best chance of getting to the rear and to a dressing station was to go on the artillery food vehicle. It had just arrived at the firing position. It was to take me with it. But it took another quarter of an hour that seemed like an eternity, until it was ready. Then I was lifted up on to the little wagon. The loading area was too small to lie down, so I had to sit up with the driver. But I hung rather than sat on the driver's seat, at the same time clinging on to the driver and to an iron armrest. A wild drive began. Enemy aircraft flew over us. The driver could not risk using roads and lanes. The horse was galloping in terror. The wagon bumped and tossed across country over meadows and fields, furrows and trenches. It was sheer torture. At the staff of another unit the driver unloaded me. A doctor gave me a tetanus injection. Sometime later I was loaded up into a *Sanka* i.e. a medical vehicle. After an absolutely endless journey I arrived at the field hospital section of the 35th Division, our neighbouring division.

There, in a small village school, the wounded as they arrived were laid on bundles of straw. A medical officer sorted us out according to urgency, not according to rank. All men are equal before God and before the court, but also before the surgeon's knife. Of the two schoolrooms, one served as an operating room, the other as a preparation room. In the latter I was undressed and, by means of injections, somehow stabilised. Scarcely had the surgeon finished with one man, than he got to work on me. Half on my belly and half on my right side, I lay on the operating table. It was only a local anaesthetic under which the operation was carried out. The doctors asked me questions and forced me to answer them. Meanwhile, I could hear my breath bubbling out of the entrance wound, and could feel them working to close it. How long that lasted I have no idea. According to what they said, they were doing plastic surgery on my skin. The effect of the anaesthetic had already begun to wear off by the time the larger shell splinter from my behind and another lodged immediately next to my spine, were taken out. The Staff Medical Officer, Dr Brunn, asked whether I wanted to throw the shell splinters away. I replied, 'Too bloody true'. The scars would be mementoes enough for me. The shell splinter in my lungs I would carry for the rest of my life.

After the operation I was moved into a small room. In one of the two beds was the man wounded in the stomach, who had been operated on before me. I was able to have a closer look at him and to recognise him. He was the commander of the reconnaissance battalion of the 35th Infantry Division. He was a *Major* and a holder of the Knight's Cross. From time to time we spoke to each other. But I had the strange thought almost immediately that there was little hope for him.

Even so, they also seemed to consider me to be a serious case. The *Major* and I were nursed by a particularly capable *Obergefreiter* medic. On his tunic was the *Kriegsverdienstkreuz* First Class, which testified to his quality. Every quarter of an hour, I estimated, he came back into the room and administered injections in my upper thigh. During the two days I spent there, I must have had, I estimated, getting on for 80 injections. For years afterwards, the area in which they had been administered above my knees was numb.

The following night the *Major* reached the end of the road. He was increasingly struggling for air. It seemed to me that he had a heart attack. The medic came with Dr Brunn and they brought an oxygen machine but could not help the poor man. I was then alone. But I was myself too weak to be significantly affected by the death struggle of my comrade. The following day the medic told me that the previous night an armoured breakthrough had been made. The enemy tanks, he said, had come very close, and they had feared that they would have to let us fall into Russian hands. According to rumour, the two chaplains from our Division, the *ESAK* and the *KASAK*, i.e. the abbreviations for Protestant and Catholic 'anti-sin guns' had been 'snatched'.

On 8 March, after four days, I was at last transported away. A medical motor vehicle drove me and other wounded men to a station. It must have been the one at Preussisch-Stargard, where we were put in cattle trucks and laid down on straw. During the loading process some wretch of a medic stole my pistol. That filled me with the overpowering fury of the helpless. I was glad that immediately after I had been wounded I had, at his suggestion, handed over my watch to my runner Franz. In Danzig, *Sankas* took us to the Technical High School in Langfuhr. It had been set up as a military hospital. At first I lay with about 50 other seriously wounded men in a large hall. I was in a pitiful state, because I was getting no air. After a short examination, I was immediately taken by porters into the operating room. The porters were French prisoners of war obediently doing what was expected of them. From the map case, which had not been stolen from me, I brought out my remaining cigarettes, that I certainly no longer needed. Gratefully, I gave them to the Frenchmen.

The operating room resembled a gigantic human abattoir. A haze of vapours of blood, pus, sweat and filth, from the dressings and disinfectants filled the room. On several tables operations, amputations, and dressings were performed. A doctor had just finished the circular cut around an arm, then began an upper arm amputation. All that I saw, though only half-conscious. Acting as theatre nurses were Dutch medical students. Doubtless, they were 'compulsory labour', and were getting some dreadful practical experience. I had to place my arm round the neck of one of these kindly and helpful nurses. Dizzy and weak, no longer used to sitting upright, I had my lungs tapped. An increasing lack of air, and the unbearable smell, had made me so apathetic that I scarcely noticed the short, severe pain when the doctor inserted the cannula. The intervention produced an aspiration of 700 cubic centimetres. It was no wonder that I had feared I was slowly suffocating. I was then able to breathe again during the following two weeks. The next aspiration produced another half-litre of fluid. After that there were only 20 cubic centimetres. Eventually the interventions were no longer necessary.

By then the hospital needed the room. So after about 10 days there was a great visitation headed by a General of the medical service. They sorted the wounded and had to empty some beds. In his numerous entourage there was one corpulent medic. He could have been a factory manager. He had doubtless only recently been caught by the *Heldenklau*, and had gone to ground in the medical service. When the swarm of doctors had passed my emergency bed, I asked that medic to hand me the inflatable pillow from the foot of the bed. He replied that I should ask someone else because he was not responsible for doing that.

I could scarcely believe my ears, and lost my temper. There I was, lying pale and hollow cheeked, hair on end from lying down, and uncut for four months, unshaven and generally run to seed, and obviously seriously wounded on a wooden bedstead. On the seat next to it was my field tunic with all its medals, including the silver wound insignia. In front of me was that fat man, with prosperity written all over him. He was all dressed up, his hair slicked down, and he had the nerve to say that he was not responsible for carrying out one small service consisting of handing over one small thing. Never before during my service as an officer had I lost control of myself before a subordinate, yelled at him, and pulled rank on him, as I had with this man.

With the last remnants of strength and breath remaining in my wretched body, bellowing, I unleashed the full fury of the frontline fighter against the 'damned' people behind the lines. 'We are letting ourselves get shot to pieces out there on the front line, and this swine, who has never heard the whistle of a bullet in his life, is not responsible for handing an inflatable pillow to a seriously wounded man!' I was going mad. Tears were choking my words. I was no longer in control of myself. Some gentlemen from the visitation at first were shocked and indignant. Then some staff came over to calm me down, while the travesty of a Samaritan hurriedly left the room.

Even more than the days, the nights in that room were full of dread. Every evening I was given morphia, but its numbing effect only lasted for a few hours. By one o'clock in the morning I would wake up in the stained bed and wait patiently for an unwilling nurse, who would get peevish having to clean things up. I had never experienced such an accumulation of misery as I had in that room. A boy near to me asked again and again for water. Shot in the stomach, he had recently been operated on and was not allowed to drink. Everybody tried to make him understand that, but failed. One moment when he was not being watched he opened his hot water bottle. I was too weak to be able to warn him as he greedily gulped down the contents. The following morning he was dead. Opposite me, another man had had both his legs shattered. Resigned and quiet, he lay on his bunk. That was the way he died.

On the other hand, those impressions, however depressing they were, gave me courage and I used them to pull myself together. I had no intention of dying. The hope of getting out was germinating in me. Certainly the town was encircled, and certainly I was not fit to be moved. In fact for days I had had a high fever, but that would pass, I hoped, and by ship or by aircraft I surely must be able to get away. I felt a hesitant joy at the fact that evidently I had got away with it again. With the greatest difficulty I managed to scribble some lines to Mother and to Gisela. Gisela received them, but Mother did not.

From there they carried me to a room on the second storey of the building. Six wooden bunks filled the room. My new comrades, all officers, were seriously wounded like me, but obviously over the hill. My right-hand neighbour was Franz Manhart, *Flak-Leutnant* from Grafenberg near Eggenburg in Lower Austria. (He had managed to reach the level of section head in the finance ministry in Vienna). His left upper arm had been shattered but he could hobble. Opposite was the anti-tank *Oberleutnant* Nabert from Schweidnitz, whose left arm had been amputated. As it turned out, we had a whole series of common acquaintances in Schweidnitz, including an actress from the *Landestheater* whom I had seen in Sudermann's *Frau Sorge*. When his dressings were being changed, Nabert's stump gave out such a stench that we regularly felt sick. On the left next to me lay a *Panzer Hauptmann*, whose right upper thigh had been shattered. He tried in vain to move the toes on his foot. Then he was taken to be operated on, and came back without his right leg. After waking up from the anaesthetic he felt with both hands to where his knee had been. He could still feel it. The realisation that he was an amputee hit him like a bolt of lightning. Gasping, he drew the air through his teeth, then, without making a sound, he put his hands over his face in horror. On the evening of 25 March he was taken away by members of his unit. A destroyer had intended to make a run for it during the night, and was to take him along.

As I found out after the war from *Herr* von Garn, our Division also sent a detachment to remove wounded men from the hospital. Obviously the group could not have carried out the order properly, because they did not find me. No doubt they had only been on the ground floor. It is idle to speculate whether I might have been lucky and subsequently reached Denmark, with the regiment, on board a ship.

The frontline was approaching. The large pocket had shrunk to a beleaguered town, and declared a *Festung*. An old reserve officer, an invalid from the First World War and teacher by profession, went from room to room. He tried, as a 'NSFO' - National Socialist officer leader - to spread confidence in victory. Nobody took him seriously any more. But I still hoped that I might be transported away. Exactly three weeks after I had been wounded, my high fever fell overnight to normal. The crisis had passed. The euphoria of the convalescent came over me. The doctor declared me to be capable of being moved.

But by then it was too late. The harbour was blockaded. Two days before, it was said, one last hospital ship had sailed out. But it had been torpedoed and had sunk with hundreds of wounded men on board. In actual fact, it was the *Wilhelm Gustloff.* It was sunk by a Russian submarine. There were several thousand refugees on board. Two days previously, when I was unable to be moved, I had struggled against my fate. Once again I had to learn my lesson and resign myself to the inevitable.

An elderly *Leutnant* from the supplies services, had been laid in the *Hauptmann's* bed. He was very drunk and had obviously been injured by a bomb splinter while in that state. Soon afterwards he died, still in the state of intoxication in which no doubt he had spent the last days and hours of his life. When he was taken out, I asked for his pistol. I still had the thought of making use of it.

In the meantime Russian and British aircraft were bombing the town. Bombs fell day and night. Heavy artillery shells landed. In the park of the high school, artillery and flak went into position. The explosions of the impacts, very close by, and the sharp cracks of our own guns and cannons as they fired went on alternately. The front was right there. We lay helpless, stuck in bed, on the topmost floor of the building. On the doctors' rounds we asked if it was possible for us to be placed in the cellar. The station medical officer replied with the words: 'You're surely not just a bit afraid, gentlemen?' Saying that, he smiled, but at the same time remained for safety's sake under the cover of the lintel of the door.

He evidently considered us to be some of those guilty for the war. He perhaps believed that we should face our just punishment in the form of a bomb. He was not allowed to gainsay it, for instance by taking us down into the cellar. Even the ward medic no longer very often summoned up the courage to climb from the cellar to the upper ward. When it was absolutely necessary he brought up food. While butter and other provisions were supposedly stored in great quantities in food depots, they dished out only thin carrot soup to us. Sometimes there were a few slices of bread spread with cheese and marmalade. Right in front of our eyes, however, the medic would still be biting pieces off a block of chocolate. When taken to task about it, he declared shamelessly that none had been issued for the wounded.

All those symptoms indicated the end to be imminent. It was a collapse that was taking place around and within us. Had we deserved that fate? Should they leave us there to kick the bucket like miserable dogs? Should they leave us to the tender mercies of the Bolsheviks? Bitterness and disappointment came over me, and doubtless also over my comrades. There was silence in the room. Nobody spoke. Everyone, lying there so wretchedly on the floor, was alone at a turning point in his life.

On 27 March 1945, the Tuesday before Easter, a bright spring morning dawned. Neither doctor nor medic appeared. The enemy artillery fire had become more and more intense. A direct hit on the wall of the building sent window-frames and panes flying crackling into the room. Then rifle fire could be heard.

Thus it was finally clear that no one else was to get out. We would be consigned to an uncertain fate. But why, I thought, should they not leave me alone there? Who was I, to be able to claim that the course of my life should be only smooth and good? I realised that I had considered myself to be too important. I realised that I had been just a tiny interchangeable part in the massive German war machinery. But by then it was obviously grinding to a halt. I reached once again for the pistol. I took hold of it, but put it down again. The thought of suicide, was at first as strong and serious as it had been that time in Powielin. But by then it was done with.

Suddenly I knew that an important part of my life was certainly coming to an end, with us losing the war. However, life even if perhaps under completely different circumstances, would go on. It would still be worth continuing to live, but not to give in to oneself. A wonderful clarity came over me. Praying, I experienced the certainty that God would not leave me in the lurch, and that he would be with us, with me. I thought long and hard about my Mother. Lost in all those thoughts I detached myself more and more, finally completely, from the situation.

Then another medic appeared. He had orders to collect up pistols and medals. He announced that the hospital had been surrendered to the Russians. He said that two doctors and ten medics had remained behind with 800 severely wounded men. 'The white flag', he said, 'had already been raised'.

Another hour passed. Franz Mahnart stood at the window and reported back on the situation. He saw our infantry retreating and the Russians moving closer and closer. Meanwhile, again and again, there were moments of anxious quiet. Finally voices could be heard, announcing an approach from room to room. Andreyev shouted out several times. They were the same dull, throaty sounds that I had heard for the first time three years before in the woods at Upolosy. The voices had exactly the same effect on me as they had then. Both wings of the door were opened as the first Russian entered. His machine-pistol at the ready, he stood at the doors and looked around. Meanwhile, outside, next to the house, German shells were still falling.

Part IV
Captivity, then Freedom

12

April 1945-April 1946: Captivity and recovery from wounds

Germany surrenders; recovery from wounds; transferred between camps; illness during autumn/winter; first year in captivity - aged 22 years

In Holy Week of 1945 the destruction of the old German town of Danzig was completed. It was the eve of that dreadful night, the 27 March. On that fearful night, the city of Danzig and all the Vistula area were in flames. An eyewitness report stated: 'From as far away as Hela, a wall of flames and smoke, 3000 to 4000 metres high, could be seen over the city'. It had been caused by air-raids with high explosive and incendiary bombs. The book *Unvergänglicher Schmerz*, or 'Endless Agony' is a record of the history of Danzig's fateful year of 1945, by Peter Poralla. The section *Das Inferno* (p. 378) reads as follows:

The enormous development of heat in burning Danzig prevented German units becoming established in the town. So it was only at the entrance to Danzig, between the Schichau Wharf, the Olivaer Tor, taking in the Hagelsberg and the Bischofsberg, that a weak defensive line was constructed. Our soldiers were fighting there doggedly against the superior might of the enemy. There was always the certainty that every minute's delay to the Soviet advance meant that some women and girls were saved from being raped. There was the possibility too that children and old people could flee. In actual fact they still succeeded in getting thousands every day across the bay to Hela and from there across the Baltic into the safer West. There are daily records showing the movement of 46,000 persons.

On the evening of 27 March the Russians succeeded in breaking through the *Schicherowgasse* to the *Hansaplatz*, and from there to the main railway station. Our soldiers were at the end of their strength. They were short of ammunition and weapons. There were no more replacements for the dead and wounded. The German Army command therefore decided to retreat to the Mottlau, and finally across the Vistula towards Heubude and Plenendorf. Danzig was occupied by the Red Army.

On Good Friday, 30 March 1945, Danzig's fate was sealed. For Danzig's population, and the many refugees from East Prussia and Pomerania, there began a *via dolorosa* of indescribable horror. The Soviets, and a little later the Poles, took their revenge on the innocents, on children, on women, on old people. That was done with unimaginable atrocity and brute force. What the people in Danzig at that time had to undergo, nobody can begin to imagine. Thousands, oppressed and beaten, committed suicide. Many women and children begged and pleaded, 'Shoot me!' Entire families were wiped out, shot or murdered, because they wanted to protect children from being raped, or were not quick enough to hand over their jewellery. Robbery, plunder and rape were committed day after day by the Soviets, and by the Poles who turned up later. They suffered death through hunger and diseases for weeks and months on end. That was the fate of the people who did not succeed in fleeing across the sea.

One in every four inhabitants of Danzig lost their lives as a result of war and from outrages committed by the Soviets and the Poles. They were starved to death during the Polish occupation. They died in forced labour camps. They died because they were not given proper help when they fell ill. At least as high must be the number of victims among the refugees from East Prussia and Pomerania who remained in Danzig.

That the city of Danzig was an ocean of fire was also described in the Divisional history. *Hauptmann* Franz Hrabowsky described it there and added to his description of the misery of the refugees: 'In addition the women, concerned for the lives of their children, begged the soldiers many times to give up the fight. So it happened that in many places the officers, even using all their authority, did not always succeed in getting their people back out of the cellars. That was supplemented by an eyewitness account in Poralla, according to which in the *Halbe Allee*, and also in the *Grosse Allee*, deserters are said to have been hanged in rows.'

During the next few hours, our rooms were entered again and again by other Russians who behaved very differently. Many threatened us with their weapons. But, in many, you could see something like pity. Young members of the *Komsomol*, perhaps 16 years old, were the worst. One waved his machine-pistol slowly from bed to bed and then stopped in front of Franz Manhardt, aiming at his head. I can still see Franz's profile with the questioning expression on his face, especially the detail of the eyelid of his left eye opening and closing while the young Russian - it seemed to last minutes, but it could only have been seconds - had him in his sights. I can still see too how another held a pistol, a German 08, at *Oberleutnant* Nabert's temple. I can see Nabert turning his eyes upwards in order, in the last second of his life, to look his murderer in the face. But on both occasions the Russians did not pull the trigger. From that I concluded that they obviously did not have a general order to kill wounded men, nor particularly officers.

Almost amusing, when compared with the situations mentioned above, in which you were hovering between life and death, was how our watches were taken away. They were collected up, in a procedure to which the main interest of the individual members of the Red Army seemed to be directed, as they said, *Uhr ist?* Because I had left my service watch behind at my unit when I was wounded, I no longer had a watch, and had to try to express this with gestures of helplessness. That seemed to be incomprehensible to one of the busy plunderers, because, with his index finger on my forehead, he pushed my head back on to the straw filled pillow. Officers also came into our room. I can clearly remember a tall, blond young major who spoke German and was an artilleryman. When he asked how I had been wounded, I replied, to please him, 'by artillery', which in fact did please him.

In conversation one of us said that the war was over for us, to which the major replied that it was only just beginning. In actual fact, at that time many Russians were convinced that with the downfall of Hitler's Germany the capitalist Western powers would then turn against Russia. I found it to be more than a friendly gesture when a captain, before the officers moved on, brought out a bottle of plundered schnapps from his overcoat and reached it over to me in bed. Of course none of us exhausted wounded men would have been capable even of taking one gulp from it. So I hid the bottle in my bunk under the straw mattress.

After some hours of continually being visited by Russians we were pleased that the last assault had passed off so lightly for us helpless men. The fact that we had not yet received any food that day was unimportant. Indeed none of us felt hungry or thirsty. After all we had escaped with our lives. We also did not see anything of the medics who had stayed behind. We understood that none of them risked coming up to us on the second storey. Similarly, little was to be seen of the two doctors. I still know their names and can remember what they looked like. One of them was the Munich surgeon Dr Stadel-Eichel. He was compact in appearance and gave the impression of being busy. The other was a senior doctor from the Greifenwald University Clinic by the name of Dr Wolf. He was tall, slim and with a relaxed manner.

Meanwhile, there was no question of a 'normalisation of conditions' so soon after the hospital was handed over. German shells were still exploding. However, a new development was that the unmistakable smell of burning was spreading through the building. The air in the house was thickening into fumes heavy with smoke. Nobody knew whether the building had been set on fire by German gunfire, or had been set alight by the Russians, or perhaps even by the Poles. It later turned out that it was arson. In fact it was said that, of the 800 seriously wounded men who had remained behind, 150 lost their lives in that fire.

The saviour of the men in our ward was Franz Manhart. It must have been after mid-day and the fumes were apparently preventing the Russians from moving about freely in the building. Franzl took advantage of the opportunity to seek out a way that we could save ourselves. He succeeded in discovering a staircase close to our ward. Although wide, the stairway itself was blocked with the furniture that had been in the rooms before the hospital was set up. Nevertheless, enough space had been left for one man to get through between the banister and the furniture. For us it was a matter of leaving our beds and struggling through that exit to freedom. For Eberhard Nabert and me - I can only remember the two of us - it was a risky undertaking. Neither of us had left his bed since we had been wounded. I was so enfeebled that I could scarcely stand. With little time, I did not know what I should take with me. I can still remember that I only had on my collarless soldier's shirt, and that I put my field tunic on over it. I needed both arms to hold on to the wall and to the banister.

Under Franzl's direction we managed to get out into the open and into a sort of yard. There were remarkable scenes that I can only recall happening in a blur. Wounded men who seemed to have just got out into the open were lying on the bare earth and only crawling or scrabbling about. Others were being taken by helpers, including Russian soldiers, to an undetermined destination. Russians seemed to be still plundering and arguing over plunder. One of them had several wristwatches on his arm. Smoke was still belching from the building. Flames could not yet be seen. The following night, according to an eyewitness account from the book mentioned above, the 'TH' went up in flames. It shared the fate of many buildings that were destroyed by fire only after they had been taken over by the occupation forces.

Free of smoke and fumes was a single storey building that had served as a physics laboratory, as could be seen from the wide windows reaching to the roof. That area had similarly been set up with basic bunks that were all occupied of course. Because of the fire it had been necessary to fill each bed with two or three wounded men. I had the good fortune to have to share such a bed with only one comrade. In the next three days and nights it was our refuge. My comrade must have been wounded in the head, because they had bandaged his skull in such a way that only one eye, his nose, and his mouth could still be seen. When he spoke, he spoke incoherently, but soon I could tell, at least by his accent, that he must be from Vienna. When during the night he was rambling in his coma, I began to recognise him more and more, and finally I was able to identify him as a comrade from my own regiment. He was *Leutnant* Robert Kelca, who had relieved me in the summer of 1944 as second orderly officer with *Major* von Garn. It was a sad, but unusual reunion.

It was dreadful that German women and girls had hidden themselves between and under the emergency beds. Of course, the Russians noticed. Again and again a Russian would come past, track down a woman and wave or drag her out. According to their temperament, the women would be led out of the room by their violators either resisting or resigned. The next day or the day after that the Russians were looking for men who had not been wounded who might have been able to go to ground among us. One Russian went from bed to bed and ordered, *Aufstehen*, which for most of us was not possible, whereupon he shouted, *Schlaffen*, after which we were allowed to stretch out again. I have to say that no healthy man was among the wounded. That was on Easter Sunday.

Women continued to hide in the room, and when their torturers had let them go, returned to us again. A certain Friedl obviously felt particularly attached to me. On Easter Sunday, after something dreadful had apparently happened to her, she came back into the room, visibly overflowing with emotion. Without a word she dashed over to me.

In the week after Easter we were transported to the complex of the Medical Academy. It seemed to be an intact hospital and not a temporary military hospital as the 'TH' had been. We were moved over there in *Sankas*. The drivers were Russians, but the porters were German prisoners. As we were being loaded up and unloaded we were surrounded by Polish civilians who followed the proceedings with hostility.

It is true that Danzig had not possessed a university, but as well as the Technical High School it had had this Medical Academy, where it was possible to study medicine before the 'collapse'. Head of Surgery was Professor Klose, an old gentleman. His senior registrar Dr Johanssen was middle aged. The rounds of those two gentlemen provided a welcome change. As civilian doctors in a university clinic, the operation of a military hospital was strange to them. They carried out their work as they had been accustomed to do and as the conquerors permitted. There were even private consultations.

Professor Klose, as we found out, enjoyed a measure of respect in the eyes of the Russians. In 1932 he had operated for acute appendicitis on the Russian State

President Kalinin who had been on a cruiser on the way to a state visit to Sweden. Professor Klose, a worthy and corpulent gentlemen, told us that he spent his summer holidays in Pechtoldsdorf near Vienna, where he had a house. One day he reported - but this was certainly not true - that the express train connection from Danzig to Vienna had been re-established. The senior registrar Johanssen was a cheerful, bright man who shared our pleasure when a cure was progressing well. From the conversations I had, I recall the theme of the future, which, in accordance with the euphoria of the convalescent, appeared to us in rosy hues. Conversing with Dr Klose and Dr Johanssen, I told them about my parents' parsonage and told them that I, too, would most want to study theology.

We did not stay long in the Medical Academy. Instead of the many Russians, who at the beginning continued to come, then it was Poles in some kind of official capacity. The hospital was evidently taken over by a kind of Polish civilian administration. Various commissions came, of which it was said that they were 'Lublin' Poles, that is, they belonged to the wing of the Polish resistance that was allied to Russia. I can recall a civilian doctor who had a seven-figure number tattooed on his lower arm. He showed it to us and said that he had got it in a concentration camp. In the Third Reich we had heard by hearsay of the existence of such camps, above all Dachau. But we knew nothing at all of their extent and of what their inmates had to suffer. At one of those inspections by Poles, a German-speaking Communist was present. He had fun rocking on my bed in order to hurt me. He succeeded, too. But I was even more astonished at the sadistic temperament of a man expressing itself in such a way.

From the shell splinter injury on my left buttock an abscess had formed. It required opening by a lengthy cut at the top of my upper thigh. Today I cannot recall whether this intervention was carried out while we were still in the 'TH' or whether it was carried out by Dr Johanssen in the Academy. But I do remember that afterwards for some weeks I was only able to lie with my leg drawn up. There was as yet no question of getting out of bed, especially as I was also really weakened by hunger. In the sick room, food was an important topic of conversation. Doubtless it was a sign that we were getting better. We imagined what sort of celebration meals we would have if, with God's help, we were once again able to eat them.

It must have been about 20 April that we were moved in cattle wagons by rail to Thorn. That was about 150 kilometres away up the Vistula. In Thorn there still remained from the war a large barracks camp, in which Allied prisoners of war had been held after the German victories. So the camp was filled with us, the final losers. As far as I could establish, as well as soldiers and officers who had been taken prisoner uninjured, the camp also came to house many wounded and sick men. Dysentery and typhus were rife. Those who had become sick with those diseases were isolated in their own barracks. From them, day after day, were brought out in the morning the bodies of those men who had died the previous night. Most of the camp inmates were dystrophic, recognisable by their oedemas due to hunger, by swollen legs and faces. On their arrival in the camp, both the healthy and the sick had to go into the sauna, the *banja*. No consideration was given to fever and the danger of pneumonia. I saw wounded men, running a temperature of 40 degrees, who had to go into the hot sauna and afterwards would lie for hours on end in the train on the way to the barracks.

The wounded not only died of dysentery and typhus, but also, it seemed to me, simply of debility due to their wounds and a lack of sufficient nourishment. In our sick barracks, in which I had ended up with Franzl Manhart, the thin soup handed out twice a day, by way of food, was distributed out of a pot. The pot, after it had been brought in, was set up in the barrack block, and then every man received his dollop from the ladle into his canteen. The many men who were confined to their beds were served their food by medics. One thing remains unforgettable to me. In that barrack block officers and men were not separated. One comrade was at the point of death. The medic, who had seen this, quickly put next to his pillow the canteen of the man who was lying at his last gasp. After the wounded man was dead, the medic hurriedly removed the canteen. In that way he got a second portion for himself. Even today I can see the scene. The medic lurked there watching the man, who was still alive. Then, after the man's life was over, he tucked into the dead man's soup ration.

After our arrival in the camp and before we were put into the barracks I had lain in one of the several Finnish tents which were provided for seriously wounded men. The Finnish tents were made of plywood and were taller than a man, so that the people lay in two layers over each other. I lay in the lower layer and I remember a Latvian *SS Leutnant* who lay diagonally above me. His arm had suffered paraplegia and dropped everything down. It was terrible, because his arm was not cleaned. Beside me there lay another *Kriegsfreiwilliger* Latvian officer. His Christian name was Antons. He had had one leg amputated and in the other had an extensive flesh wound. But he had still kept his leg. As well as his native language, Antons spoke fluent German and Russian. So I was able to have some good conversations with him. He was completely without illusions in contemplating his future. He was enormously collected and self-controlled. As a Soviet citizen who had opposed the Bolsheviks, he might expect their revenge and a completely uncertain future. The Russian medical officer, a major, who came on his rounds once a day, was called Raskolnikov. His hair was already grey and he had a moustache. We could tell how to a certain extent he 'put up with' the misery which surrounded him. But he clearly regretted that he was not able to give better help.

Time alone had been left to heal my wounds. There were neither medicines nor fresh dressings. I was urged by the German doctor to diligently practise stretching my left leg. A final test tap revealed that there was no more coming from the injury to my lungs. In Thorn, in the barracks, I was allowed to get out of bed and could move around the camp with a single crutch. As the doctor had threatened that he would sit on my crooked leg if I did not soon stretch it out again, I carried out the exercise diligently. Slowly the condition of my leg returned to normal.

In the camp at Thorn for the first time we came into contact with political propaganda. On large banners were written so-called 'sayings'. They were mostly words of Lenin or Stalin, with which we were confronted. 'The Hitlers come and go, but the German people, the German state, will remain', went one Stalin quote. It had a surprisingly prophetic ring to it. As we received no kind of news or situation reports, we knew nothing of the progress of the war or even about the death of the *Führer*.

Towards noon on 8 May 1945, it is true that the camp loudspeaker quite unexpectedly announced to us that the war was over. Germany, it said, had 'unconditionally surrendered'. Sometime afterwards the sentries appeared also to have heard the news. They celebrated the event in their own way, by firing their ammunition off into the air. For us, this was not without its dangers, because ricochets were buzzing through the air and bullets came through the wooden walls of the barracks. We, the conquered, meanwhile, lay on the floor of the barracks or on the sandy ground of the camp, scrabbling for safety on the ground. Hopefully it was for the last time.

The camp complex included a sports ground, at the edge of which the convalescent officers lay in Finnish tents. I often visited them to get a change and to exchange ideas. They were waiting to be transported away. No-one dared to think that some would be released and sent home. Perhaps one small *Hauptmann* would be lucky. Both his lower legs had been amputated below the knee, and he had thus become even smaller than he had otherwise been at his scant 5 foot 2 inches. He moved around on his hands and knees and made tiny leaps just like a sick frog.

Among the closed circle of the officers there was still the accustomed politeness. You addressed each other with *Herr*, whereas elsewhere it was soon the fact that you were addressed as *du* by a 'class-conscious proletarian'. In the company of those officers was a girl of 20, pretty as a picture, dazzlingly blonde, with bright blue eyes. She was the daughter of General Lasch, the commandant of *Festung* Königsberg, who had surrendered there. I wondered where and how such a girl could have survived the first assault.

The Thorn camp was so gigantic that, with my limited sphere of movement, I was not able to get an idea of the extent of it. It was said that 30,000 men lay within its barbed wire fences. Every few day transports of ambulant prisoners left. They had been gathered into groups of a few hundred men and had left the camp. In Thorn, incidentally, I had met another man from Stockerau by the name of Franz Heinz. We had exchanged addresses and I had given him a slip of paper for my relatives, as I suspected that he, because he was only a private soldier, would be released earlier than I would, because I was an officer. It actual fact he was released as early as 1945 and my parents received the news I was alive only on Christmas Eve, 24 December.

As it turned out, the next destination of the marching column was Graudenz, some 55 kilometres away. But the march had to be made on foot. There could have been 500 to 1,000 men who set off, after the fashion of the Red army, each section consisting of five men. At the head there marched some 30 officers from *Oberstleutnant* to *Leutnant* with quite varying amounts of baggage. The gentlemen who had surrendered and had been taken prisoner uninjured had generally a lot of baggage. I and others only possessed the little we had been able to salvage from the military hospital in Danzig and had been able to supplement during the course of the following weeks. I had only the underclothes I was wearing, my uniform tunic and trousers, a haversack and canteen and an overcoat. Added to those, I believe, were a toothbrush, my pay-book, my identification disc and a couple of photos in my old plastic wallet.

Franzl Manhart had already been allocated to an earlier transport and we had therefore been separated. Another comrade whom I had found in Thorn I had lost again. He was Dr Walter Rath, a Viennese whose home address was *Hütteldorferstrasse* 333. Rath had studied Latin and Greek, was an educated

Mittelschule teacher, but in the bad times before 1938 had been unemployed. He had therefore become a leader in the Labour Service. At first he was in the Austrian Labour Service and afterwards in the Reich Labour Service. Towards the end of the war he had been transferred to the *Wehrmacht* as a *Feldmeister* and had thus become a *Leutnant.* In the hospital barracks in Thorn he had been in the next bed.

In about 1960 I met him again in the Salzburg officers' mess. He had transferred into the Austrian *Bundesheer* and then, as a major, he was commandant of the Telegraph Battalion. He regretted that he had not met me years earlier. He had had trouble in proving his officer's rank, something to which I could have attested, at least for our time in Thorn, when we were still wearing badges of rank.

The highest-ranking officer and therefore the right-hand wing man in the first unit was *Oberstleutnant der Reserve* Dr Josef Deckwitz. He was a lawyer from Münster in Westphalia. From then on until I was released, with some interruptions, I was always together with Deckwitz. I shall speak of him many more times. Although by age, he was born in 1896, and could have been my father, we had a close comradely relationship with each other. I owe him much for expanding my horizons. Deckwitz had been a flak officer. He had a huge ribcage and possessed a loud voice. He had, he said, been much in demand as a defence counsel in criminal cases and his legal pleas were something worth hearing.

Once, he said, in a trial before a jury, knowing that from midnight of the next day an amnesty would come into force, he had pleaded for many hours to benefit his client. The court, he said, had patiently tolerated his constant repetitions. Before 1933 Deckwitz had been a Social Democrat. His wife was the niece of an SPD, if not a Communist, member of the *Reichstag* who had emigrated to the Soviet Union. (After graduating to my doctorate in 1952, I visited him in Münster and was delighted to see him again. His wife was interesting and clever. The great misfortune of the two of them was that their son, their only child, had 'completely ruined himself' with drink.)

Although many healthy men capable of marching were in the column, it was still an unparalleled trail of misery. The armed sentries walked on all four sides of the column, but took careful notice of the many weak and feeble men. The distance of 55 kilometres, which healthy troops could have covered in one day's march, was tackled in three stages. Half was done on the first day, something that made demands on many men, leading to exhaustion. The other half was tackled in two days' marches each of 12 kilometres. Obviously the weakest men did not have the strength to walk further. I had recovered to such an extent, and had in the meantime learned again to stretch my left leg, that I managed all right. The worry of every man was always not to drop out of the column or be left behind, in order not to be shot by the guards, as had often happened. We spent the nights in barns on farms. If the sentries had not just dug out some women and the women were not screaming out for help, you could get a bit of rest and sleep well in the straw.

On the first day's march we passed through the little town of Kulmsee. It had obviously been taken without any fighting. We were stared at by the Polish civilian population without visible hostility. I saw it as a particular irony of fate that on the last day of the march we moved along the very that five months before had been one of the roads along which we had been retreating. That was before we had crossed the Vistula over the ice bridge to the south-west of Graudenz. It was a particular sign of our having been beaten. In Graudenz, so word had gone round in the meantime, the transports were being assembled that would take us by railway into the interior of Russia. In Graudenz we were gaped at by the civilian population. They were evidently more hostile than the population of Kulmsee, but there were no incidents. Our destination in Graudenz was a barracks complex. We were placed in groups of many men, in completely empty rooms. But they were dry and everyone had enough room to be able to stretch out. We remained in the barracks for two or three days and nights. Then it was time for us to march to the railway station to be loaded on to the trains.

Today I can no longer remember whether the railway in the area occupied by the Russians had at that time already been converted to the Russian gauge or whether this was not yet the case. But I do know that 20 men were stuffed into one goods wagon. Half way between the floor and the roof a shelf had been placed on both sides of the wagon doors. There we lay on the bare wood. There was no kind of comfort, neither straw nor hay, to relieve the hardness of the floor. The only necessary luxury was the availability of a hole in the floor of the wagon, some 20mm in diameter, that served for the purposes of defecation. It was a simple solution, but an unpleasant one for those who, like me, were lying near to the hole. Fortunately it was not necessary for urinating. That was done through the open wagon door.

The transport train left Graudenz about 20 June. Nobody knew what its destination was. The rumour was that we were heading for Murmansk. It was one of the many topics of conversation in our officers' wagon. Nobody had been on the Murmansk front. But many of us knew what had happened there in the First World War. 70,000 of the German prisoners of war and 20,000 of the Austro-Hungarian prisoners of war set to work on building the Murmansk railway had died. But as things turned out everything was quite different than the *Parolen*, that is the rumour, would have it.

After a relatively short journey, via Deutsch-Eylau and Allenstein, the transport came to a halt. It was the time before and during the 'Potsdam Conference'. That was to be the last summit conference of the 'Big Three' of the anti-Hitler coalition of the Second World War. It was held in the *Schloss Cäcilienhof*, in Potsdam, from 17 July to 2 August 1945 and was between Truman, Stalin and Churchill or Attlee. The result of that conference was the 'Potsdam Agreement'. In that agreement, subject to a final settlement of the territorial questions in a peace treaty, the town of Königsberg and the adjacent district of East Prussia were placed under the administration of the USSR. The border had hitherto existed between the USSR and Poland and ran approximately along a line between the towns of Braunsberg and Goldap. The area to the north was allocated to the USSR. For our transport and us it resulted in our destination being the part of East Prussia occupied by the USSR. We were not sent further on into the interior of the Soviet Union.

The train was on the tracks for five weeks. I recall the summer of 1945 as being very hot. During those five weeks it did not rain on one single day. For a fortnight no one was allowed to leave the wagon. Only after that, during the remaining three weeks, did the guards allow us during the day to camp in a meadow alongside the train beside the tracks. Being allowed to do this made our stay more bearable than the first fortnight had been. The constricted conditions and the heat had thoroughly irritated us prisoners. Many of them worked themselves up into a proper fury. In our wagon, too, hostile words were exchanged. For instance, men who were on the lower bunks were disturbed by the feet of those lying above them. One man complained that, when eating it was so dark that 'you couldn't even find the way to your mouth'. He who said it was a *Leutnant* Dr Hess from Frankfurt am Main. He worked as a translator at IG Farben, spoke fluent English, French and Spanish and had some interesting things to tell about his job. Hess was my neighbour and we were both lying directly beside the notorious hole.

Then there was a *Hauptmann der Reserve* Stölzner. He came, I believe, from Upper or Central Franconia. He was about 40 years old, and told of an elder brother who during the First World War had been taken prisoner by the Russians and had been sent to Siberia. From there he had fled to China and had attached himself as a military adviser to Marshal Chiang-Kai-Shek. His brother had married a Chinese woman, a fact that led in the wagon to a debate over the virtues of the women of another race. With the most earnest face Stolzner told of a peculiarity of Chinese women. His assertion caused among some men a short astounded amazement, until the laughter of the other men told them that Stolzner had been leading them 'up the garden path'.

As one of the naive and, moreover, still visibly fearful comrades, I recall Staff Paymaster Uhland. He was a descendant of the poet of the *Schwäbische Kunde*, but evidently was not so fearless as his ancestor was supposed to have been. While the war was still going on, rumours had been circulating that the poor quality soap there was at that time had partly been produced from human bones. That was something that seemed completely incredible. But then after the war had ended, assertions concerning the atrocities practised in German concentration camps were doing the rounds. It is true that our fear of being shot had in the meantime abated. But the future was completely unknown and it seemed quite probable that we would be consigned to years of forced labour under inhuman conditions. It was therefore black humour when, in order to worry *Herr* Uhland, a man in the wagon asserted that the German officers who had been taken prisoner were going to be taken and turned into soap, and that well nourished paymasters, such as Uhland, would be made into toilet soap!

During the time we were kept in the transports there were some deaths. The causes of death could not be established. Since there were no lists in existence, the only responsibility of the guards was to replenish the number of prisoners being transported. That was achieved by the guards swarming out and grabbing male German civilians, of whom there were still a few, there in Masuria. During the first period of our captivity in the East there were no lists and the prisoners were not recorded by name. The many who died of epidemics and hunger were never recorded. In my opinion the real reasons that many years later, long after 1955, when the last prisoners were released, that people believed in the existence of so-called *Schweigelager*. Meanwhile, it is a fact that one in three soldiers who had come into the custody of the USSR did not survive his captivity, and never returned. From my personal experience I attribute that to the reasons I have mentioned above and to the wholly insufficient medical care which they received initially.

Before the summer of 1945 I had not been acquainted with East Prussia. If there had not been the sadness that we experienced at the loss of a land through which we slowly travelled, it would have been a pleasure to see this friendly and cultivated land. From the train, as it travelled past the settlements and even the town of Allenstein much seemed to have remained intact. But everywhere was depopulated. Only the summer sunshine stopped the landscape from giving a ghostly impression. Wistfulness seized the sensitive ones among us, as we travelled through the station at Tharau, because many knew the song *Ännchen von Tharau*.

I must mention one more stop in Deutsch-Eylau, where several thousand prisoners of war were encamped in a meadow. It was there, and not in Graudenz, that the final allocation and assembly of the transports for the East took place. In that meadow, as elsewhere, the officers were separated. It was there, completely surprised, that I met some gentlemen from our Division. They were *Major* Östreich, the Divisional Adjutant, and *Hauptmann* Franssen, the commander of the signals battalion.

From the latter I learnt that the Division, before the surrender, had got to Bornholm by ship in a fairly good condition. They had thought themselves to be safe, when two Russian torpedo boats appeared. The Danish island was occupied by the Russians, and all the Germans were taken prisoner. Östreich did indeed know that Regiment 7 under *Oberstleutnant* von Garn on the destroyer *Karl Galster* had not made for Bornholm, but had set course for the Danish mainland. But it was not known whether the destroyer, and with it the remnants of the regiment, had got through. Östreich, Franssen, and the other *Bornholmers* had until then been able to keep all of their baggage. They had evidently until then not been searched and not been plundered. A not so pleasant memory is that none of them offered me even a cigarette. Compared with them I had nothing. I enjoyed smoking again, ever since the senior registrar Johanssen in Danzig gave me a cigarette. He had said, with a smile, that I could forget my fear of not being able to smoke after the injury to my lung. But I could once again have that pleasure.

In Deutsch-Eylau I also saw again the medic who had shamelessly bitten into the full block of chocolate in front of all the hungry men in our room. I refrained from speaking to him. Elsewhere on the meadow a soldiers' choir was singing a song which at that time belonged to the firm repertoire of German *Gesangvereine*: *Wenn ich den Wanderer frage, wo gehst du hin? Nach Hause, nach Hause, spricht er mit frohem Sinn*. ('If I ask the wanderer, where are you going? I'm going home, home, he says cheerfully'). Here at least the German spirit, which had evidently remained intact, was still alive and kicking.

We stayed a week in the area of the border that had just been drawn in Potsdam between Russia and Poland. There would not be a journey into the unknown lasting for weeks, as many men had feared. In Insterburg we had already reached our destination. I recall marching past the huge undamaged Martin Luther Church. Then the column moved along the road over a valley bottom lined with poplars that stretched for a few kilometres. Our destination was the Georgenburg camp, an old estate. In previous decades it had been home to a stud farm. Georgenburg was the home of the Barrings and was known to the educated German middle-class from the novel of the same name. It was only after I returned home that I read *Die Barrings* and its sequel *Der Enkel* by William von Simpson. But even in 1945, without knowing the novel, I could imagine clearly enough how things had been before, and the defeat that had taken place. We marched along the drive and through a gate on which there was the date 1268 in old figures.

There in Georgenburg was Main Camp 445. Later it was called 7.445. It was the headquarters of the prisoner of war camps in the Russian-occupied part of East Prussia. From there, camps were established in Königsberg, in Tilsit, and in other locations in East Prussia. At that time there was still the infectious diseases hospital in Insterburg that was later closed down. I cannot recall many facts from our short first stay there in Georgenburg in the summer of 1945. The main thing I recall is the soup made out of turnip scraps. They constituted the main part of our food. The turnip scraps had been used as fodder for horses on the stud farm, and I cannot believe that this was unknown to the Russians.

Then I recall that many officers, particularly staff officers, were there. Amongst them, was an *Oberst* Remer, the elder brother of *Major* Remer. After 20 July 1944 Remer, on Goebbels's orders, had occupied the *Bendlerstrasse* with the Berlin guard battalion. He had crushed the rebellion, and for that had been personally promoted by Hitler to *Generalmajor*. By contrast to that Remer, who was said to have been something of a simple unit officer, our Remer was a real man of the world with the best address and international experience. He had himself been military *attaché* in Spain or had been attached to the military *attaché*. He could speak several languages. As once many Russian noblemen and *Tsarist* officers had done, after the First World War, he had hoped to be able to see out the rest of his life as a hotel porter. I also recall the appearance of a quartet of men who sank the famous French hit song *Parlez-moi d'amour* to great applause. 'Tell me of happiness' was the first line of the song in German. That much I understood.

But I also recall some political speeches made by officers. They were attempts to come to terms with the new situation. They were completely apolitical men. Their world, their only world, had collapsed. Finally, I can still remember that there in the Georgenburg camp all insignia of rank had to be taken off and all heads had to be shaved. We officers found that to be an additional humiliation. It was the intention that its main purpose was a hygienic measure to prevent epidemics. In the Red Army shaven heads were the regulation, even if not for officers. Most of the prisoners in any case were suffering from diarrhoea mixed with blood, like dysentery, for which there was no kind of help.

Among the most significant industrial plants in East Prussia, where there was little industry, were the pulp factories attached to the Feldmühle concern. In Königsberg they were the *Werk* Sackheim and the *Werk* Zosse. Those factories were supposed to be rebuilt by German prisoners of war as part of the restitution process. For that reason there was a camp in Sackheim and another in Holstein, below the town, where the Pregel emptied into the freshwater lagoon.

We had been transported on lorries from Georgenburg to Königsberg. The town appeared to have been dreadfully destroyed. In Danzig, while being transported from the Technical High School to the Medical Academy, I had happened to get a glimpse of the *Marienkirche*, the landmark of the town. There on the journey through Königsberg was offered sufficient opportunity to imagine how beautiful that town must once have been. We drove past the destroyed castle and a comrade from Königsberg showed us where Kant's grave was.

The British air-raid of 30 August 1944 had turned the inner town into a heap of rubble. Before the town surrendered on 9 April 1945 the Russians had circled it to the north. The first suburb they had taken was Metgethen. The Russians were in fact driven out of there again. But the fate of the inhabitants and of the refugees who had been caught by surprise was a terrible indication of what was waiting for the German civilian population. General Lasch, conscious of his responsibility for a large civilian population, and for his troops who were uselessly shedding their blood, had surrendered the town on 9 April. He may thus have saved the lives of countless other people. But Hitler personally sentenced him to death by hanging, because he had not fought to the last man. Unspeakable things had then indeed gone on. In their despair, women and young girls had thrown themselves into the Pregel, or committed suicide in some other way. After the rapes, murders, arson, and plundering, there came hunger and many deaths.

Hugo Link, one of the few Protestant pastors to stay behind in Königsberg and survive, tells in his book *Königsberg 1945 bis 1948*, that in autumn 1945 the number of Germans in Königsberg was still 96,000. The number of civilians in Königsberg during its last period as a *Festung* had been 126,000. Thus, in the course of half a year 30,000 people must have died. Epidemics and hunger decimated the population still more, so that finally only 24,000 were left. They were to be transported away. According to that, more than 100,000 must have been snatched away by death.

The prisoners of war were hermetically sealed off and guarded so intently, that for most of them or even all of them, no contact was possible with the civilian population. I cannot recall any particular occasion, even if now and again news of the civilian filtered through. The German camp leader of our small Holstein camp, which was supposed to hold 200 men, was *Oberleutnant* Kahl from Königsberg. It was said that his family was still in the town. The process of living, suffering and dying thus went on unseen by the prisoners of war.

Meanwhile, they had the certain feeling that their life was no longer directly under threat. I also, looking back, cannot say for certain that we were systematically exposed to starvation. The dreadful turnip scrap soup of Georgenburg was replaced by *sauerkraut, kapusta*. There was a litre of that soup twice a day. The calculated ration of meat and fat, both of which were mixed into the soup, was 9 grams for meat and 12 grams for fat. There may well have also been at that time, I cannot now recall exactly, a tablespoon of sugar and bread, the ration for which was 600 grams per day. But the sugar, it was always unrefined sugar, was hardly ever edible, but mostly damp and heavy. It was generally known in all camps that the Russians responsible deviated from the set ration of food for the prisoners of war.

The calculation was simple. If you mixed to the quantity of 10 grams of sugar 1 litre of water, you had got an additional kilogram left for private barter. It was a similar case with the bread, the *khleb*. There was an unimaginable difference, even while the war was still going on, between what we considered to be bread, and the bread that the Russians provided. It must have been baked in moulds, in tin boxes, because with the unimaginably high water content the dough would have run away. But the moulds had to be lubricated, and we never got to the bottom of the question as to whether this was done with petroleum or with engine oil. The crusts, the only parts that were baked through, sometimes tasted disgusting and smelled unpleasant. From time to time a lot of oats were also mixed in. Many could not face the damp, badly baked bread, and for that reason often, if an oven was nearby, it was toasted, which gave off quite considerable clouds of steam. The weight of the toasted slices was considerably less than it had been before.

'Camp Holstein' was in a plant that had been built in the inter-war period, probably after 1933. It had housed an 'Army Optical Research Institute', or something of a similar name. Two buildings measuring some 20 by 10 metres stood at right angles to each other. They had two storeys and were built of red brick. The area was no larger than 2,000 or 3,000 square metres and had been securely fenced in by the builders. The building to the right of the entrance, ran at a right angle to the road, and had been a workshop. From its roof you could see across the freshwater lagoon far to the west and to the south. The plant lay alone outside the settlement. In the first building there was still a lot of equipment from the time of its earlier use, in particular binocular periscopes, for which the Russians obviously had no use.

The other building, lying parallel to the road, was where we were housed. The officers were quartered in some smallish rooms on the ground floor and on the first floor, and the other ranks in two large rooms. We officers had individual wooden beds, whereas the other ranks lay on bunks one above each other and subdivided. The German camp leader, *Oberleutnant* Karl, had a room of his own in which he lived with his assistant, another officer. In front of the accommodation building was the kitchen block from the time when the plant was in German hands.

The running of the kitchen was the responsibility of two officers. They had been taken prisoner unwounded and were a picture of enviable strength and health. They used their position to divert rations to themselves. From the roof they had thoroughly observed the terrain, and one day in the spring of 1946 they disappeared. Many months later there was a rumour that their escape attempt had succeeded and they were supposed to have written from Germany.

Our workplace in the Holstein factory was about three-quarters of an hour away. We went there on a country road and passed a solitary house, that had earlier been a simple inn. *Oberleutnant* Kahl told us that, on our road over 200 years earlier, Immanuel Kant, the Königsberg philosopher, had gone for walks. He was said never to have left Königsberg, and yet in his lectures had been able to give exact descriptions of London and Paris etc.

The factory was already partly in operation again. We prisoners were detailed, in the Russian fashion, into so-called brigades, groups of about 10 men each. My brigade worked on making multi-layered wooden trestles that were used in the construction of a larger container. We worked under the direction of Russians, who were all members of the technical units, as shown in the names of their service ranks. So, for instance, the normal sub-lieutenant was called *Mladschy-Tjechnik-Litenant*, in German *Unter-Technik-Leutnant*. The so-called *Natschalnik*, the commandant in our area, was an elderly first lieutenant, of good-natured appearance. He was a teacher from Tambov, a provincial town halfway between Moscow and Samara. The foreman was a sergeant-major from Tomsk in Siberia, a skilled craftsman as far as I could judge. He must have been a mix of Russian and Mongolian. With him I had the impression that it embarrassed him that officers were performing menial tasks for him as prisoners.

During the fighting the high factory chimney had received a direct hit from an anti-tank gun. But it had only made a hole and had not brought down the chimney above it. To all appearances the Russians had suspected there was an artillery observer on the flue and had wanted to clear him out. A topic of conversation was how, and by whom, the hole could be repaired. Rumour had it that a specialist, a Russian buzz-word, had been offered 8,000 roubles to repair it. Such a specialist had been requested from Moscow and was already on the way.

It was autumn. We had been working for some weeks in the factory. Our working hours were 10 hours a day, only Sunday was a day off. But one Sunday there was a 'voluntary' work detail in which every prisoner capable of working had to take part. However, the unusual thing about it was that we did not have to go to work in the factory. We were loaded up on lorries and driven into the area of the new frontier between Russia and Poland. The process of drawing the frontier had apparently not yet been fully accomplished.

In the frontier area we had to gather up stinging nettles and similar weeds that were supposed to serve as fodder for horses. On that work detail I must have caught cold. The following Monday I felt ill. With difficulty I dragged myself to work in the factory. I was completely weak on the march back. I felt a stabbing pain in the right side of my chest that I could not explain. The lung that had been injured had been the left one. My strength deserted me more and more, and I was in danger of being left behind. The men next to me and behind me had apparently not noticed, and gradually I had reached the end of the column. I was afraid that I would soon collapse, when quite unexpectedly I got a hefty blow on my back.

The frequent cries of *dawai, dawai* by the sentries who brought us, or rather drove us, to work, was something that we were used to, and were part of the prisoners' every day experience. Until then and, I have to say, also later, there had not been any mistreatment. I fell, and it was only with difficulty that I could pull myself up again. But two comrades got hold of me under my arms, and supported me on either side. They saw to it that I did not drop out of the column again. It was not the physical pain that hurt me and brought tears to my eyes, it was the mental torture I suffered through the degrading and humiliating mistreatment. I can still see the guard who hit me with the butt of his rifle in the small of my back. He was a young chap with a pretty face, if it had not been disfigured with pockmarks. Back in the camp I reported the incident, but *Herr* Kahl could do nothing. The only thing was to be treated by a doctor. By the evening it was obvious that I was running a fever.

Meanwhile, there was no doctor in our camp. Only a 'field medical assistant' who was a medical student without qualifications. As best he could, he fulfilled the function of camp doctor. It is true that he had a thermometer, a wooden stethoscope, a few dressings and iodine. He was an Upper Silesian by the name of Lebek. He listened to my chest and diagnosed an inflammation of the lining of my lungs and my ribs on the right hand side, but could only prescribe 'bed rest' for me. Of course I was incapable of working. I had a fierce stabbing pain in the right side of my chest. The only treatment Lebek could give me was repeatedly painting that side of my chest with iodine. He monitored my temperature and my general condition, but apart from that had to leave me to my fate.

During the following weeks I ran a heavy fever. I lay on my bunk without straw mattress or blanket, dressed in my uniform and covered with my old overcoat. The days were bleak while my comrades were at work and, God knows, I felt myself to be abandoned. There were no scales in the camp, so that it was only by seeing my bones protruding more and more, that I realised that I was losing more and more weight. We did not have a mirror in which I could have seen what I looked like. One time, when I had got out of bed, I saw that my knees were thicker than the bones of my upper leg. I was wasting away to a skeleton. I presented a similar picture to those I afterwards saw in photographs of the inmates of concentration camps. Night and day I used an empty jam tin as a urine bottle. I had to stand it next to my head, so that I did not accidentally knock it over, and I could reach it with less effort.

Throughout the winter, sick and weak, I remained in the camp. I could not and did not work. The winter, with temperatures as low as minus 15 degrees, was said not to have been a harsh winter for East Prussia. We had a stove in the room, so that at least cold was not added to hunger. There was also a good feeling of camaraderie in the cramped room. There was no one who acted in an underhand way, with one exception. He was, of all people, a circuit judge and a Reserve *Oberleutnant*. He was once seen drinking a comrade's soup as he brought it from the canteen. Everyone could see how he was tortured by shame over this lapse, and so the incident was passed over in silence.

It was a different kind of anger for the community when *Herr* Rauchfuss, in civilian life a police official from Potsdam, sold his watch. He had been able to hold on to it through several 'friskings'. But then he did a deal with a Russian sentry who obtained for him some additional rations. In particular he paid for a tin of American corned beef with a label in Cyrillic script. It was as painful for the rest of us to know of the existence of that supply, as it must have been for Rauchfuss to eat those additional rations alone! He knew how much the others envied him. But camaraderie no longer extended to giving to other people even a bit on the end of a knife.

Another man in our room was an artillery *Oberleutnant* Theo Krühne. He came from Leipzig, was a junior lawyer, and the son of a *Reichsgerichtsrat*. He occasionally spoke with pride of his father, who in his job was a leading jurist. After I returned home I found out through Paul Eberhardt what a dreadful fate Krühne's family had met. In the artillery school in Jöterbog he had become acquainted with and married a girl from the nearby small town of Kalau, from where the *Kalauers* come. In the little town near Berlin the family thought they would be safe and had fled from the bombed city of Leipzig to Berlin to his young wife's parents' house. Krühne spoke with great pleasure of his wife and his small son. He had a red moustache and had striking blue eyes. It was a cruel stroke of fate that the house in which the family was living, including those who had fled, received a direct hit. A total of nine people lost their lives as a result.

Paul Eberhart, whom I have just mentioned, was Krühne's close friend. He came from Augsburg and had relatives in Bregenz. This had given him the idea of passing himself off as an Austrian. It was not important in the Holstein camp, but only later in Georgenburg. In Holstein I was already instructing Paul about the importance and the significance of the *Heimatschein* for him, as an Austrian. In actual fact he did succeed in getting released with us and in getting back home to Augsburg.

In later years, after my studies, I met him in Munich, where, with a PhD, he was working as an occupational psychologist. Paul Eberhart was the same age as I was, but he looked a lot younger. He had a somewhat round face with blue eyes, and for a grammar school boy he was very well educated. In fact he had already studied philosophy for one semester. He spoke about the art historian Worringer in Munich and about other professors. He was acquainted with publishing houses and had an eye for valuable books. It was he who brought back to the camp many books while on work details in Jüditten and Metgethen.

One day Paul had been in the library of a Königsberg lawyer, Egon Fridell. He turned up with a three-volume cultural history of modern times from the C.H. Beck Verlag. It was a large first edition in greenish yellow. He worked his way through those volumes during the winter. He always underlined important parts as he did so, somewhat as my father and his father too had done. He also let me work on Fridell. I can still remember how we both agreed that we had found studying the introductory chapter particularly difficult. Of the books that Paul brought back with him, and which I then read for the first time, Rudolf Georg Binding's *Erlebtes Leben,* and Hans Carossa's *Führung und Geleit,* were the best known.

Other comrades in our room were *Herr* Straub, a lawyer from Düren near Aachen, and *Herr* Korte, who was a singer, a bass or baritone. I can remember that Korte would toast his bred on the stove in small strips and slices, and carefully distribute his sugar ration over them. A particular personality was *Herr* Böhm, a Reserve *Hauptmann* who had taken part in the First World War. Böhm called himself a lyricist, but I can no longer remember the quality of his poems. He was a gentleman of refined appearance with excellent manners and a cultured way of expressing himself. His *Hochdeutsch* had that certain East Prussian ring to it. I had the feeling that the downfall of his home city was a dreadful blow to him. I can still hear his voice when, in his East Prussian fashion, he would say to me *Härr Schejderbauerchen.* I had the impression that he was a prosperous man and a bachelor. One time he gave us a laugh when he sang a popular song, full of black humour, from the period after the First World War. *Wenn der weisse Flieder wieder blüht* ('When the white lilacs bloom once more'). Remarkably, I can still remember the title of one of his lyrical poems. It would have marked him out as an East Prussian dialect poet. I do not know whether that was really the case, but the poem was called *Schalche Flack,* in *Hochdeutsch, Ein Schälchen Fleck,* or 'a little bowl of *Fleck*'. It referred to the sour *Kuttelfleck,* a favourite East Prussian dish.

When my 22nd birthday came round, on 13 January 1946, I had recovered sufficiently to feel able to walk. It was a Sunday. I can remember it clearly because for the first and only time there was meat in the soup for lunch. Because it was my birthday, like all birthday boys, I received an extra helping by order of the camp leader. I devoured it with the greatest enjoyment and without the slightest prick of conscience towards my comrades!

After the meal I realised that Fritz Seyerl, a staff vet and Sudeten German, had not eaten with us. No one could explain why he was already full, but he was occasionally taken out of the camp by the Russians as a vet. So we thought he must have already eaten. On closer questioning he replied, after the meal, clenching both hands into fists, *Solche Kavernen.* He meant the state of the lungs of the horse he had been treating, and at the slaughtering and inspection of which he had been present.

My first trip out beyond the camp fence may have been in January or February. In the camp a comrade had died who had to be buried outside the camp. *Herr* Kahl, the camp leader, took me with him a few steps outside the camp. There the grave had already been dug. It was by a hedge. The body was laid in the flat grave. *Oberleutnant* Kahl said an 'Our Father', then the grave was filled in. Then we went back to the camp. We were the few prisoners who were capable only of working inside.

My last recollection of Holstein dates from March or April 1946. At that time we had received orders to erect round the camp a fence that was to some extent permanent. The Russians provided posts of over two metres high and many rolls of barbed wire. The posts were dug in or even concreted in, and then the wire was stretched over them. Stretching the wire with a tool designed for the purpose, I was able to get to work again for the first time. Slowly I felt my strength returning, even if I was still only capable of working inside. I even felt a certain satisfaction when I saw how tightly I had stretched the wire after the staples had been hammered in. But by the next day the tension had slackened because the material was already over-stretched.

The man directing the work was a Russian captain by the name of Mironov. He was the friendliest Russian that I met in captivity, not yet 30 years old, good-natured and kind. Blue-eyed and black-haired, he was smaller than me. He spoke a little German and was polite, almost comradely. But the notorious *Skogo damoi*, i.e. 'home soon', was no more convincing from his mouth than it was from other Russians. Doubtless it was decently and sincerely meant.

Meanwhile, we certainly were not going home soon. Although one day in April, we officers, with what little baggage we had, were loaded up on to lorries. But I was to encounter one more grotesque episode in the Holstein camp. For years I had carried in my right hand top pocket a marching compass. It was the compass that had, in February 1945, prevented me from going in the wrong direction with my men. But then I thought that the possession of it might lead people to think that I was planning to escape. It was too risky to keep it, even if my physical condition ruled out any thought of escaping. On one occasion as I went into the unused building in the camp where there were various types of optical equipment, I simply hid it. I decided I would certainly not need it any more. In the event that it was found on me during a frisking, it would lay me open to extreme unpleasantness.

But I was plain astonished when, a few weeks later, that very compass of mine was offered to me 'for sale'. A *Landser* had been rooting about in the building and had found my compass. He decided that it was very likely that an officer might be interested in acquiring it as such an instrument would be necessary in any escape plan. Thanking him, I declined, without batting an eyelid.

Soon afterwards our miserable time in Königsberg came to an end. We officers were transferred back to the Georgenburg camp. Of course, once more we were completely unsure as to what was going to happen to us. Indeed, right up to the last day of our captivity, there was complete uncertainty, and unending anxiety. By then, the spring of 1946, the general situation had to a certain extent stabilised, if not improved.

Our return to the 'main camp' of Georgenburg, which was probably better organised than the Holstein camp, seemed at any rate to be advantageous to us. In fact the organisation and accommodation in the many barracks did indeed seem to be better. That was evident even as we arrived. We were subjected to a thorough 'frisking'. My pay book and my New Testament were taken away from me. Losing my pay book felt to me just like losing my identity. From then I no longer had any document that could show who I was. I had nothing to show my name and rank, my date of birth, nor any other important dates. The seizure of my New Testament also hit me hard. It was the small pocket edition with the psalter I had received as a present from Father. It had his dedication, 'A thousand shall fall beside thee, and ten thousand at thy right hand, but it shall not come nigh thee'. From then I had to summon up from my memory the consolation I had often felt in reading it. But I had to continue to trust in my Father's dedication. The Russian guards evidently had orders to confiscate all written and printed material. Even my request for them to leave me with my New Testament 'for cigarette papers' met with no success.

We new arrivals were also given an immediate medical examination. The examination was not even 'purely clinical', but really consisted in viewing the naked prisoners and pinching their backsides in order to determine the degree of dystrophy. Since I was extremely emaciated, I could not be put down as capable of working. I was quite happy about that. But I considered myself to be even more fortunate not to be placed in the tuberculosis barracks. The 'pointed' noses of the men who were in the process of slowly dying there, beyond recovery, were frightening enough.

In the spacious barracks where we Holsteiners joined the other officers in the camp, there was at last enough room for an individual to lead an existence that was halfway human. We slept on single beds placed in the room either individually, against a wall, or in twos next to each other. Every bed was provided with a straw mattress and a blanket. Among the inmates of the barracks I was reunited with a whole series of acquaintances. Above all was *Oberstleutnant* Joseph 'Job' Deckwitz, whose *Obermann* in the bunk I was to be for a long time.

Another sign of the organisation in force was the fact that we were recorded on a register. That involved, at least for all officers, filling out questionnaires of several pages. Everyone had to answer 42 questions concerning his personal dates and, above all, the activities in which he had been engaged in the military. Our answers, in conjunction with denunciations by informers, provided the material that served as documentary evidence in the many war crimes trials that resulted in their cursory sentences of 25 years' hard labour. From the start I had provided true information. For instance I had not concealed my rank as an officer, as many had done.

Even in the camp at Thorn, when informally that was still possible, officers who had 'lost' themselves in the ranks had acknowledged their rank. The constant fear of discovery, by comrades or fellow-countrymen, in which those men lived, would have prevented me from taking such a step. That was quite apart too from the fact that it would not have been in line with my natural honesty. As long as I had been with my unit nothing had happened that could not be militarily justified or that could have qualified as a war crime. So I was confident that no undeserved fate would overtake me. In actual fact I had had nothing to fear.

Even during our first stay in Georgenburg in the summer of 1945, the heads of men and other ranks had been shaven. What we took to be a measure intended to humiliate us, had obviously been necessary due to the completely unsatisfactory hygienic conditions. Many others suffered under such degradation. However, I resigned myself to the measure as a fateful means of enforcing conformity. I can still remember how many of us looked at each other in surprise. The disappearance of their hair had significantly altered the appearance of many men. The shape of the skull became a particular distinguishing feature. But we did not have to be subjected to that procedure a second time.

Our insignia of rank had long since been removed, and a man who had previously been an officer could only be recognised by the material and cut of his uniform. But nevertheless there were other signs too that distinguished the prisoners of war from each other. We could not believe our eyes when we saw on some caps small red, or white and red coats of arms and even some others of different colours. As it had been ordered by the camp authorities, it was pointless to let oneself be upset by it. It was an expression of the existing political situation, as it was known to us, by hearsay.

The German Reich, Greater Germany, had been completely conquered and shattered. Germany and Austria had each been divided into four zones of occupation, and no one knew what the borders of Germany would be in the future. So the Sudeten Germans cherished the illusion of eventually returning again to their homeland that had once again become part of Czechoslovakia. That was the case with Staff vet Dr Seyerl and another comrade. *Herr* Grün, a qualified businessman from Saarbrücken, had studied in Paris before the war. He was distinguished by his knowledge of French food, and reckoned that the Saar would become French. Thenceforward he considered himself 'French'.

For most Austrians the situation seemed to be simple and clear. Of course many of us could not hide the feeling that it was a shabby trick, after our common defeat, now to separate ourselves. Should we follow the motto 'every man for himself', and abandon our German comrades-in-arms to their fate? I also remembered literature concerning the First World War. The members of the successor states of the Austro-Hungarian monarchy had then deserted the flag that they had once served in common. I recalled the snide commentary with which that act had been portrayed.

So now we were in the same situation. We deserted our common flag and for this were given dirty looks by many of our 'German' comrades. But no one knew how to answer the question as to what else we Austrians could have done. The thought that the Austrians would generally be released earlier than their comrades from the old German *Reich* was also by no means irrelevant to this issue. Who could have been criticised for trusting in that hope? Should we be like Paul Eberhart who, in the light of it, passed himself off as an Austrian? The fate of the Sudeten Germans had no doubt long since been decided. None of them knew what that decision was. We were cut off from our homeland. Until then we had not even been allowed to write. The coats of arms on caps indicated at a stroke the problems thrown up by that completely new situation. The Greater German Reich no longer existed. Hitler, to whom all of us had sworn an oath, was dead. It was therefore morally right, and even necessary, to declare our allegiance to our small Austrian homeland.

We prisoners were each assigned to work details, according to our physical constitution. Work details 1 and 2 were completely capable of working and had to work outside the camp. Work detail 3, to which I belonged, was only capable of *Innendienst*, that is, we could only be used for work within the camp. We still had a few Staff officers in the camp, including Dr Deckwitz, and they too had to be employed within it. Of those, I can recall an *Oberst der Reserve*, about 50 years old, by the name of Kassl. He was a pharmacist. He had lost an arm and feared that he would not be capable of carrying out his profession, because he would no longer be able to mix up ointments.

The oldest was *Major* Kischke, owner of a small East Prussian estate. I thought him to be between 60 and 70, he appeared old to me. Then there were a few gentlemen from Peenemünde, the experimental Army rocket station. They had not been able to get to safety in time before the Russians arrived. An 'old' *Major* and former '12-Ender' was called Hinz. He had been the so-called *Platzoffizier* in Peenemünde. He had the furrowed face and the tanned skin of a native of the Alps, but in actual fact he was not.

The most distinguished among the officers present was *Oberleutnant* Jürgens, a fighter pilot with, it was said, 88 victories. A young East Prussian was 'Hänschen' Wieberneit. The nerves in both his lower arms had been damaged, but all the same he was capable of working.

There was an established hierarchy in the camp. At the head were two former officers who had already been prisoners for some years and who had been in the *National Komitee Freis Deutschland.* That *Nationalkomitee* had come into existence under and promoted by the Russians. It was composed of Communist *emigrés* such as the writer Eric Weinert and other prominent officers. It became well known after the disaster of Stalingrad, and especially through the name of General von Seydlitz. It claimed to be against fascism in the form of the Hitler dictatorship, and in this sense claimed to be collaborating in the political reconfiguration of the Germany of the future. Under the name *Antifa* the group developed anti-fascist activities, in which, speaking reasonably, there was nothing to object to. The fact that it was actually the activity of a communist cell was something which, in my youthful naivety, I neither recognised nor realised, particularly since its officials with whom I came in contact were, to all appearances, reasonable and decent human beings. The two officers just mentioned were called Kubarth and Gless; one of them was the first camp leader, while Willi Gless was in charge of political indoctrination.

Among the camp officials there were also three Austrians. They were Alois Strohmaier from Donauwitz, a Styrian Communist, Karl Koller from Eisenstadt, the son of a Social Democratic member of the *Landtag,* and the camp clerk Oscar Stockhammer, an active *Unteroffizier* in the Austrian *Bundesheer,* who later became a police official in Salzburg. Stockhammer was not a Communist. He had an unhappy marriage, but was a good Catholic. Until he died he could never bring himself to get divorced from the wife whom he did not love and who was considerably older.

I came into friendly contact with Stockhammer who was my elder by 10 to 15 years. It was with his help that I became involved in the area of managing the camp. There were many German books in the camp, and many more had been brought into the camp from outside, by the work details. Orders were then issued that those books should be checked, in order to weed out not only National Socialist literature, but also literature that did not accord with the anti-fascist ideology. All that came about as the unexpected result of contact with the camp leaders. In my naivety, that was something I had not reckoned with. It meant that I was then morally compelled to take part in the recruitment, and educational events, organised by the *Antifa*.

13

April 1946-January 1947:
Prisoner of the Russians

*Work in prison library; allowed to write to relatives, June 1946;
first letter from Mother, January 1947; forestry work; given new
uniforms; moved to Tilsit*

The word *Weltanschauung* had until then meant virtually nothing to me. The word implies and includes 'a coherent, scientifically or philosophically formulated, i.e. represented in a philosophical system, an overall view of the world and human beings, itself directed towards action'. (*Meiers Enzyklopädisches Lexikon*, vol 25, 1975, page 184). Until then, when there had been talk of the National Socialist *Weltanschauung*, I had connected it with phrases such as *Blut und Boden* i.e. blood and soil, and with slogans such as *Recht ist, was dem Volke nützt*, i.e. justice is what serves the interests of the *Volk*, and *Du bist nichts, dein Volk ist alles*, i.e. you are nothing, your *Volk* is everything.

My 'service' in the Hitler Youth had never taken the form of ideological education, because my parents had not allowed me to go to camps. It is true that I had participated in the afternoon *Heimabende*, but all I had taken away from those was, at best, a form of pre-military training, not associated with any ideology. The fact that National Socialism, as it asserted, had introduced a new epoch in the history of the world, that the *Volksgemeinschaft*, i.e. 'community of the people', could be an important philosophical concept, was something that I had never known, nor would I have believed it or considered it to be correct.

The Christian faith, and the traditional middle-class way of life on the one hand, and the force of what was happening in the war had hit me hard. On the other hand, there was the undefined feeling that it was not unconnected with the *Weltanschauung* that so many villainous types had surfaced. In any case, it prevented me from getting more closely involved with it. Adolf Hitler's *Mein Kampf* was something that I had never read.

In the camp, things were completely different. My mind was full of uncertainties. My untrained intelligence was exposed to everything that streamed in on me under the apparently scientific cloak of Marxism. Marxism, the whole of the teachings of Karl Marx and Friedrich Engels, concerns 'a theoretical interpretation of historical development, and in particular, of the motive laws of the capitalist means of production. That facilitates and accelerates the struggle for emancipation of the working class'. It was 'the doctrine of dialectical and historical materialism. It led to a critique of political economy, a critical representation of the dialectical structure and motive laws of the capitalist means of production. It led to scientific socialism, to its statements concerning the future social order and the means of struggle leading to that social order being implemented'. Marxism starts from the basic premise that the material world is the only real world, and that human behaviour, thought and will, can be understood only in the context of material production. In its view, consciousness is 'nothing other than material being, transferred into the mind'. Nature is interpreted as a unity based on its own materiality, which develops from the lowest forms of material being (and material movement), from dead material, through living material up to material which is capable of consciousness. The transition from one stage to the next occurs by means of a 'qualitative leap', so that this materialism is not required to reduce higher forms of being to those forms of being which are lower, but is capable of acknowledging the qualitative differences.... The historical function of the dialectical-materialistic theory of historical development principally consisted in the ideological confirmation of a belief in the progress of the working class' (see *Maiers Enzyklopädisches Lexikon,* vol 15, page 693).

Quite simply, it was impressive, and entirely new to me concerning materialism and dialectic, their essence and subject matter, concerning the law of coherence, evolutionism, its necessity and the 'leaps' and the law of opposition. No less upsetting for me was what I learned of historical materialism, of its basis, the doctrine of basis and superstructure, the doctrine of development, theory and practice, and ideology with its general features and its influences on philosophy, science, morality, and also on art and religion. My mind was not equipped with the weapons to make any kind of sound objection to what was being drummed into me. It was simply new territory into which I was being led at that time.

But course it was not as if those new ideas occupied my mind day and night. Our existence was too hard for that. The harsh reality we experienced, in the prisoner of war camp and outside it, was too much at odds with the theory that was being put forward. Once it was announced that a lecture was to be given by Strohmeier, entitled 'What is to be done?' It recalled one of Lenin's writings of the same name. Even Communists, for whom this was right up their street, had to smile to themselves at this surreal question, to which there was only one answer, that was, 'Go home'! But everyone was exposed to the suggestive effect of the slogans, and it affected many men as it did me. 'The doctrine of Marx is all powerful, because it is right', was one of the slogans, but there was also another Marxist slogan that said, 'The idea becomes material power if it seizes hold of the masses'. Lenin's slogan, 'Learn, learn, learn!' not only hung over the camp like a watchword, but it was ever-present at all the *Antifa* events.

Only many years later, after my own studies, when I was already working in my profession, did I find the time to come to grips intellectually with Marxism, and in particular to study controversial literature. I did that with the aid of the *Handbuch des Weltkommunismus,* published by Bochensky and Niemeyer, 1958. I used the judgement of the German *Bundesverfassungsgericht* (Constitutional Court) of 17 August 1956 concerning 'The prohibition of the *KPD*', or German Communist Party. It was a special printing of the judgement from the third volume published by C F Müller Karlsruhe. That judgement (pages 655-656) contains the following notable passage:

> An overall assessment of this intensive work of training, recruitment, agitation and propaganda by the *KPD* compels recognition. There is careful harmonisation of all these actions with each other and in the efforts to include all classes of people. It uses the methods of propaganda and agitation that are most suited to

each of them. There is an integrated plan that is directed towards weakening, as 'the social order of a bourgeois-capitalist world', the free and democratic order of society. It aims to bring about the time for the proletarian revolution. The particular danger that this disruptive propaganda poses to free and democratic social order results from the fact that the apparent 'aimlessness' pervading free democracy as a result of mutual tolerance is confronted by a coherent system of organising the world. It claimed to be based on clear scientific principles, that provided clear answers to very complex economical and political questions and thus attracts the attention of the person to whom such matters are otherwise very difficult to understand. Instead of a hard, never-ending struggle with other social groups, and progress in the direction of greater social justice and freedom in the State and in society, one is presented with the picture of a 'paradise on earth'. That is certain to be attained only if the clear scientific perceptions of the *KPD* and the rules for political behaviour, deduced from these, are followed. The conclusion, that the 'bourgeois-capitalist social order' stands in the way of this development must be eliminated, should be self-evident.

In our Russian captivity in the Georgenburg camp, Lenin's slogan 'Learn, learn, learn!' was exclusively restricted to the 'all-powerful' teachings of Marx. In the camps run by the Western Allies, especially before the end of the war, it went without saying that the prisoners were given the opportunity to learn. That was not the case with prisoners of war held by the Russians. The 10-hour day on our work for 'restitution' did not allow tired bodies and minds to concern themselves with anything else. It was not even possible to hold Russian language courses. Remarkably, among the many books in the library there was no Russian language primer. Thus, almost no prisoner of war was able to learn Russian. I, in my two-and-a-half years as a prisoner of war, was scarcely able to learn more than 200 Russian words, 'parrot-fashion'. There were indeed other comrades who, thanks to their basic knowledge of Polish and Czech, easily mastered Russian. I came across two comrades who could speak Russian but only because they had spent some years in Russia.

One of them was Willi Jelinek who came from Stockerau. At the end of the 1920s and beginning of the 1930s, as 'companion' to elderly rich Vienna Jewesses, he had spent some time on the Riviera. He had then taken himself to the 'Workers' Paradise', from where, after a few years, he returned disillusioned. He made no secret of how disappointing his time in Russia had been. The other man was the Viennese *Reservehauptmann* from the *Luftwaffe*, Alfred Tunzer. Taken prisoner by the Russians during the First World War, he had learned Russian. On his way home he had got caught up in Moscow, and had lived there until the 1930s, working in the 'Many Peoples Publishing House' of the USSR. He spoke excellent Russian. But because of that, and because of what he had done in his life, he was, in his own words, an object of suspicion. He was often taken to night-time hearings and was actually held back when we others came to be released. Tunzer had to remain in captivity until 1949. I chanced to meet him after 1950 when I was studying in Vienna. Characteristically he did not say much about how things had gone with him. In 1947, in the camp, he had suffered from painful facial erysipelas. His whole attitude, and the expression on his face, gave away the fact that life had given him a bad deal. Fate had not looked kindly upon him.

For almost a year, as a member of work detail 3, I worked in the camp library. In the circumstances that work had been a stroke of luck for me. I always had something to do. Many books from the abandoned houses in Insterburg came into the library. To recognise National Socialist literature was not difficult. Whether my work was in line with the censorship measures that had been ordered, I must most conveniently doubt. It was not only that I knew too little of the Marxist class struggle, but in the field of literature, and above all of *belles-lettres*, I was not sure enough of myself to be able to judge whether a book would be 'acceptable' in the context of the class struggle. Of course I kept *Die Barrings* and *Der Enkel*. I owed that to the spirit of Georgenburg - but not in the sense Karl Marx meant!

The library was located in the single-storey house beside the offices of the camp leadership. The bookbinder there always had plenty to do because the books were subjected to a great deal of wear and tear. He was the former *Feldwebel* Hans Adam. Slowly and deliberately he carried out his work, and made the best of the scanty possibilities for his beautiful handiwork. He had cardboard and glue, together with some presses and clamps. He did not need anything else.

In the autumn of 1946 the camp pulled off a great achievement. They got hold of a X-ray machine, which made it possible to X-ray the sick men. It was an old model, and of course was not able to produce photographs. The doctors in the camp were Dr Eitner and another with a thin face, glasses and dark hair, whose name I have forgotten. The two of them used the machine to prepare drawings of the chest cavity and hand those out to their patients. The inflammation to my ribs and the linings of my lungs, that I had suffered as a result of my wounds during the previous winter, were set down on the drawing. Because of the massive lesions in the lining of my ribs, the doctor had sketched the lower halves of both my lungs. That made a great impression at the frequent examinations under the supervision of Russian medical officers and assistants. Thus, doubtless because of my condition, I continued to be excused from heavy work.

At about the same time, the infectious diseases hospital was closed. Until then it had been used in Insterburg. The remaining personnel joined us in the camp. Among them, were the surgeons Dr Walter and Dr Drechsler, the pathologist Dr Schreiber, and a certain Dr Kindler. However, they were not employed as doctors any longer, as there was obviously no need for them. With the exception of Dr Kindler, I came across those doctors again, while I was studying in Vienna. Another man who had arrived from the infectious diseases hospital was the pharmacist Wilhelm Cellbrot. He became a close comrade and friend, and has remained so to this day. I will be speaking of him again. From Dr Fritz Walter I learnt that he was one of the many pupils of the surgeon Eiselsberg.

I must add that the doctor who had X-rayed me ordered me not to expose myself to the sun. His advice clearly indicated that I had contracted tuberculosis. At that time tuberculosis was still a disease that was feared, and was often fatal. I was shocked. But that was mitigated by the fact that I was not running a fever, and did not have to go into the *Tuberer* barracks. Thus I could evidently consider myself to be cured.

Uncertainty about what was going to happen to us was characteristic of our time as prisoners of the Russians. It lasted from the first day almost to the last day. It was gradually alleviated, but never quite eliminated. A great relief, and a great step towards certainty and towards the hope that we might some day be able to go home again, was the fact that in June 1946 we were allowed to write to our relatives. For many men that raised the question as to whether their relatives were still alive.

I too was uncertain. Both Rudi and I had urged Mother, if the front was getting closer and there was real danger of being occupied by the Russians, to flee to the West in time. To whom and where, was I to write? My feelings for Gisela had cooled. In the light of what we had heard about the political situation in eastern Germany, and since the last time I heard of her she was in the labour service in Saxony, it seemed pointless to send post to her. Therefore I addressed the postcards that were handed out to us to my mother. I sent them to our home address in Stockerau, and to Aunt Ilse Steinbach in Vienna.

The first news that my relatives received was the postcard sent to Aunt Ilse on 27 June. She received it on 21 September, nearly three months later. She immediately sent it to my parents. But it was to take until January 1947 until the first reply arrived. On 20 January the first prisoner of war postcard from my Mother reached me. She had written it on 20 October 1946. The postcards were in Cyrillic characters, that is, in the Russian language, and each was subtitled in French. The name and the address of the recipient had to be printed in Latin characters. A Red Cross worker, who knew the language, added names and addresses in Russian. The large heading referred to the organisation of the Red Cross, and the Red Crescent in the USSR. My address as a prisoner of war was *Moskau UdSSR, Rotes Kreuz, Postfach 445*.

The news that post was coming had already been rumoured for weeks. Waiting for the first post, for half a year and more, was agonising. Who would receive post? Would it be good news? When the time came and I recognised my dear Mother's handwriting, I was glad. But I gathered that news from my father had been sent previously.

We thank God that you are still alive and well. We long for you to return home soon. Löhners, Richards and Aunt Lotte in Dresden have lost everything. Löhners are now living in Aachen with friends, but things are not going well for them. Gisela Pittler is living in Oberlind and has asked after you. Things are going really well for us here, even if our flat is small. Today Father had a lot to do and is very tired. Heartfelt greetings from us three! Your Mother.

To my great surprise the address from which the card had been sent was Braunau am Inn, in Upper Austria, Linzerstrasse 41. But what really disturbed me was the fact that Mother wrote nothing about Rudi. I immediately had the ominous suspicion that he was no longer alive. My suspicion was confirmed six days later when I received Father's first card, undated. He wrote that they had not received the news I had written to Stockerau, but only that which I had sent to Aunt Ilse. The one and only piece of news that they had had from me was the slip of paper which I had given to my fellow *Stockerauer* Franz Heinz and which the family had received with great joy on Christmas Eve 1945. Then came the shattering news.

At that time we did not yet know that our dear Rudi had been called to his heavenly home six months earlier. He had been killed in action on 10 April 1945 at

Haubinda/Thuringia, between Sonnenberg and Coburg. Even though it is difficult not to have him with us any more, may you nevertheless be consoled by the words that we put on his obituary notice: 'I have loved thee from everlasting to everlasting, therefore I have drawn thee to myself from pure goodness'. We cannot doubt that God, even if he has laid heavy suffering upon us, has shown Rudi the greatest blessing by calling him home out of this life into a better world. Be consoled with this, and pray that God may keep us all in true faith, so that one day we may meet our dear Rudi again and all be reunited in glory. We are glad to have news from you at last and long for you to come home. We have been here since 20 May 1946.

I received the third card on 16 February 1947. In it were more details about what had happened to the family. On 15 December 1946 it had been Father's induction. In Braunau, the card said, there was no grammar school, only a high school. Liesl was in primary school and in addition she was doing a Latin course. Otherwise, it said, many things were better there than in Stockerau. They were not able to continue to live there because of the bomb damage. In Korneuburg both the vicarage and church were totally destroyed on 20 March 1945. Frau Spindler, Rudi and Christl were killed. 'Father came home on 9 March 1945. The burial of Frau Spindler and her children was his first official duty. On 2 March 1945, after a day's leave, Rudi left home for the last time. Your Father never saw him. Now he is resting so close to places we know so well. He is in *Kreis* Hildburghausen, near to the Gleichberge. Fräulein Weidmann has visited his grave. It is being loyally taken care of by the teachers and pupils of a rural grammar school. May God protect you and send you home soon'.

I deeply regretted the loss of my brother, companion of my youth who was always so cheerful, with whom, particularly during the last years, I had had such an excellent understanding. Aunt Ilse too, deeply disturbed, had informed Mother that Jörg, the father of her three children, had been killed at the end of the war. So, after the death of Uncle Erich Scheiderbauer, in November 1942 at Lake Ilmen, three men from our closer family had been killed in the war. In the light of what had happened to them, at the same time I felt myself to have been unjustly treated. Because those three had not been so often and so continuously in mortal danger as I had, in all probability I felt it should have been me killed before them. Not they, but I had been held and protected by the invisible hand of God. I had felt it over me so often during the war and in my captivity.

Nevertheless, I knew that my good parents and my little sister were alive and had a roof over their heads. I knew also that they did not have to suffer hunger. All things being well, I knew that I would be able to return home to them. Compared with many other comrades who had not received any news from their dear ones for a long time, things were all right with me. It had been two years since I had heard anything from the family, and everything might have been a lot worse! The postal connection, which was functioning again, even if only very unreliably and incompletely, was a contributory factor in strengthening the new feeling of life that I felt within myself.

I believed that at any rate after my happy return home, a completely new and completely different part of my life would begin. Everything that I had gone through would drop away from me without leaving behind any noticeable traces. It is true that soon after I returned home I realised my mistake. But at that time I did not see it. The *Antifa* propaganda had raised in me the expectation that the future of Austria lay in a form of democracy under Socialist leadership. As a person interested in politics, I might play some part. The fascist dictatorship was dead and the restoration of earlier conditions, i.e. those which I had known in the Third Reich, were out of the question.

In the camp there was a modest 'cultural life', in the organisation of which Dr Deckwitz was involved. One day a competition took place. It resulted in an exhibition of artistic creations such as drawings and literary productions. Few took part, and interest in it was small. I can remember none of the works exhibited apart from my own productions. Those were two poems, one of which was a love poem. It spoke of longing for an unknown girl. I know that in it I was no longer thinking of Gisela, but of another girl, unknown to me, to whom I would give my love. The other poems had been entitled 'On looking at the last photograph from the old times'. It said that everything that I felt when I looked at my uniform, like a dream, was lying behind me. Everything was past and gone like the glimmer of joy on my cheeks, and now everything was new. 'Now everything is new' was the last line of that simple poem. My poems caused no sensation. They only received one vote each, from Dr Deckwitz.

The main attraction of our 'cultural life' was the orchestra. During the course of time they had succeeded in getting hold of instruments and in forming an ensemble of about 20 men. The conductor was the trained conductor Kurt Forst. He looked quite pleasant, and had a gentle appearance. The musicians had the advantage of not having to go on work details. They also had special clothing, namely a kind of shirt that they wore, in Russian fashion, over their trousers. It was made of heavy material and replaced the uniform tunic. Apart from the musicians and the tenor, Benno Stapenbeck, only the leading camp officials, Gless and Schubert, had such shirts. The last two also wore newly tailored breeches to indicate their positions of importance within the camp.

The orchestra gave occasional concerts, some even outside the camp for the Russians. It was also involved in the so-called *Bunte Abende*. As had been the case in frontline entertainment, individual artists of different kinds, mainly non-professionals, did their bit. Such a non-professional was Gottfried Stadler from Timelkam near Vöcklabruck. As he had already shown in his unit, he was a gifted compere. The programmes for these *Bunte Abende* were very mixed. Of course they also appealed to the emotions, for instance when the tenor sang the Italian song of the Chianti wine. It was popular at that time, as were other songs that 20 years later would be called 'schmaltzy'.

Gottfried Stadler had been assigned to a work detail involved in unloading duties at the Insterburg railway station. He and his comrades worked for months on end loading on to trains of Russian gauge for transport to Russia, vehicles that had been plundered or had been requisitioned by the Russians. Many a time, with anger or shock, he said that, from what he saw every day, the whole of eastern Germany under Russian occupation must be in the process of being plundered. Sewing machines and bicycles, crockery and other household goods, furniture and machines, pianos and such like from private households were all there. But the objects were mostly in a poor state, having stood for weeks or months on end out in the open. They seemed to have been randomly and aimlessly snatched together. One day he told us of the stock from the Weimar National Library. Unbelievably, he had held in his hand a folder with line drawings by Goethe. Other museum objects too, confiscated by the victors, were there in Insterburg, passing through German hands for the last time.

In the spring of 1947, soldiers fleeing from other camps who had been taken prisoner again were often brought our camp. According to their accounts, in the interior of Russia they were not guarded as strictly as we were. Some of them had travelled unmolested among Russian civilians, by railway, to the area of the border. Since the new border with Poland had for a long time been strictly guarded, they had easily been caught and were with us in the camp. Among them was a man who, with some thousands of others, had succeeded at the end of the war in fleeing across the Baltic to Sweden. As is generally known, Sweden, contrary to all the provisions of international law, responded to Russian pressure. They handed back those interned German soldiers to Russia. Some of the men had been forcibly loaded on to ships and carried across the Baltic. Our man came from a camp at Libau in Estonia. He had also been picked up close to the border.

I only knew of one man who escaped from our camp. He was the former *Major* Witzel, whom I have mentioned before. He was brought back after three days. He was given a few day' solitary confinement, which he had to sit out in a so-called bunker. Then he was brought out to the camp company, who were assembled to be counted. After that he took up again the quarters he had had before he escaped. He was with the group of former staff officers who worked inside the camp in a primitive workshop making nails.

I have not yet spoken of the daily counts. Morning and evening, the camp had to assemble and form up into ranks of five. Then the Russian who was on duty walked through the ranks and if the numbers agreed, the count was quickly concluded. Once there was an amusing incident. Because smoking in the ranks was of course forbidden, burning cigarettes had to be put out at the beginning of the count, during which we had to stand to attention. Once, in the winter, a man near to me had not properly put out his roll-your-own *Kippe*, i.e. fag. During the count, smoke was visibly coming from his overcoat pocket. The comrades standing around him had long since spotted it, but he himself had not. The incident had no unfortunate consequences. Probably the Russians carrying out the count had appreciated the comedy of the situation.

In Georgenburg the food situation in the second half of 1946 had improved and it remained that way. I have already mentioned that in the daily sugar ration a distinction was made between officers and other ranks. It was the same with tobacco. For the officers there was only rarely the usual crumbly *makhorka* often given to the men. For the most part we had fine cigarette tobacco, sometimes even the black Caucasian tobacco. Ready-made cigarettes, *papyrossi*, we never received. Only the guards smoked them. Also there were never any cigarette papers or pouches in which you could put your tobacco. But in Georgenburg we had enough newspaper and were all old hands at rolling our own cigarettes.

Of course everyone had to be careful to keep back a certain small supply of newspaper, because that was also needed for toilet purposes. Mostly the 'business' had to be done in the so-called *Dutschlandhalle*, a simple barrack block about 30 metres long, through the length of which ran a *Donnerbalken*. On it prisoners usually sat really close together. It would never have occurred to anybody to feel disturbed by his neighbour. We had long since had to accustom ourselves to such sensibilities. The art of switching off and keeping oneself to oneself, even if everybody could be seen by everybody else, was something that we had long since learned. The most popular method was to pull the blanket over your head when you were lying on your bunk.

After the turnip scrap soup of the summer of 1945, there followed, for at least a year, cabbage soup twice a day. Then, in Georgenburg, twice a day, one litre of soup made from cabbage or various types of grain and in addition a quarter-litre of *kascha*. That was a moderate, sometimes very glutinous brew, mostly made from buckwheat, and also, rarely, from millet. In the morning there was one litre of tea, and those of us who were good managers still had left a remnant of the *spelty* bread from the previous day's bread ration. In Königsberg there had still been the risk of starving to death. But that was not so in Georgenburg. In 1947 some comrades even succeeded in bringing in with them, from places of work outside the camp, provisions that they had exchanged or that had been given to them. Of course nobody knew how long we would be staying there, or when our captivity would come to an end.

Little was known about the situation at home. Remarkably, at about the turn of the year 1945 to 1946, the results of the first election of the Austrian *Nationalrat* had trickled through. I can still remember today, that the *ÖVP* received 85 seats, the *SPÖ* 76 and the *KPÖ* 4. But it was particularly the bad result for the Communists that no-one had expected. We did not dare to believe it, so reassuring was the result. At that time, the sentences in the main war crimes trials in Nuremberg were also being talked about. I recall that I felt it to be light at the end of the tunnel. There was a glimmer of hope that such distinctions were made in those sentences. Papen, Schacht, and Fritsche had even been released. Also from the *Tägliche Rundschau*, a newspaper that appeared in the Soviet occupation zone of Germany, much could be picked up concerning the general situation. Generally speaking, it had an anti-fascist, that is a communist slant.

All the time I worked in the library and was exposed to the *Antifa* influence, I struggled with myself for a new, correct view of the world. It was not an easy job for me. Traditional *bürgerlich* values had been handed down to me. My deep-rooted child's faith, it is true, was based on no firm certainty of belief. So I struggled with what I had recently heard. It seemed to sound so simple and convincing, supported by my dull imaginings of a new life. What Father had written about Rudi's death did not fit in at all with all the talk of the 'superstructure'. I simply could not believe that 'spirit' came out of material. What moved me was what I talked about in long conversations with Dr Deckwitz. He understood my needs. He offered me something of a way out. He referred me to the religious socialist movement of the Swiss Protestant theologian Leonhard Ragaz. Fortunately, in the meantime, the problem soon sorted itself out.

My days in the library were numbered. All in all it had been a good year spent in that work. With the help of many books, I had been able to keep my mind fresh and active and to acquire a bit more learning then I had already. I had read Goethe's *Faust* in a connoisseur's pocket edition, bound in dark red leather. On the inside of the binding in front of the title page the owner had stuck a photograph. It was the picture of a young woman, obviously his own. She was standing naked on a beach by the sea, behind her waves were curling; she was happy and ready for love. She must have been very fortunate and the owner of the book must have been very fortunate too. When the book, the contents of which had been spiritual nourishment for him as they had for many Germans, was taken away from him, he must, in the face of this double loss, literally have felt himself to be, like Faust, a 'poor fool'.

I have already spoken about the *Deutschlandhalle* as the camp's great public lavatory. I must add to this by telling of the large tin drum that stood outside the barracks door for use at night. Since it was in the evening that we had the greatest intake of fluid in the daily rations, the drum, which once had served to carry petrol, was often used, particularly during the late hours of the evening. On cold days my bladder was particularly sensitive, and for a long time, two to three times a night, I had to get out of my bunk and run outside the barracks until my bladder was emptied and I found peace until the morning.

It was particularly during the warm seasons of the year that bugs made their unpleasant presence felt in the barracks. In the last summer, 1947, Willi Cellbrot and I had an idea. Instead of sleeping in the barracks, we would sleep outside in the open air. The barracks containing the kitchen and canteen, had a front building with a roof that was ideally suited for our purposes. For some weeks of the very warm summer we slept on our straw mattresses with blanket and overcoats over our old uniforms, free from bugs, that alone was some pleasure! Out there in the open air we were also not bothered by rats. They occasionally made their disturbing presence felt during the night. Sometimes such a creature would take a nibble at your bread ration kept on the board over your head, or give you a shock by running over your feet.

I had a remarkable experience the night before New Year 1947. Just as I was standing for the third time at the drum, I could not believe my ears. From far away, coming from Insterburg, there was the sound of music. It must have been an Austrian transmitter that was broadcasting it, because the music was unmistakably that of the 'Blue Danube'. This seemed to me to be a hopeful omen that this was the beginning of our last year in captivity, and this was in fact the case.

It must have been in May when my everyday life suddenly completely changed. In all the regular physical examinations I had always been put down for work detail 3, but all of a sudden I was designated as completely capable of work. That was in line with my general physical constitution. For some time I had no longer felt my knees trembling, and by and large felt that I had recovered my strength. So I had to give up the work in the library that I had come to like. But it was the right thing for me. From then on I was no longer close to the *Antifa* officials, who always, so to speak, forced me to think and speak in 'political' terms. From then I joined the so-called forest commando.

The forest commando consisted of the few Hungarians in the camp. There were about 15 of them, including a lieutenant. He had remained to his fellow-countryman their superior, a person whom they respected. He was called Nyiri Antal, was about 28 years old and came from Budapest. Amongst his men there were some ethnic German farmers, including a father and his son. Nyiri spoke a little German. With him and with the Hungarian soldiers of German ancestry I could make myself understood very well. Also members of the forest commando were the Austrians amongst the officers. There was Willi Cellbrot and me, but Paul Eberhart belonged to another commando. Every morning at 6 o'clock our small group got into a rickety lorry. When it had barely reached the road to Insterburg, it turned off sharply to the right to drive along the highway to the woods in which we carried out our tree-felling work. Those woods must, at one time, have been the pride and joy of their owners and of those who took care of them. In the meantime the bark beetle had infested wide stretches, and we prisoners had to chop down kilometres of forest.

Peace and quiet reigned there in the forest. The only sentry, who drove with us and stayed with us after the lorry gone, was just as peaceful. Boris would immediately find a sunny spot for himself, while we spread out over a small area and got to work. Boris more or less dozed away the rest of the day. Lack of movement and at a lot of *kascha* made him drowsy. He always looked as if he was just about to fall asleep and could only with an effort keep his little brown eyes open. He came from around Gorki, the earlier Nizhni-Novgorod. If there had still been peasants there one could have spotted him a hundred yards away as a peasant lad. His vocabulary was no more than 400 words, and it was simple Russian that he spoke. But for the most part he was quiet. He only occasionally summoned up the effort to make a necessary announcement that his position as sentry required of him.

I was not in a position to judge Boris's linguistic knowledge, because I only knew about 200 words of Russian. But Willi Cellbrot, who had studied at Polish universities, was in a better position to judge. He spoke excellent Russian, which was obviously attractive to Boris. Probably because of that, and not because we represented any particular risk of escape, he liked to sit near to us. Perhaps he was also amazed that we two and the Hungarian officer as the only officers, had no fascist brutality. We worked hard to boot. We always fulfilled our norm, although that was not small.

The forest commando was organised in such a way that two men always sawed with a bow saw, while the third, with an axe, took care of removing the branches. It was amazing how quickly we mastered the rules of tree felling. At first you had to assess how the tree was to be felled and accordingly how the saw was to be placed. The trunks, 20 and more metres long, then had to be cut up into pieces four metres long. They were then piled up at the edge of the road ready to be loaded up. While our young Hungarian was engaged in removing the branches, Willi and I were sawing at the next trunk.

Once there was a short-lived misunderstanding that spoiled Boris's rest. Willi and I were supposed to be cutting up gigantic oak trunks that had been felled years before and had been dragged to the edge of the road. With our relatively short saw blade the work would not have been pleasant, even with softer wood. The hard oak of the thick trunks, however, made our progress very slow. Because of that, Boris thought we were lazy and cursed us. He grunted curses at us, culminating in a shout of *Sibir nada.* He said our laziness should send us to Siberia, and that was what he wanted say.

We were furious and Willi began to argue with Boris. He told him that he did not understand anything of working with timber. He challenged him to pick up the saw and to try it himself. That would convince him that oaks are harder than pines. Boris put down his rifle and loosened his belt. Sweeping his arm right back, he waved Willi over and said *Dawai!* They knelt down and began to saw. Boris, from his little eyes, threw half mocking, half poisonous looks at Willi. The unaccustomed work quickly got him into a sweat. He also expended too much strength on it instead of matching the regular strokes of Willi, the trained forest worker. The tense situation was resolved when the lorry arrived. *Afto gommt* said Boris relieved, and stopped what he was doing. He got up, put his belt back on and picked up his rifle again. From then on there was no more talk of cutting oak trunks into smaller pieces.

The 'Afto' was sometimes a rattling 'Sis', but often also a heavy German artillery tractor. But instead of pulling a field howitzer, it was fully loaded with trees. On the last run of the evening the prisoners got on. As had happened to me in the war, sometimes the heavy vehicle from time to time sank into swampy areas of the forest floor. Then the driver brought out the steel cable, tied it round the nearest thick, firmly rooted tree trunk and turned on the motorised windlass, with the aid of which the vehicle pulled itself out.

By the time it was evening, the norm was fulfilled and tiredness would overcome us. We the prisoners, and Boris too, would listen for the 'Afto'. Mostly it came at 5 o'clock as planned, but sometimes it was delayed until 8 or even 11 o'clock. Then we arrived in the camp towards midnight and received our mid-day and evening soup all in one. After that our bellies were so full they hurt. No food was brought to us in the forest, so it took a while until our stomachs had got used to not having the midday meal. But just as sore muscles had gone after a few days, our bodies also adjusted to this. In the lunch break for the most part we would swarm out and go in search of berries. Once Willi caught frogs, roasted the legs over the flames of the fire, and he and I devoured the few tasty delicacies.

If the place where we were working was close enough, we visited abandoned foresters' houses. In their gardens, wild and overgrown with weeds, there were sometimes berries and green fruit. It was unbelievable how good that tasted when we were short of everything. After the monotonous diet, low in vitamins, that we had had for two years, it was invigorating to feel the effect of those 'shots' of vitamins. In the houses everything made of wood, doors, lintels, windows, stairs, everything flammable had been destroyed, or torn out and taken away. It had been done by the Russians and the civilian population, scanty numbers of whom had settled near and further away.

Boris had another two surprises for us. One particularly sultry June day, on the drive home he had the Russian driver make a detour that took us past a little pond. It was an incomparable joy and pleasure that we had long done without when he let us take off our sweaty old clothes and go into the water. He too allowed himself the pleasure of bathing, without paying any attention to his rifle while he was doing so.

The second surprise was quite different. One lunch break he took us, without saying anything about it beforehand, to a forester's house about a kilometre away from where we were working. The red brick building, still clean, at first looked to be in no way different to the other houses and farms that we had seen in the district. Shell splinters had left deep gashes in the walls. The garden was growing rampantly in luxurious green. Boris's destination was a store not far from the house. We went down into the half-buried vegetable cellar by a few steps. It was roofed by a brick

vault. The wooden door, pushed outwards, lay on the ground in front of the entrance, in the middle of it there was a sharply jagged hole. Anxiously we went in
and peered into the dark interior. We could see the dull gleam of steel helmets.

It was a day sultry with the threat of thunder. Outside it had become weirdly
dark. There were black clouds in the sky over us, pushing themselves together into
a huge pile. Then there was a gust of wind and lightning flashed luridly. After it
came a huge thunderclap and from the clouds burst streams of water. The rain-
drops crashed into the ground and exploded like little bombs. We fled into the cellar. Carefully and curiously our eyes got used to the darkness and we could look
about us in the room.

On the floor men were lying soldiers, stiff and motionless. They were dead,
but looked as if they were still alive. They had not decomposed, but had only dried
out, in full equipment. The scanty military, half-civilian clothing showed that they
had been men from the *Volkssturm*. Some had artificial limbs. They were invalids
from the First World War. But they were lying there, 2, 4, 6, 10, 20 altogether.
What had happened?

They may have had a kind of command post in the cellar. Probably the
bunker, at that time in the winter of 1945, after they had stood guard in the cold,
was where they had got warm again. The door of the cellar had been facing in the
direction of the enemy. Obviously that had not bothered them, perhaps because
they did not know of the danger. Perhaps they knew but did not take account of it.
Perhaps it was all the same to them if only they could find a little warmth, shelter,
concealment, even if that had been deceptive. Their attacker's shell, which may
have come from a tank, had hit the door and burst through it. No doubt it exploded on impact. The massive blast of the explosion had suddenly and painlessly
killed all the men in there.

The event was two years in the past. In the meantime we had been weaned
away from death. That evening, depressed by what we had seen, we drove back into
the camp crouching on the high laden tractor. Along part of the way we could see
the last rays of the sun in the west transfiguring the image of the town of Insterburg.
It lay on the other side of the valley. The tower of the Lutheran Church stood on a
hill, towering up alone. Was the Prussian eagle that had once adorned it, still sitting
on the top of the church spire?

But physical work in the forest commando, which in a certain sense had made
me 'free' and had contributed towards my regaining my self-confidence, was soon
at an end. It seemed as if the Austrians among the prisoners of war would soon be
released. In July something actually happened that pointed in this direction. Even
the Russian camp personnel appeared to be remarkably busy. The captain with the
German name Enter, and the dreaded sergeant major from the *MVD*, often stayed
in the camp. They came from the successor organisation to the feared *GPU*, and
following Stalin's example, mostly worked at night. Accordingly they were pale in
appearance and spread fear about them.

We Austrians were kitted out with fresh clothes. By this I mean that we received new field grey tunics with Navy buttons, and trousers from clothing stocks
of the former coastal artillery. It was almost painful when I had to take my leave of
the three-year-old tunic in which I could still see the holes made the last time I had
been wounded. In addition there were two sets of underwear of Red Army pattern.

They were vests and underpants made out of thin linen, provided with laces to tie them on, the vest on the chest at the front and the underpants above the knees. The Austrians were supposed to be assembled in Tilsit, the former border town of the Reich, which by then was called Sowjetsk, hopefully the last station of our existence as prisoners.

14

January-September 1947:
Freedom - Aged 23 years

*Physical work continues; leave Tilsit; the journey home; captivity
ended after two and a half years - aged 23 years*

In 1939 the town on the Memel had been home to 58,000 inhabitants. Then it had been completely deserted by Germans and only a few Russians had settled there. We came across the wide town square. There was a memorial to Max von Schenkendorf, the poet who wrote the song *Die Wacht am Rhein*, a son of the town. Here too was a pulp factory that had belonged to the Feldmühle concern. But we did not think that we would be set to work again, because it had been said that we were actually going home. No fighting had obviously taken place around the town. Even the barracks in which we were quartered was intact, but indescribably bug-ridden. The nights were sheer torture. On the walls there were spots of blood in abundance, the remnants of bugs, gorged full of blood that had been squashed to death. We tried to counter the scourge by moving our bunks away from the walls, but of course it was in vain. Faces and hands, the parts of the body that during the night were not covered, the vermin could gain access. We were studded by lumps left by the bites. Some could count themselves fortunate whose blood did not attract the bugs that supposedly only went for 'sweet' blood.

There in the Tilsit camp, the great brick barracks from imperial times, I had once again met and got to know, other Austrians. From Georgenburg I already knew Franzl Reisegger. He was born in 1914, a master-shoemaker from Ranshofen near Braunau am Inn, who also worked as the camp cobbler. Franzl had married young. But with his first post he learnt that the child conceived on his last leave, his wedding leave, had died after it had been born. I became friends with Franzl because we were to be released to the same place, Branau am Inn. It was the same with Othmar Hadaier. He was born in 1926, and from Ranshofen. However, I did not have as close a friendship as I had with Reisegger.

After we were released I often met with both of them. Othmar, who still had to complete his degree, lives as a tax adviser in Ried in the Inn district, Franzl in Ranshofen. I became a close acquaintance, if not a friend, of the Protestant pastor Ernst Hildebrandt. He was some 10 to 15 years older, and had also been a *Leutnant*. He had managed until then to hold on to his New Testament and occasionally I was able to borrow it from him. But the religious discussions to which it had prompted me did not come about. The exertions of our work left us too tired.

It had been wishful thinking that we would not any longer be assigned to work in Tilsit. First of all there was a sawmill, in which the officers' brigade had to work. For a week, Willi Cellbrot and I stacked five metre-long beams. It was hard work and demanded all our strength. But we managed well, and I can still see our muscu-

197

lar upper bodies. Apparently 'sweet on us' was the 20 year old Russian girl Veronica, who worked in the office of the sawmill. She was a pretty girl, who looked at us half mistrustfully, half pleased, when she was checking whether we had fulfilled the *Schto prozent*, i.e. the hundred per cent of the prescribed norm. After our work stacking planks we were detailed to work on lathes. I worked on one with which I made chair legs and chair backs, and also the frames of the seats that were later filled in with plywood. The work involved a certain craftsmanship or even sense of taste, needed to ensure that uneven parts were avoided. Of course you had to take care not to get too near the electrically driven blades. I learned to take a certain pride in my work. It was not just unskilled work but already skilled work, which pleased me more than the other kind.

Other kinds of work to which we were assigned were unloading small freighters that brought timber for pulp and paper production from Finland or Sweden. We unloaded railway trains that brought coal, no doubt from the Upper Silesian coalfield. While unloading those trains, we discovered one day a wagon bearing the inscription *Österreich*. We felt that to be not only a greeting from our native land, but another good omen that our return home, even if it was obviously to be drawn-out, might be soon. Unloading the charcoal and the coal demanded all our strength.

With coal, the norm for the 10-hour working day was, for two men, to unload a wagon of 20 tons. Whether you finished in time depended upon the kind of coal. It had sometimes been cut in large pieces that you could only get hold of with your bare hands. It could be relatively easily pushed out of the wagon. The work was also easy when the coal was in small pieces about the size of an egg. Then you could get a reasonable pile on the big shovel. The most unpleasant and the most unpopular work was when the coal was in medium-sized pieces, about the size of a cobblestone. Then it was difficult to get several of the pieces on your shovel or to throw or push them individually out of the wagon by hand.

But the hardest work was in the factory boiler house. There, work went on non-stop in three shifts and our brigade had to take over the night shift for a week. We had to shovel the coal with which the several furnaces were heated. It went into tippers and we pushed them to the furnaces. That was a very hard kind of work that not only called for strength, but also cost a lot of sweat. But, like the images of the forest commando, I recall the scenes from Tilsit, especially those from the night shift in the factory, before my mind's eye. It still fascinates me today to see the dark figures, their faces wet with sweat, in front of the bright flames of the furnace. I can still also remember the tiredness and exhaustion that set in towards morning and that everyone could feel as they marched back to the camp. Yet how releasing and healthful the sleep was, on the bright day after the night shift and before the next one.

At that time I thought that I had recovered my strength, that I was fit and that I had nothing more to fear from my last wound and its consequences to the lining of my lungs and my ribs. But one day I suddenly got quite a high fever and I was brought into the barracks' sick bay. I had, it was ascertained, contracted *malaria tertiana*, which also occurs in temperate zones, where the attack of fever follows a fever free day. I must have been infected by a mosquito of the genus *anopheles* in the East Prussian woods in the forest commando. That explanation was consistent with the one to six week incubation period. I was not the only one who was treated in the sick bay for *malaria tertiana*. The sick bay was equipped to provide the proper treatment, because it had atebrin. After about a fortnight, I believe, the illness was cured. In the sick bay I had been cared for by a Brother of Mercy from Vienna, by the name of Maly. (I chanced to meet him years later near to his hospital in the Second District of Vienna, wearing the religious habit of his order.)

The high fever of over 40 degrees, affected me every other day and of course brought with it renewed debility. For the next few days, the last in Tilsit, I was no longer capable of work. In the sick bay Willi Cellbrot, who during that last year had become my closest comrade, visited me after work. Once he brought well-nigh a miracle, a fresh hen's egg that he mixed up with my sugar ration. In doing that he gave me an indescribable pleasure such as I had not experienced for years.

It was the beginning of September! We set off from Tilsit. The journey was partly made in open wagons without sides. I had the bad luck of sitting on one of those wagons which only consisted of a platform. Everyone who sat on it was blackened by soot from the steam from the locomotive. It took hours and hours for the men who had been affected in that way to get their uniforms even half way clean. In Georgenburg there was a great process of registration, parading and frisking. We were called by name several times. When our surnames were called out we had to answer, Russian fashion, with our Christian name and that of our father. To the guttural shout 'Scheiderbauer', I replied loud and clear, 'Armin Anton'.

No one doubted any longer that those whose names were being shouted out were going *damoy*, home! Those who remained behind looked wistful. I could not refrain from sadness. I was particularly sorry for Dr Deckwitz and Alfred Tunzer. From July, Deckwitz had been working on a version of *Fidelio* that could have been produced without female parts. A camp choir assembled for a short time under the direction of Kurt Forst had been practising the 'Prisoners' Chorus'. *Oh, welche Lust, oh, welche Lust, in freier Luft zu leben.* 'Oh what joy, Oh what joy, to live in free air' I had sung. Even years later, when I was at home with my parents, I had played variations on the theme on the piano. Because of that chorus I had taken my girlfriends to the *Theater an der Wien* to see *Fidelio* when I was a student. The emotion it raised in me was something that for years never left me.

During the last great process of 'frisking', every prisoner had to spread out his possessions in front of him. The Russian guards and the officers of the *MVD* carried out a precise check of what everyone possessed. In the case of Oskar Stockhammer, the camp clerk, they discovered his pay book that he had held on to until then. He was separated from us. I can still see him today, pale as wax and bereft of all hope, sitting staring into space. (Later he became a police inspector in Salzburg. When we used to meet, we always thought of those 20 sad hours.) But he was then allowed to rejoin the column.

When we at last formed up to march out of the camp, the camp band had taken up position beside the barbed wire at the gate. Marches were not part of their repertoire, and to play a march would no doubt have been out of place. So they played the American popular song whose German title was *Wochenend und Sonnenschein*. The 'wing' man on the bass drum was a certain Paul Padurek. He looked like a Sicilian, but was a homespun Saxton from Grimmitschau in the

Vogtland. When we were already far beyond the camp fence, on the march to the station, the jaunty notes of the song kept reverberating within me.

It was inconceivable that this captivity, after two and a half years, was to come to an end. Many could simply not believe it. I was exceptionally sceptical. Indeed the feeling had begun to set in that I could not have stood it for one day longer. However, I knew that none of us, if we had had to stay behind, could have done anything about it. There had been the constant uncertainty about what was going to happen to us, and what the future would bring. If we had possessed the fatalism characteristic of the Russians, then camp life might have been tolerable. But we could think of many things that could have been improved. Still, no one knew whether our journey was really taking us home or whether some developments in world politics, of which nobody knew, might not influence our fate. The orders over the camp loudspeaker and the daily playing of the martial Soviet anthem in the evening at 10pm would, it was clear, not have been missed by any of us. But would the journey really be taking us home?

Our mistrust grew after we had been loaded into the goods wagons and the train had begun to move. It was not westwards or southwards that the train was going but, to our horror, it was going eastwards. Only when we were not far from Minsk in White Russia did it to turn southwards and we went as could be seen from the landscape, through the Pripet marshes. Then we went south-westwards towards Galicia. Lemberg, Kolomea and Stryi were the stations that we reached after many stops, often lasting for hours.

It was in Kolomea or Stryi that a check was carried out of a type that we had not seen before. All the men on the train, each with his baggage, had to parade on the embankment in front of the wagons. Then they had to pull their trousers down, everyone had to turn round and, bending over, present their naked backside to the authorities carrying out the check. The most fanciful rumours rushed in a flash through the ranks, all more so since some poor devils were separated off. People suspected that they had had special tattoos, similar to those carried by the *Waffen-SS* showing their blood group, although no one had heard of such measures being taken before. Gradually the opinion grew that it must have been a sanitary check. The Russians had been looking for men with crab lice or in any event for men whose buttocks marked out their owners as suffering from dystrophy. It was an unmistakable sign that we were going home. It indicated that the Russians were concerned that their prisoners did not arrive home like walking skeletons.

The mood improved as our train approached the Carpathians. We went on many double bends through green woods and past picturesque villages. In one of those villages, one Sunday, we saw men and women standing in bright coloured costumes in the church square. It was a totally unaccustomed picture of the deepest rural peace. In a high pass we had a shocking experience. Our train was standing beside another one that was heading in the opposite direction. In the same kind of cattle wagons that we occupied there were, in the other train, German women and girls from Transylvania who were being transported to Russia for forced labour. It seemed incredible that we 'Plenny's' were travelling home to be released, whereas those young German women did not know what fate awaited them.

Through the Carpatho-Ukraine, which before the war had belonged to Czechoslovakia and by then had been annexed to the USSR, the journey went further southwards. After Tschop, which in Hungarian was called Csop, the train left the Soviet Union. It was night when we crossed the border. The wagon doors had to remain closed. Scarcely did we seem to have passed the border when from wagon to wagon the doors were opened. But at the first glance out into the darkness of the forest a Rumanian guard could be seen. It was a further step closer to freedom, although we continued to be under Russian guard.

Marmarosch-Szigeth, the Rumanian border town with a Hungarian name, was the destination of this penultimate stage of the journey home. A gigantic barracks area built in the old Austrian style received us. Thousands of Austrians from the former German *Wehrmacht* and Hungarian prisoners of war were held there. We stayed there for some days. The main purpose of the stop seemed to be relaxation and food. There was plenty of food. It was Hungarians who were doing the cooking, because it was an excellent peppery millet *kascha* that was served to us. There was a more or less happy atmosphere and you were reminded of Wallenstein's camp, although there were no camp followers.

The transports of Austrians going home were supposed to depart daily. The first and the second transports had already left. We should have been on a third, but, by way of a last minute fright, we officers were kept back. It was uncertainty, literally until the last minute, that dominated that period of captivity. Carelessly I had done a deal with a Hungarian officer. I had swapped my rucksack, an item of *Luftwaffe* equipment, for a simple Army haversack and 100 grams of fine cigarette tobacco, because I had thought that I would not need the rucksack any more, and I could carry my few possessions in a haversack. Indeed, apart from what I was wearing, I possessed very little. I had a second set of underwear, a tin of tobacco, my three-year-old toothbrush, my eating irons, and, the most important item, a spoon. Many prisoners carried one in their outside left top pocket so as not to lose it, and to always have it ready. But we had a rucksack at home, I knew. If this had not been the case, it would have been a poor swap.

A fortnight had passed since leaving Insterburg. With the fourth transport, we officers were also allowed to travel. In broad daylight we went across the Hungarian plain through Szolok and Debreczin. Everyone who caught sight of our train, which was not travelling very fast, waved to us. When we stopped, Hungarian women brought to us watermelons in large slices. The pleasure that the civilian population shared with us seemed to us like a foretaste of our reception in our native country. The train remained in Györ (Raab) overnight in order to ensure that our arrival on Austrian soil would be in daylight.

In Raab we also changed locomotives. It seemed to be a first greeting from home when, from there on, an Austrian engine driver drove the train. When the train started off from Raab and the Austrian border was coming closer, the excitement was well-nigh unbearable. We arrived at Nickelsdorf. You could tell that you were on Austrian territory because the second track of the line had been dismantled. That was part of the reparations that the Soviet Union had demanded. Well, that did not bother us. Wherever civilians caught sight of the train they waved to us. It was harvest time and many men and women were in the fields. They stopped their work and waved to us joyfully. It seemed almost too good to be true.

Meanwhile, we had heard that the station at which we would arrive was Wiener Neustadt. There the formal process of release was to take place. The closer we came to that destination, the more emotional did the mood become. It was on the morning of 19 September 1947 when our train reached Wiener Neustadt. Of the partially destroyed city you could see very little. Our attention was directed to the reception that was awaiting us. Many hundreds of people had turned up at the station. After we had got out of the old familiar cattle wagons, the column formed up to cover the short distance to the barracks in which the *Heimkehrer-Entlassungsstelle Wiener Neustadt* was located. The way to the barracks was lined by relatives of *Heimkehrer* or those who hoped to see them. It was clear that many Viennese had come to meet their *Heimkehrer*. It was shocking that many women and also many elderly men were holding photographs in front of them, and placards on which was written something like 'Who knows him?' These were relatives of people who were missing, asking for information, but none of us *Heimkehrer* had the time to carefully look at the pictures and the names individually.

It took hours until the release certificates were issued. In the meantime we were fed. We had our first meal on our home soil. If I remember rightly, it was a goulash, the first meat we had had to eat in two-and-a-half years. The '*Heimkehrer* Release Certificate' I of course still have today. At the top right-hand corner of it there is a stamp 'Declaration on Oath. I declare on oath that the information given is the truth'. Under that is my signature. As profession I gave 'student'. Under the rubric 'Return from captivity, from which captivity, when captured', are the dates 19. 9. 1947, in Russian 27. 3. 1945. The release address is shown as Braunau am Inn, Linzerstrasse 41. The day of release is 19. 9. 1947 at Braunau. A further stamp certifies that I was free of lice and infectious diseases.

On the back of the release certificate there are many stamps. From the date of release they go on for several weeks. They indicate that I received 50 schillings federal assistance and 10 cigarettes. Again, on 20 September from the *Heimkehrer* control point Bahnhof-Linz, I received loose change, cigarettes and a brochure. I was fed until the evening of 20 September. On 23 September an identity card was issued to me by the town of Braunau. On 2 October I received vouchers for two pairs of socks, two pairs of underpants and two vests.

The *Heimkehrer* who arrived on our transport were during the course of the day sorted into groups according to the places they would be released in the various *Bundesländer*. They were assembled into small groups. So, within our small group of officers, it was time to say farewell. Willi Cellbrot was going to Styria, Paul Eberhart to Vorarlberg and the Vienna doctors, I remember Fritz Walter, Kindler and Drechsler, to Vienna. The men from Upper Austria, including me, were travelling on overnight. So we were put in passenger carriages. The train drove through Vienna at night on the connecting line from the southern to the western railway. I recall passing the level crossing on the main Hietzing road. There I thought of Aunt Ilse, who lived not far away from there in Ober-St.Veit.

But we were not yet completely free. That became apparent to us when on the Enns, the demarcation line between the Russian and American zones of occupation, there was a last stop. For one last time we had to get out and form up to be counted, even if it was without the familiar and yet so annoying *dawai*. That last count has remained unforgettable to me to this day. Every time I cross over the Enns bridge, I look at the place not far from the large farm, where the small barracks of the Soviet border guards used to be. That time the Russians were friendly, there was no longer any reason for them to object, and we were allowed to get back into the train. On the western bank of the Enns the American guards were waiting for us, without us having to get out of the carriage. They went from compartment to compartment and looked at us half curiously, half with pity. Their casual manner and the jaunty cut of their uniforms were in striking contrast to the usual appearance of the Red Army troops.

In half-an-hour we had reached Linz. The train drove in to the ruined station. It had not yet come to a halt when a band, probably that of the railwaymen or of the police, was already striking up *Oh, du mein Österreich*. In front of the railway building, in the midst of the rubble, an area had been cleared into which we were led through a cordon of people. Here too, many were happily excited and many looked anxiously and searchingly, holding their pictures and placards of their missing relatives before them. I can still exactly recall the feeling of wonderful release and relaxation. Even as we were passing over the Enns bridge a final weight was lifted from me, and the tormenting uncertainty that had weighed heavily on us during our time as prisoners of war of the Russians, was at last gone.

As we walked through the cordon to the station, I literally had the feeling of being outside myself, of standing beside myself and observing everything as a spectator. The province of Upper Austria greeted its sons through the representative of the *Landeshauptmann*, Dr Lorenzoni. I can recall nothing of his speech. But I do know that Lorenzoni spoke warmly and kind-heartedly. I can still see before me the distinguished head of the speaker with his silver hair. Afterwards the three Pichler sisters sang the *Hoamatland* from the text by Franz Stelzhammer, Upper Austria's provincial anthem. That too was deeply moving.

In Linz the *Heimkehrer* were sorted into groups according to their districts of residence. From the *Bezirkshauptmannschaft* Braunau am Inn a young official by the name of Bautenbacher took charge of us. Later I often used to meet him and he told me of his remarkable war experiences. He had been the pilot of one of the three gliders, loaded with members of Otto Skorzeny's *Waffen-SS* unit, that had landed in September 1943 on the high plateau of the Gran Sesso and had freed Mussolini who was being held prisoner there. In Bautenbacher's charge, Franzl Reisegger, Othmar Hadaier and I travelled from Linz to Braunau am Inn. In Wels, Grieskirchen and Ried im Innkreis we left the *Heimkehrer* who lived there. From Ried im Innkreis the journey took about another three-quarters of an hour.

It was on 20 September 1947 when my journey home came to an end and our train arrived in Braunau am Inn. Then, at the end, anxious questions had surfaced. How had the family survived the time during which the Russians were in Stockerau? What was known concerning Rudi's death? But I would soon know. It was certainly a different kind of homecoming from anything we had imagined. But it was good for all that. I was lucky to have come through. At the station about 100 people were waiting. As soon as I got out I could see my family. My Father, was bearded as ever, but older. My joyfully excited Mother was looking youthful. Liesl was now 13 years old. After we had greeted and hugged each other, we *Heimkehrer* were taken into the small waiting room of the station, where *Bürgermeister* Fageth welcomed us home. After a while we went from the station, outside the town, into the town where at that time the Protestant rectory was in *Linzerstrasse* No. 41. It was located within the medieval centre of the town in a narrow row of houses. Over the front door there was written, in white on a red background, *Herzlich Willkommen*, surrounded by a garland. I was moved that it was there for me.

My homecoming was described 40 years later by my sister Liesl as follows:

> We had always worried about my brother Armin. Firstly, because things were dangerous on the Eastern Front, secondly because he had been seriously wounded twice. Then we had news that he was alive and was a prisoner of the Russians. When we received it, I can't clearly remember, because at the time I was only 11 years old. I presume that Mother told me of it. But the joy that my parents and I felt was enormous. Our fears were then at an end, because, as we thought, Rudi was completely safe at the war school. It is true that it was a long time until Armin returned home in autumn 1947. The radio announcements concerning the *Heimkehrer* had probably been heard by somebody from the parish who had passed it on to us. I don't remember them, only the great feeling of joy that my brother, whom I had not seen since Christmas 1944, was coming home.
>
> The train carrying several *Heimkehrer* arrived at the station in Braunau. While I had not even been afraid during air-raids and had been interested watching the aeroplanes, the sight of those figures was depressing. Grey, emaciated, exhausted, and looking the worse for wear, carrying nothing, only a bundle of possessions, but with the most precious possession of all - life. I especially remember that Armin seemed to have lost the power of speech concerning what he had experienced in the war and as a prisoner of war. He would say nothing about it and we were not allowed to ask...

I went into the house. It was a different house from the one I had left in July 1941. But it was the goal of my homecoming, after six years, one month and twenty days of war, and as a prisoner of war.

Thus ended the adventure of my youth. I was not yet 24 years old.

Glossary

Abteilung / Abt.	Battalion / department / section, dependent upon context
alte Hasen	*lit.* 'old hares', i.e. 'old hands'
Baubataillon	Construction battalion
Ersatz	Replacement
Etappenschweine	*lit.* 'Rear-area pigs', contemptuous term used by frontline soldiers for men who populated rear-area postings avoiding seeing action
Fahnenjunkerunteroffizier	Non-commissioned officer cadet
Feldgendarmerie	Field police
Feldwebel	Sergeant
Festung	Fortress, or more usually referring to a 'fortified place'
Gebirgsjäger	Mountain troops
Gefreiter	Lance-corporal
General der Artillerie	General of artillery
Generalfeldmarschall	Field Marshall
General der Infanterie	General of infantry
Generalleutnant	Lieutenant-General
Generalmajor	Major-General
Generaloberst	General
Hauptfeldwebel	Senior sergeant
Hauptmann	Captain
Heeresgruppe	Army group
Heimatschuss	Soldiers' term for a wound that would require its recipient to be shipped home for treatment
Heimatkehrer	*lit.* 'Homecomers', used to refer to German soldiers returning from captivity after WWII
Hilfsarbeiter	Labourer, possibly foreign
Hilfswilliger	Auxiliary, usually non-Germans assisting military formations in a non-combat capacity
Hochdeutsch	*lit.* 'high German', equivalent of 'the Queen's English'
Infanteriegeschütz	Infantry gun
Kampfgruppe	Battle group
Kreis	Administrative region, approximately equivalent to a county in size
Kreisstadt	Chief town in a *Kreis*
Kübelwagen	Jeep, command car
Landesschützen	Regional defence troops
Landser	Nickname for German soldiers, equivalent to the British 'Tommy' or US 'G.I.'
Leutnant	Lieutenant
Marschbataillon	Personnel replacement transfer battalion
Nebelwerfer	Rocket launcher
Oberfähnrich	Officer candidate
Oberfeldwebel	Master sergeant
Obergefreiter	Corporal

Oberleutnant	First lieutenant
Oberst	Colonel
Oberstleutnant	Lieutenant-colonel
Panzer Abteilung	Tank battalion
Panzerjäger	Tank hunter
Ratschbum	German slang term for the Soviet 76mm gun
SS-Unterscharführer	SS sergeant
SS-Untersturmführer	SS second lieutenant
Stadtkreis	District formed by a town
Stahlhelm	Steel helmet
Stellungsbaustab	Trench construction staff
Sturmgeschütz	Assault gun
Sturmgewehr	Assault rifle
Unteroffizier	NCO/sergeant
Volk	*lit.* 'People' but in German the term encompasses a pseudo-mystical reference to the way that the people, the land they live in etc. are inextricably linked
Volksartilleriecorps	People's artillery corps
Volksgrenadier	People's grenadier
Volkssturm	German equivalent of the Home Guard
Wehrkreis	Military area/district, a German administrative area for military purposes

Related titles published by Helion & Company

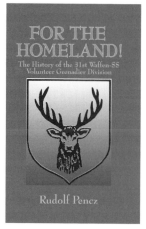

*Last Laurels. The German Defence
of Upper Silesia,
January–May 1945*
Georg Gunter
320pp, over 170 b/w photos,
20 maps. Hardback
ISBN 1–874622–65–5

*For the Homeland! The History
of the 31st Waffen-SS Volunteer
Grenadier Division*
Rudolf Pencz
288pp, 26 b/w photos,
11 maps. Hardback
ISBN 1–874622–01–9

A selection of forthcoming titles

*Elite of the Third Reich. The Recipients of the Knight's Cross of the Iron Cross 1939–45:
A Reference Guide*
Walther-Peer Fellgiebel   ISBN 1–874622–46–9
*Hitler's Miracle Weapons. Secret Nuclear Weapons of the Third Reich and their Carrier
Systems Volume 1: Luftwaffe and Kriegsmarine*
Friedrich Georg   ISBN 1–874622–91–4

SOME ADDITIONAL SERVICES FROM HELION & COMPANY

BOOKSELLERS
• over 20,000 military books available
• four 100-page catalogues issued every year
• unrivalled stock of foreign language material, particularly German
BOOKSEARCH
• free professional booksearch service; no search fees, no obligation to buy
Want to find out more? Our website is the best place to learn more about Helion & Co.
It features online book catalogues, special offers, complete information about our own
books (including features on in-print and forthcoming titles, sample extracts and
reviews), a shopping cart system and a secure server for credit card transactions, plus
much more besides!

HELION & COMPANY

26 Willow Road, Solihull, West Midlands, B91 1UE, England
Tel 0121 705 3393   Fax 0121 711 4075
Website: http://www.helion.co.uk